MANAGING MANAGEMENT TIME™
Who's Got the Monkey?

William Oncken, Jr.

Prentice-Hall, Inc.
Englewood Cliffs, NJ

Prentice-Hall International, Inc., *London*
Prentice-Hall of Australia, Pty. Ltd., *Sydney*
Prentice-Hall of Canada, Inc., *Toronto*
Prentice-Hall of India Private Ltd., *New Delhi*
Prentice-Hall of Japan, Inc., *Tokyo*
Prentice-Hall of Southeast Asia Pte. Ltd., *Singapore*
Whitehall Books, Ltd., *Wellington, New Zealand*
Editora Prentice-Hall do Brasil Ltda., *Rio de Janeiro*

©1984 *by*

William Oncken, Jr.

20   19   18   17   16   15   14   13

10   9   8   7   6   PBK

Library of Congress Cataloging in Publication Data

Oncken, William.
  Managing management time.

  Includes index.
  1. Time management.   I. Title.
HD38.053 1984   658.4′093   84-11659

ISBN 0-13-550690-5

ISBN 0-13-551086-4 PBK

Foreword

To say that I was pleased when Bill Oncken asked me if I would be willing to write the foreword for his book is an understatement. I was thrilled. In fact, I was honored.

Every once in a while someone comes along in a field who sees things clearer and more accurately than others in the field. Ted Williams was always considered that kind of hitter in baseball. The reason he hit for a higher average than anyone else was that he seemed to see the ball better. Well, Bill Oncken is that kind of person in the field of management.

The reason Bill Oncken has been consistently in such high demand as a teacher of managers for over twenty-five years is that he sees what's going on in organizations much clearer than anyone else in our field. The loud bursts of laughter that continuously echo from his training sessions are sounds of recognition. Since crying in public is not an accepted practice for managers, the only thing left for them to do is laugh. And laugh they do. Why? Because Bill Oncken, time after time, hits both the absurdities and realities of organizational life in America with such accuracy that it hurts. That is why I am so excited about this book. Now what hundreds of thousands of managers have learned in "Managing Management Time" seminars is being made available for every manager in America to read in the quiet of his or her office. Get out the handkerchiefs because this book reads as accurately and humorously as Bill tells it "live." This is vintage Bill Oncken with the "bite" and the insight left in.

There is one other reason I am excited about *Managing Management Time* appearing in its entirety in print. It shows the depth of knowledge that Bill Oncken has about management and organizational behavior. For years, everyone has known him for his "monkey-on-the-back" analogy either from hearing about it in a training session or reading about it in his classic November 1974 *Harvard Business Review* article, co-authored with Donald Wass, entitled "Management Time— Who's Got the Monkey?" Fewer people know the depth and breadth of Bill Oncken's knowledge and understanding. While I know practicing managers all over the world will "lap up" this book, I think it would be a shame if it were not required reading for all students of management in our colleges and universities. It certainly will be in my courses. *Managing Management Time* is not just about time management, it's a complete course in management.

"Why is Bill Oncken so insightful?" you might ask. First of all, he is one of the few people I've known who went to Princeton who was able to "get over it." Most people can never seem to "shake it." Recognizing that that comment comes from a Cornellian, we can get to the real reason—he paid the price. He spent over twenty years as a practicing manager before he decided to teach managers. Most management consultants and trainers, including myself, started as academics—students and teachers of management behind the "hallowed halls." While we were getting our lumps trying to publish so we wouldn't perish, Bill was out in the real world learning from experience. While our articles and books might have gotten us promoted, Bill's bruises got him a graduate degree from the "School of Hard Knocks." That is something I have learned to respect. In fact, I think Bill Oncken has probably forgotten more than most people in our field ever knew. After you finish reading *Managing Management Time*, you will know what I mean.

I know you will learn from and enjoy this book. That is a given. But what I hope you will do is use what you learn. The truths that Bill Oncken will give you can set you free and make your organization a more productive and satisfying place for everyone to work.

KENNETH H. BLANCHARD
Professor of Leadership and Organizational Behavior
University of Massachusetts, Amherst
and
Chairman of the Board
Blanchard Training and Development, Inc.
Escondido, California

Introduction:
An Ongoing Exercise in
Time Perception

Could you increase the value of each hour you put in

- If your boss delegated more responsibility and assigned fewer tasks?
- If the paper work you do added up more often to something important to you, and not just to someone else?
- If you could successfully anticipate, and not have to wait for, the decisions of your boss and those of other departments? And if your subordinates would similarly anticipate you?
- If your own subordinates would assume more responsibility for day-to-day operating decisions—so they wouldn't even reach your desk?
- If you could ask for—and get—the operating information you need instead of having to dig it out for yourself?
- If you could deputize your subordinates to represent you—within clearly understood limits—at many meetings you now attend in person? And if your boss would similarly deputize you?
- If you could sign more documents prepared by your subordinates with full confidence that you were underwriting better papers than you would have time to produce yourself? And if your boss would more often do the same with documents you prepare?
- If your subordinates were already on top of more of the problems you now get called about? And if your boss were less often called about problems you already have well in hand?
- If your absence from your office for a month would delay only *one* aspect of your job—namely, planning?

- If you could maintain performance standards high enough to encourage your weakest subordinates to move on and challenge your strongest ones to stay?

- If your subordinates had routine ways for finding answers to more of the questions they now interrupt you for?

- If you could rely on your subordinates for more of the decisions they now depend on you for? And if your boss would rely on you for more of the decisions he or she now reserves for him- or herself?

- If interdepartmental conflicts and differences were resolved more often at those levels in the organization where they initially arise?

- If the reports you get from the field were more timely and meaningful? And if you got faster feedback from reports you send "up the line"?

- If sales, production and accounting (for example) could get together on more things that you now have to arbitrate?

- If you could become more accessible to your subordinates *and* have more time to yourself without having to put in longer hours?

- If information you need from other departments was in a form more useful to you (rather than in a form more convenient for them)?

- If others would stop bypassing you for decisions that are your prerogative to make? And if your boss stopped preempting you by making such decisions on his or her own?

If so, then this book will be invaluable for you.

When you have finished reading it, go over this list again, and notice the difference in your perceptions.

Review this list regularly thereafter—say, once a month. You will find that the progressive difference in your perceptions will materialize in the increasing value of each hour you put in on your job.

The ball is now in your court.

William Oncken, Jr.

Preface and Acknowledgments

This book has been more than a quarter of a century in the making, although it was less than six months in the writing. Along the way there were many individuals who, unbeknownst to them, helped shape its philosophy, its central theme, its vocabulary and its imagery. I wish to acknowledge here those whose identities are still lodged in my memory.

Michael J. Kane, now deceased, was one of the "four horsemen" (Kane, Dietz, Dooley and Conover) of the Training Within Industry task force commissioned by the federal government during World War II. He used the "boss-imposed, system-imposed, self-imposed" trilogy in his oral presentations but never reduced it to writing. A close friend to me during his lifetime and especially during the early 1950s, he would have been gratified had he lived to see his insight become the backbone of the philosophy underlying this book.

James L. Hayes, chairman of the board, the American Management Association, used the leaping monkey analogy in his platform presentations during the mid-1960s for the President's Association to illuminate the subtleties of "reverse delegation" (introduced here in Chapter 4) and the management/vocational trapezoid that I make use of in Chapter 3. They, too, are indispensable building blocks in the structure of this book.

Michael Kami, long-range planning consultant, in some of his lectures used as a prop an actual mechanical gear train, much to the enlightenment and amusement of his audiences. I have made use of it in Chapter 3 and occasionally later in my treatment of organizational leverage.

David Ewing, managing editor for *The Harvard Business Review*, labored long and hard in restructuring my article (co-authored with Donald Wass) entitled "Management Time—Who's Got the Monkey?" to render it fit for publication in the November 1974 issue. Most of that article is repeated verbatim in Chapter 4.

Lawrence A. Apply, now retired as board chairman of the American Management Associations, held a unique view since the early 1950s of management as a *professional* activity and planted the seed from which grew the professional versus amateur contrast that underlies every page in this book.

As for the many "original" concepts I introduce—the management molecule, the "up needle-down needle" phenomenon, the intracompany economic system, the managER/managEE role conflict, the managerial freedom scale, the intracompany credit rating and many others—I am unable to trace their conceptual lineage, if any. Not yet ready to concede that I conceived them unaided, I am attributing them to Benjamin Franklin's grandfather until such time as their true parents come forth to claim them. Notice is hereby served that they must do so now or forever hold their peace.

Except for *Douglas McGregor* and *Abraham Maslow,* behavioral theorists (who often prefer to be called behavioral scientists) have produced little specific source material relevant to the message of this book. Either they have not been asking the relevant questions or their research methodology has been less than responsive to them. Not surprisingly, their principal impact has been on the academic rather than on the business community; witness the courses in "Organization Behavior" that MBA candidates must pass to earn their degrees. This book is thus unlikely to become required reading for academic credit. I hope the absence of the jargon of contemporary management theorists will not trouble those to whom the *practice* of management is now, or is soon to become, the principal source of their livelihood.

The message underlying this book has evolved since 1961 through the development and marketing of three educational vehicles: (1) a two-day seminar conducted initially from 1961 through the early 1970s by myself and subsequently also by *Donald Wass, Hal Burrows,* and *Richard Hagener,* who today conduct about 125 such sessions between them annually, (2) a video-assisted version of the "live" seminar produced by The Hewlett-Packard Corporation in 1976 and subsequently edited and marketed internationally by Deltak, Inc., and (3) an audiocassette version produced and marketed by *Charles E. Becker.* Donald Wass contributed to the structure of the "live" seminar as did Hal Burrows, the latter also contributing to the structure of the video-assisted version. All these contributions had a decisive influence on how this present book is organized.

More specifically, Donald Wass, Alan Boal and Allan Baker each made detailed suggestions on the first draft of the manuscript. Wass made some sections easier to read, Boal suggested I change the order of the first four chapters—which I did—and Baker rewrote many key paragraphs, most or all of which I adopted. My son, *William III,* made a key-point analysis of the text for consistency and continuity. It is a much better book as a result. *Bette Bond Hurst,* as a self-appointed archivist, preserved and made available the bulk of "The Collected Sayings of Benjamin Franklin's Grandfather" that appears in Appendix D, and *Patricia MacKay* reviewed the manuscript for those troublesome writer's devils—syntax and usage.

Finally, the manuscript would not have been ready for the publisher on time had not *Edwina Danley* of my office "ridden herd" on the typing and retyping that had to be done, often donating evenings and weekends voluntarily to this labor of love. Nor would it have been acceptable to my editor had not both she and her colleague, *Ramona Neel,* edited the manuscript so that, if any errors or omissions were later found in the proofs, it would be the typesetters, and not they, at whom the accusing finger would be pointed!

William Oncken, Jr.

Contents

Chapter 3:
PRINCIPAL *SUBJECTIVE* **SOURCES OF THE**
MANAGER'S TIME MANAGEMENT PROBLEMS........... 67

Getting the Subject Squared Away   68

Efficiency vs. Content; Comedy and Tragedy; Management
Time vs. Vocational Time; How to Recognize Vocational
Time; Explaining vs. Rationalizing; Deviant vs. Normal
Managerial Behavior; Professional vs. Amateur in
Management; Example from the Medical Profession.

Management—An Acquired Discipline   75

The Lures of Vocational Work; Identity: The First Lure;
Pride of Craft: The Second Lure; Instant Feedback: The
Third Lure.

School of Experience/Hard Knocks   85

Doing Battle with Administrivia; The Trapezoidal
Subterfuge; The Truncated Career; Where Professional
Management Begins; Resisting Deceptive Counter-
Propaganda; Caught Between a Rock and a Hard Place;
Are Boards of Directors Fair-Minded? Archimedes' Insight;
The Art of Fulcrum-Moving-Overmanship; The
Professional Moves His Fulcrum Over; The Name of the
Game; The Left-Leaning Trapezoid; The Mechanical Gear
Train Analogy; The Three Constraints on Managerial
Leverage.

Chapter 4:
BUILDING MOLECULAR SUPPORT 103

Your Boss   104

Your Boss's Anxiety Index; The Managerial Freedom
Scale; Image or Reality?; Authority vs. Freedom; Climbing
the Freedom Ladder; When the Pro Works for the

Optimizing Value   209

Practice Makes You Competitive, Not Perfect; Don't Give
Routine Treatment to Nonroutine Things; The Executive
Rat Race; "Shooting the Sun" with Your Managerial
Sextant; The Value Line; The No-Orange Juggler;
Managerial vs. Operating Decisions; Five Minutes a Day
That Could Move Your World.

APPENDIXES

1

Principal *Objective* Sources of the Manager's Time Management Problems

Much of the wheel spinning in management ranks is due to the time that managers spend trying to reconcile management's requirement for *compliance and conformity* with its expectation of—and the need for—*creativity and innovation*. Resolution of this dilemma is, for each manager, the first precondition for effectively managing his or her time. Six widely followed but futile approaches to this problem are described and shown to be characteristic of management's also-rans.

KEY DILEMMAS OF ORGANIZATIONAL LIFE

"Where did my time go today?"

Tens of thousands of managers are asking this of their secretaries around quitting time every day. Because these dedicated and perceptive assistants typically want to hold their jobs, they won't risk an honest reply.

And yet upon the answer—and upon the remedy—may hinge the difference between career success and failure for these same managers. So let us take a serious stab at the answers to managing *your* management time here and now.

Downward-Pointing "Needles"

The obvious place to begin is with the organization chart, because it helps us understand the first and principal objective source of our time management problems. This is what we prefer to call *boss-imposed time.* It is the time you spend doing things you would not be doing if you did not have a boss. The basis for it is clearly expressed in the popular theoretical model of organization, the ubiquitous organization chart that, prominently displayed on office walls, serves notice on all passersby as to who is entitled to needle whom about what. The needles all point down!

However, this model fails to account for where all the time is spent in the organization. It does not even *imply* that anyone has any right to impose on the time of anyone outside of his or her chain of command. Yet, as anyone who has worked in an organization knows, many people other than their boss can claim their time. Charts with dotted lines crisscrossing in apparently random fashion give pitifully eloquent testimony to this fundamental inadequacy. What is needed is not a patching up of a model that works well enough to explain the time generated by bosses, but a model that explains time taken up by others not in a direct superior/subordinate relationship to us. For instance, what right has the assistant to the general sales manager to make a direct incursion on the shipping room foreman's time?

In all modesty, we have discovered, if not invented, the long-awaited model of what we prefer to call *system-imposed time*. It is the time you spend doing things you would not be doing if you were not just one of a seemingly countless number of pulleys on an endless administrative transmission belt crisscrossing the corporate organization chart. Let me illustrate:

Imagine, if you will, a bed built for three in which nine men are trying to sleep. Since this is to be our model for organization in its system-imposed (as against its boss-imposed) aspects, let us suppose that we've given each man his job description that states, first, that his job objective is to get eight hours of sleep. Second, because no man can sleep that long without being able to turn over several times, the means he will use to gain this sleep will be to turn three times during the night. Each job description will thus read:

OBJECTIVE: Get eight hours of sleep.
METHOD: Turn three times.

Administrative Coordination

We see to it first that the men are settled and have read their job description. Then we tell them that we will be back in eight hours to pay a day's wages to each man who has earned it by achieving his job objective.

No sooner have we left than each one of the nine realizes instantly that he cannot turn without the cooperation of the other eight. A huddle is spontaneously called at which they decide that when any one of them feels a turn coming on, he should shout, "one," "two," and that on "three," they would all turn in order to enable *him* to make *his* turn. Having made this procedural decision, each returns to his own preoccupation for the night.

Eight hours later we return, payroll in hand, to reward the successful ones. Addressing the nearest, we ask him how he made out. He confesses that he came nowhere near achieving his objective.

"Did you turn over three times?" we ask.

"Twenty-seven times," he replies. "Three of which I initiated (as I was expected to), but I had to charge off the other twenty-four to *administrative coordination*. I did more things last night, but I still didn't get anything done."

"Things" referred to means (turns) and "thing" referred to ends (sleep). This phenomenon has a name—The Triumph of Technique over Purpose. It is a phenomenon peculiar to formal organization wherein the pursuit of individual ends is thwarted by the very means established by the organization for their collective attainment. This model thus provides as adequate a theoretical basis for system-imposed time as the organization chart does for boss-imposed time.

We have so far identified two key areas where time is spent: boss-imposed, which is due to our responding to the downward-pointing needles, and system-imposed, which is due to our accommodating others. However, these two kinds of time in themselves pose two significant dilemmas for anyone interested in making their own work and that of their organization more innovative and effective. The dilemmas are these:

1. The *boss* requires compliance (the downward-pointing needle). He or she must, or the accountability structure of the organization falls apart. Yet *you* feel that, to get things done, the needle must at times point up, a self-imposed necessity for which there is no theoretical basis or model.

2. The *system* requires conformity (individual ends thwarted by organizational means). It must, or the team structure of the enterprise falls apart. Again, *you* feel that, to get things done, you must occasionally override the system, a self-imposed necessity for which once more there is no theoretical model.

Yet the company itself *expects* innovation upwards and sideways in all job categories. It must, or it will fail to be sufficiently adaptive to survive. How can it get the innovation it so desperately needs and still maintain both its accountability and its team structures?

In its attempts to resolve these dilemmas, the company is perceived at times to be saying that it wants innovation and at other times implying that it can't tolerate it.

It, too, feels locked into the same two dilemmas!

Self-imposed time holds the solution to both dilemmas. Being itself the means to the solution and therefore not posing an additional dilemma, it needs no model. It needs only application. But application poses a problem, the correct solution to which distinguishes the professional manager from the amateur.

Whence comes self-imposed time? Not everyone generates it during working hours. But those who do so successfully will generally get promoted.

Self-imposed time is the result of certain personal qualities such as initiative, drive, enthusiasm, loyalty, resourcefulness, guts, imagination, foresight and so on. (If you are interested in extending this catalogue of virtues, refer to your company's merit rating form or to either the Boy or the Girl Scout Oath.) The value of self-imposed time generated by these attributes depends on three other personal qualities: character, personality and competence. (We all know, for example, of the resourceful knave, the imaginative fool, the energetic incompetent, etc.)

These qualities are in greatest demand when a vacant position has to be filled. Remember when *you* were selected to fill such a vacancy? Although it was still *unfilled*, the personnel department was working around the clock to find a competent man or woman of requisite character who was a veritable dynamo of drive, imagination, enthusiasm, initiative, etc., etc., and they finally picked you. They had high hopes for you. You shared them.

But now you are not so sure.

You have since acquired bruised shins in trying to get about the organizational maze whose channels are labeled "boss-imposed" and "system-imposed."

Having said this, we are ready to deal with some misconceptions made popular by authors who have set the so-called "Protestant ethic" against the "social ethic" in a way that encourages readers to take sides between them. In his *Organization Man*, William H. White played up to the traditional disfavor with which Americans have reacted to attitudes of compliance and conformity. You need only to get a discussion going in a management development seminar on "compliance" and "conformism," and it won't be long before the consensus holds these qualities in contempt—when found in managers. References to Horatio Alger, Andrew Carnegie, and Henry Ford will abound, punctuated with "free enterprise" flag-waving over "what made America great."

We all despise the *compliant* manager wherever he may be found *except* when he happens to be one of our *own* subordinates. Then he is worth his weight in gold. Not that we *want* it that way—we're helpless to act otherwise.

Compliance, Conformity and Innovation

Suppose I am an overworked boss who has just come to the point where I must either delegate some of my projects immediately or get so far behind that I'll never catch up. The only two men to whom I can confidently delegate are yourself and Jones. I am so pressed for time that I'll have less than five minutes with either of you to get you started. Who gets the assignment, you or Jones?

Watch me make this decision.

You and Jones are very different people, although you are both equally competent, thorough and reliable once you take on an assignment.

Jones always takes on assignments from me with words to this effect: "I'll handle it. Consider it done. *You* just forget about it." In less than five minutes he'll be out of my office, and I'll be confident he'll get the matter taken care of just as I would have.

But *you* always have an idea about how to do it *better.* I always have to take time to hear you explain it, time that I never have. Since in the past you've always been right, I can't afford not to listen. But neither can I afford the time to listen. It's bad enough that you are innovative; it is insufferable that you are always right. My only recourse is to evade this painful dilemma—so I give the assignment to Jones. I can better afford the loss of your brilliant ideas than the time necessary for you to get my approval in advance. My number-one problem is my time, and my number-two problem is the project I want you to take on. But you can always be counted on to reverse that priority!

Why Yes-Men Get Ahead

Jones gets the assignments because he is compliant. (He also gets the promotions!*)

Do not misunderstand me. I don't want it that way. I am deeply disturbed that it is working out that way. I recruited you because I wanted someone with originality, drive, imagination, initiative—but now that you're on board I haven't the time to take advantage of these very same qualities. (Want to change places with me? It's not a happy dilemma to be in.) Yet I can find no way out except to encourage and reward *compliance* despite the contempt with which I view "yes-men" in my more reflective moments.

It's the same with *conformism.* There is hardly anyone with a responsible management position who would have a good word to say about the conformist. We'd denounce conformism as a management attitude or philosophy after our first get-together in a hotel room talkfest. The truth is, however, that we unanimously despise it everywhere except when it appears in other departments on whose administrative support we depend. Then—once more—it's worth its weight in gold!

---

*If you are in a similar dilemma in relation to your own boss, take heart; Chapter 4 will show you the way out.

Why "Mere Administrators" Survive

Ask the sales force to name the most valuable employee in the Accounting Department. They'll name the accountant who, as a good "team player," pays off on expense accounts immediately upon receipt—asking no questions. (The fact that the company inevitably fires such accountants merely convinces the sales force that "outstanding talent" often goes unrecognized!) Guess whom the Accounting Department would pick as the best salesman in the company? Why, the salesman who "conforms" by always getting his expense account in on time, filled out the right way, on the right form, in accordance with the "procedure spelled out in The Accounting Manual, Chapter IV, Section 5, Paragraphs 2, 7, 8 and 15 (second half) as amended in Supplement No. 2 dated October 19, 1982, rescinded in January, 1983, with the proviso that in the event the total exceeds $500 in any one month the former shall still apply, in which case Chapter VI, Section 3, Paragraph 49 shall also apply, unless it falls in the last month of the fiscal year, in which case it must be dated one month in advance unless the books have not yet been closed in which case etc., etc., etc." (That such a salesman gets fired more often than not once again convinces the Accounting Department that the company does not recognize "rare talent" when it sees it!)

We all look for conformity in other departments on whose cooperation we depend and despise it in our own. Departments all create "systems" for each other, and *systems don't work* without conformity. We insist on freedom to innovate with the "system" originated by another department but do not condone innovation on their part with the "system" *we* originate. Intellectually, we reject this paradox but practically we have learned to live with it as a dilemma by voicing such rationalizations as the personnel people saying that "the Personnel Department understands the needs and attitudes of research people," or the production people saying that "the Production Department realizes that if there's no delivery there's no sale and eventually no jobs for anybody." To each rationalization, of course, there exists an equal and opposite rationalization. So the dilemmas live on.

Thus the *requirements* of compliance and conformity come into daily conflict with *expectations* of innovation. To make matters worse, it is difficult to find the three corresponding qualities equally developed in any one person. They clash, especially the first two with the last.

Obviously, career success in management falls to those who can negotiate all three. To do so requires, respectively, the ability and willingness

1. *to comply,* for without this the leadership structure of the organization will fall apart;
2. *to conform,* for without this the team structure of the organization will deteriorate;
3. *to innovate,* for without this the goals of the organization will fail to materialize.

Most of us therefore find ourselves in the position of a novice trying to learn to juggle three oranges without dropping any or letting them clash in mid-air.

If you don't have this problem, read no further. You are not in management.

THE ADMINISTRATIVE JUGGLING ACT

It is one problem, not three. You solve it in its entirety. *Only the amateur tries to solve it piece by piece.* Let's watch him or her work:

The amateur decides to simplify the problem by laying one orange on the table so he or she can first master the art of juggling *two.* Which one will the amateur lay down?

Not the first, obviously. Swift and obvious penalties pursue those who deal with the boss's requirements in a lighthearted, cavalier fashion. Boss-imposed time is thus penalty time and demands compliance.

Not the second, just as obviously, for although the wheels of the gods grind more slowly, they grind just as fine. The "system" penalizes the nonconformist much as the human organism expels foreign bodies from its bloodstream. System-imposed time is also penalty time and therefore requires conformity.

But how about the third? The longer the novice considers this alternative, the more attractive it becomes. He knows that neither the boss nor the system can penalize him for having failed to do something that neither of them knew he had intended to do! Since self-imposed time is nonpenalty time, it invites procrastination.

So attractive, therefore, is this third alternative that most amateurs decide—consciously or unconsciously—to forget about innovating until they have mastered the twin arts of conformity and compliance. And few there are who ever find the need to pick up that third orange again.

Years later they are retired, and honored by their colleagues for their years of loyal, faithful service—loyal to the boss and faithful to the system. (They are often affectionately referred to as Old Hound Dogs.)

The Fate of the Two-Orange Juggler

A tragedy, of course. First for the company, because it was denied the innovative potentialities of those who never progressed beyond the amateur state. But more so for themselves. Life yields many satisfactions, some during working hours, some outside. The only satisfaction available during working hours is in the work. Work without innovative accomplishment is drudgery, and drudgery produces boredom. To spend the best part of one's waking hours for the best part of one's life in boredom is an incalculable tragedy. One's salary is, in such circumstances, little more than compensation paid for damages done to one's career. This type of amateur therefore acquires the habit of getting to work under the wire, leaving on the dot, and of not being caught in the act of either doing nothing or of doing something wrong. Job security is his or her only reward. But its price is out of proportion to its benefits. The utopian theorists can be counted on to blame this outcome on the "dehumanizing" nature of the "oppressive" corporate working environment, rather than on the choices made by this individual during the course of his or her managerial career.

It is for precisely this reason that the "pro" decides to juggle all three oranges from the start.

To do so the pro knows that he or she must satisfy *simultaneously* the following:

1. The boss's requirement of compliance
2. The system's requirement of conformity
3. The company's expectation of, and his own need for, innovation

This is the make-or-break problem in his or her management career. It is peculiar to the professional practice of *management*. It has no counterpart in the practice of any of the vocational professions. Indeed, there is nothing in the vocational training of doctors, engineers, accountants, toolmakers, or salespeople that even suggests that their ability to solve this problem may in years to come be more critical to their career success than their ability to solve any of the problems they are to face vocationally. Some may eventually achieve such a high degree of excellence in their vocations that, through a succession of promotions, they may reach high managerial positions without ever recognizing this problem for what it is. This is why we find amateurs in management at all responsible levels in business, education, government, industry and the military.

It Is a Three-Orange Juggling Act

It is not enough to recognize the problem for what it is. Many amateurs are able to do this. You must also *solve* it like a pro. There are at least five additional ways in which amateurs characteristically solve the problem—ways that create additional problems without solving *anything*. We shall also describe the one professional solution that you should recognize from your own personal experience.

"What about subordinate-imposed time?" you impatiently ask. "Much of my time is spent taking care of problems and questions my subordinates constantly bring to me." This is the problem of the "upward-pointing needle," which has, as noted earlier, no theoretical model to justify its existence.

That is why subordinate-imposed time is but a symptom of the three-orange problem and is not one of its elements. When you have solved the basic three-orange problem, your subordinate-imposed time will all but vanish. This leaves the "needles" pointing *down*, as they should be. Sound incredible?

Then read on!

THE AMATEUR'S SOLUTION TO MANAGEMENT'S DILEMMA

Let's examine in detail some of the other solutions to the three-orange problem characteristically resorted to by amateurs. As noted, the amateur attempts to solve the problem piece by piece. Thus there are six ways the amateur goes about it; he or she can juggle any one of the three *pairs* or any *one* of three oranges. To do the first he need only lay down any one of the three oranges (three separate solutions). Of these six possible solutions open to the amateur, we have already described the most popular solution—the two-orange solution in which the third orange (e.g., the self-imposed) is set aside. That this approach creates a serious career problem for the amateur while solving nothing is painfully clear.

This solution is most popular because it has general application. Each of the remaining five solutions can be employed only in *specially favorable circumstances.*

Thus, if you have a boss whose first and only instruction to you was to "get lost," you could easily lay aside the first orange (e.g., boss-imposed) with impunity and concentrate on the other two. Admittedly this situation does not occur often, but when it does, the amateur is alert to it and is quick to capitalize on it. If he or she is really "on his toes," he will also drop the third orange and devote all his energies to juggling the remaining (e.g., system-imposed) orange. This is amateurism in management at its classic best.

The Bureaucratic One-Orange Juggler

With neither shame nor apology I will here and now confess that I know whereof I speak. I was once a master one-orange (system-imposed) juggler.

It happened years back when the Eisenhower Administration first took office in Washington, and I was a federal Civil Service employee in one of the government agencies. The top structures of most of the agencies were in the throes of shifting around their administrative and bureaucratic "furniture" in response to the "new brooms" that showed up in the secretariats as a result of the Republican victory. In this process organization charts were changed, some jobs abolished and others created. Alert, career-minded civil servants watch these changes like hawks and apply for any openings that appeal to them. I was no exception.

(What I am about to describe also happens in business and industry, especially in large organizations. The fact that what follows took place in a government agency is incidental. I have no choice but to refer to my own personal experiences since they are the only kinds I've ever had. But those of my readers who are employed in America's 500 largest corporations may read what follows with profit to themselves. Having spent ten years in businesses both large and small, plus an additional twenty-three years as head of my own management consulting business, I have concluded that bigness is bigness no matter what the business or who foots the bill.)

I singled out the job I wanted and applied for it in competition with many others.

What I didn't know was that this job was created by a newly appointed assistant secretary who had just interrupted a brilliant career as an executive in a nationally known department store chain to serve his government at a considerable financial sacrifice. He soon noticed that the agency was run very differently from the retail merchandising business (in which he had spent all his working life) and set about to correct the deficiency. The creation of this job was one of his first moves, and it was met with serious opposition from all the career bureaucrats in the top echelons. When the question arose as to where to put the job, no one wanted it in *his* department. Again the assistant secretary had to overrule; he arbitrarily assigned the position to that department head who had opposed him most aggressively when he decided to create the job at the beginning.

I was the lucky appointee. On the day I reported for work I asked to see my department head and was ushered into the office from which he administered his bit of the larger bureaucracy. A very engaging fellow, he asked me whether I preferred sugar or cream, or both, or none, in my coffee. Having settled that backbreaking issue, we took our well-deserved coffee break together, exchanging pleasantries from the upholsteries in which we were embedded.

"What's my job?" I asked, respectfully.

"Damned if I know," he replied with a yawn.

"Then perhaps you'd like to give me a special assignment to work on?"

"Gladly. Your first assignment is to find out what your job is."

"How long do I have for this?"

"Would six months crowd you unduly?"

"That would be fine," I replied, with no idea of the magnitude of the task I had just taken on.

He wheeled around in his chair toward his desk, seized his appointment calendar, flipped its pages to a date exactly six months hence and wrote on it in red pencil these words: TODAY ONCKEN WILL REPORT HIS FINDINGS.

Our meeting having thus served its purpose I left for my office. After several false starts I found it—on the first floor—and, after introducing myself to my secretary, who had been hired for me the day before, I strode into my office closing my door behind me.

The room was barren except for my desk, my chair, a conference table and chairs, and a bookcase. I sat down, casting about for a clue as to how I might gainfully employ my time for the benefit of the taxpayer. My roving eye caught the bookcase, which was empty except for a single volume. Its title read, *Organization and Procedures Manual Governing the Administration of the Office of the Secretary.* Sensing no help from that source, I pushed the volume back in place.

My eye moved next in the direction of an administrative tool that had never failed me and which simply must not fail me in this hour of my deepest need—my in-basket. With a sigh of unutterable relief I saw that it had *come through*! It was the closest shave of my career, for it had but one piece of paper in it. But *one* was all I needed. From even the smallest in-basket acorns, the mightiest administrative oaks can grow. I seized it. It was a three-hole-punched piece of paper, obviously intended to be filed in a ring binder. There was a buck-slip stapled to the upper left-hand corner addressed to me with the notation, "This is the revised page 22 of page 22 in your copy of The Organization and Procedures Manual. Please remove and destroy the old page 22 and replace it with this revision."

That did it! I had my morning's work cut out for me. I immediately unsnapped the just-obsolete page 22 from the binder and compared it with the new, revised page 22 to see what the crisis was all about. Each was an organization chart of the Secretary's Office, identical in every respect except that the box representing my job was on the new one but not on the old one. Looking more closely I found a brief thumbnail description in very fine print of my functions written into my box right under the boldfaced position title. This was my first clue to what my job was. (I later learned that it had been written by a clerk in the comptroller's department—whose job it was to write such statements because the Secretary couldn't approve organization charts without them.) As I contemplated these words, I soaked them up into my consciousness to the point where they remained with me for my next three-and-a-half years with that agency. (Oddly enough, I never met that clerk.)

Three hours later it was lunch time, and I had successfully performed my task vis à vis the two page 22s, since by Parkinson's famous Law, anything you have to do will fill the time available.

I went up to the Executive Dining Room, had lunch and returned to my desk two hours later. To my utter surprise—and satisfaction—my in-basket was now six inches deep in incoming paper. The reason did not elude me for long. Two hundred and fifty other people in the agency had just gone through the same exercise as I had with the page 22s and simultaneously discovered a new mailing address (mine!) that bid fair to solve one of their pressing problems. Had my job been in existence years sooner, they would not have accumulated so many incoming papers for want of an appropriate forwarding address. The creation of my job thus opened the sluice-gates through which most of their files marked "Miscellaneous" would be emptied on the installment plan.

As you might expect, I rose to the challenge.

I took the top piece of paper, noted its subject and compared it with the functional statements of other people's jobs on the aforementioned page 22, selected a likely individual, forwarded (or "bucked") the paper to him with the notation "See me about this," initialed it and placed it in my out-basket. I went through the remaining papers the same way with similarly appropriate notations, such as "Call me about this," or "Cease and desist from any further activity along this line, for this is MY (repeat, MY) jurisdiction." (This last notation is, in government circles, called *carving out your mission*. It can be more fun than working!)

It was a race to get to the bottom of the basket by quitting time, but I made it and left for home with a triumphant spring in my walk. I knew that for every administrative action I had just taken there would be an equal and opposite reaction the next day.

An Eye for an Eye

When I got to work the next morning I found several people waiting urgently outside my office to see me. On my desk were, as expected, a dozen phone messages urgently asking me to return the calls. And, of course, I viewed with the deepest satisfaction another six-inch installment of paper in my in-basket, which I would manipulate to create even greater system-imposed demands upon my time.

I was definitely in business within twenty-four hours of reporting to the agency for work. Few ever get their feet on the ground in so short a time.

That day was not long enough for me to meet and talk with all those who had to see me, to answer all those incoming phone calls and "process out" the papers from my in-basket. The latter *had* to be kept current in order to maintain my backlog of system-imposed time.

Within six weeks I became so far behind in my work I began to take it home nights just to stay even.

Within twelve weeks I got permission to hire two assistants.

Four months after my initial (and only) interview with my boss he came down to see me in my office. He had noticed that I was so overloaded I was now working weekends. He asked me whether there was any way he could be of help.

...l the assignment you gave me the day I
...d the time to get to it."

... replied. "Now that you have become
...r any need to find out what your job is."

...atched him leave—a truly sensitive and
...agement theorist would have loved him!

...d in your work every day within ten
minutes after you ... re is no need to know why you came. For
three-and-a-half years I commuted to and from the job, never needing
to know why I went.

My work had interfered with my job.

Means Are Ends-in-the-Making

This is one-orangemanship at its best! I had no boss-imposed
time; that was *his* doing. I had no self-imposed time; that was *my* doing.
I was on my way to a long career devoted exclusively to the *system*.

Today there are fourteen people in that same government office.
Occasionally, when I go back and visit them for old times' sake, I ask
them, "Have you yet formulated your mission?" They shake their heads
and say, "We've never found the time."

It is popular, of course, to make fun of the government because of
a bias in our society that people who work for it are "feeding at the
public trough." I think that is beside the point. It is not the fact that it's
government that this happens; it's the fact that it's people that this
happens. And in each of the jobs represented by my readers there
must be at least one segment that is just like this. You are so far behind
in your work that you have not had time to find out why you do it.
Welcome to the club!

The Amateur's Other Options

Let us next look at the four remaining "one-orange" and "two-
orange" solutions.

To ignore the "system" requires special conditions to which the
amateur in management is always alert. Such special conditions offer
him the opportunity to juggle the boss-imposed orange and (if he
chooses) the self-imposed orange, ignoring the system-imposed orange
with careless disdain. Such opportunities most often occur in positions
attached, stem-winder fashion, to key executive jobs, with titles such as
"executive assistant," "assistant to," "coordinator," "special assistant"
and so on. Amateurs in these positions think nothing of making

impulsive guerrilla raids on the most remote parts of the organization in complete disregard of "channels," shouting, "The boss wants it." The hapless individual bearing the brunt of this reference to authority may have every reason to doubt its validity, but he is generally in no gambling mood.

The Fate of the Boss's Hatchet Man

It is interesting to observe how often such stem-winder positions are occupied by the physically handicapped, e.g., the hard of hearing. They somehow never hear the clicking of the bolts in the gunstocks under the desks of their fellow employees when they walk by. These employees watch the newspapers every day for news that the stem-winder's boss has gone to his Reward, because on that day our stem-winder will be running for the border in search of asylum.

This is a tragic outcome, although in many cases long delayed. As always, it is the price of amateurism in management. In this two-orange version, the self-imposed orange aggravates the situation because the human targets of his zeal never know which of the things he demands are truly boss-imposed and which are simply his self-imposed brain-children on a psychedelic trip.

The second two-orange solution is the combination of the system-imposed and self-imposed. Here, too, a special circumstance is required, one in which the boss has plainly abdicated, thus relieving you of any boss-imposed concerns. You are now free to embark upon a career of making your job an end in itself (the self-imposed orange) and building a strong network of political support in the rest of the company (the system-imposed orange) to protect you in the event your boss should suddenly wake up to his supervisory responsibilities. If you pursue this form of amateurism with purpose and dedication you will become known throughout the company as an "institution." You will have built your job into what it is to the point where no one—not even the president—would dare change it as long as you are in it. Of course, on the day you retire or die the company will abolish your job without ceremony, and those persons from whom you had horse-traded their legitimate responsibilities will grab them back. This prospect does not bother you, because the security of being indispensable now fills you with a warm glow every time you are called to a meeting, or the phone rings, or someone walks in seeking your concurrence.

Irreplaceable and Nonpromotable

The tragedy attending this form of amateurism is that higher management cannot risk promoting you. Having built your job around yourself instead of around a rational organizational concept, you make yourself irreplaceable. No one else can (or would even want to) fill the job. Nor can you risk resigning, because your career has lost its marketability. Your track record of amateur two-orangemanship has limited the possible demand for your talents. What you thought would become an impregnable wall of job security has finally become an impenetrable ceiling on your future.

You Can't Live with Him
but You Can't Do without Him

The one-orange version of this, namely, ignoring all but the self-imposed, requires that you build your security in some other way than through the system. Sheer competence in your vocation is the only means open to you (unless you marry the boss's daughter or stumble upon some equally effective subterfuge). And you will just about *have* to be in the genius category if you want to achieve freedom from both the boss and the system. In this category are the commission salespeople who can look his or her salaried boss in the eye and say, "If you're so smart, why aren't you rich?", the brilliant scientist who can say to his or her boss with confidence, "I'll do it my way, or I'll pick up my marbles," or the crack production foreman who can tell the president, "If you don't like the way I run the line, you can get somebody else," and get away with it. To survive this kind of one-orangemanship, it is not sufficient that you *be* a genius in your line of work; you must also have a lot of others in the company *believing* it and, more important, afraid to challenge it. The long-term career outcome is nevertheless tragic even if you survive to retirement. Life is too short to do things under continual stress.

You Can't Live with Them
So You Can Do Without Them

We need not dwell long on the situation of the person who *thinks* he or she is a vocational genius but is alone in this opinion. Attempting the kind of one-orangemanship that only the acknowledged genius can get away with, they are taken aback when the system and the boss clamp down on them. They are referred to behind their backs as "prima donnas" and are looked upon as those who "make waves." Their refusal to *comply* and *conform* is not compensated for by their vocational competence. When they are finally disposed of, they blame their demise on "the dead hand of bureaucracy" or "managerial myopia" or "entrenched interests" or "superannuated deadbeats" or some other cliché out of the also-ran's cynical lexicon of corporate malaises.

Whether they are acknowledged geniuses or just self-styled ones, there is no reason why they cannot learn to juggle all three "oranges" and thus reduce the limitations on their careers in management. There is every reason why they must.

To summarize: In this chapter we revealed that there are three objective sources of a manager's time management problems:

1. Boss-imposed time
2. System-imposed time
3. Self-imposed time

This analysis left us with the three-orange problem, which is how can one comply, conform and innovate all at the same time, which is surely necessary for success. We saw that the amateur could, under especially narrow and favorable conditions, keep one or two of the oranges in the air, but that the professional worked on all three at once.

In the next chapter we will define the manager's objective environment in more detail to set the stage for how he pulls off keeping all three oranges airborne.

2

The Management Molecule

Additional wheel spinning results from the *frequent and random intrusions* upon the manager's time by superiors, peers, and subordinates (to say nothing of customers, suppliers, union representatives, and the like), thus making a mockery of the well-worn aphorism, "Plan Your Work, Then Work Your Plan." Learning to capitalize upon rather than to become dominated by such intrusions is the second precondition for effectively managing one's time.

YOUR BOSS

Of all the objective sources of your time management problems—namely your boss, your peers, your subordinates, as well as people at a comparable level to your own in other organizations (customers, suppliers, government agencies, unions, etc.) with whom you must deal—your *boss* is the principal one. He or she may not be the most frequent source, especially if your offices are hundreds of miles apart. He or she may not be the most disruptive source, especially if the two of you enjoy a high degree of rapport. But your boss is nevertheless the *principal* source simply because he or she is the principal source of your *priorities*. If you were in business for yourself, you would work to your own advantage as *you* saw it. If you work for someone else, you work to his advantage as *he or she* sees it. Your boss, likewise, works to his or her boss's advantage as *he or she* sees it. Ultimately, the board chairman works to the advantage of the shareholders as *they* see it. This chain linking you to the owners of the enterprise is called the *chain of accountability*. This same chain makes the president accountable to the board for how his vice-presidents prioritize their time; it makes his vice-presidents accountable to him for how their general managers prioritize their time; that's why your boss is accountable to his or her boss for how *you* prioritize your time. Management graveyards are full of the stymied careers of managers who had been persistently mixed up on this point.

The Chain of Accountability

Granted that what is to someone else's advantage as he or she sees it is a judgment call and is therefore subject to challenge; but the judgment call must nevertheless be made, not just now and then, but often many times a day, day after day. If your boss and you are in disagreement as to what your priorities must be, you are obligated to do your best to persuade him, but only if you know it would be to his or her advantage, as he or she sees it, to see it your way. If you fail in this, his or her priorities must continue to be yours until you succeed.

The foregoing can be summarized in the familiar Golden Rule of Management: "He who has the Gold makes the Rules." Although the imagery of this rule may be outdated, its application is not. In our enlightened industrial society your boss cannot, as in an earlier era, *make* you do anything; but he or she has both the obligation and the power to make you regret that you didn't. Management theoreticians who are contemplating taking an "honest job" for the first time should take note and spread the word!

The organizational climate characterized by the Golden Rule of Management can cause serious time management problems for individual managers who react to it in an amateur fashion. For example:

Although the term *management* has many valid definitions, this one is widely used: "Management is getting things done through others." In this definition, "others" obviously refers to the manager's immediate subordinates. If your boss happens also at this moment to be contemplating this definition, your name will surely come to his mind when his eyes light upon that word "others."

Therefore, if management for your boss is literally getting things done through you, then management for you is bound to become "just one damned thing after another."

Just One Damned Thing after Another

To illustrate this, let us imagine that you are a manager with a few years' experience and who is a product of one of your company's management training programs. In one of those sessions on planning, you learned that the management process consists of planning, organizing, leading, coordinating and controlling. You were given an aphorism to display on your office wall, the familiar, "Plan Your Work, Then Work Your Plan," which no one had gotten worked up about because it seemed so banal. Nor had you gotten around to applying it, simply because you could not count on having enough time free of interruptions to perform the first part, the planning. So what planning you did was on your own time, usually at home.

One Sunday afternoon you were doing that very thing in your living room with the TV set turned to a program you were ignoring. Your spouse was down the street gossiping with the neighbors, your youngsters were up the street doing their "thing," and you were making the most of your solitude to do some planning.

First your mind went quickly through tomorrow's (Monday's) scenario. This was easy, because you had spent the last hour before quitting time on Friday getting organized for Monday. What you ended up with was not a plan for Monday but a very tight *schedule*.

Next your mind scanned the entire week. You knew better than to schedule that far ahead, for Murphy's three famous laws would have made shambles of it. But you did have a tactical plan for getting a number of issues squared away that had been hanging fire for too long. Finally, your mind, like a radar beam, scanned the entire upcoming month. This, you recognize, is long-range planning, in which one can easily lose sight of both the forest and the trees. The scenario you developed emerged only with great effort because you have a low tolerance for ambiguity.

"Plan Your Work, Then Work Your Plan"

Driving to work Monday morning, you quickly reviewed once again your day's schedule, your week's tactical outline and the month's scenario. You entered your office at 8:30 A.M., sat down behind your desk and for last-minute inspiration before you got down to work you took in that aphorism on the opposite wall: "Plan Your Work, Then Work Your Plan." You had already done the first part; you were ready now to dive into the last part.

But there was another person on your company's payroll who had an unquestioned right—without warning or apology—to call you on the phone and knock all your planning into a cocked hat.

It was your boss, and this was how she did it: After she had exchanged pleasantries with you, she informed you that yesterday afternoon she too was sitting in her living room with the TV set on when she got to thinking. Sensing your incredulity, she then lectured you that you did not hold a monopoly on planning and, so as to emphasize the point, she instructed you to take out your pencil and take notes on what you would be doing for the rest of that day, for your week and for the rest of the month!

As you rapidly took down those notes, *your* plans crumbled before your mind's eye and finally wound up in shambles. Your only response was an occasional, "Yes, m'am." This response did not indicate that you were a yes-man, decidedly not! However, it did demonstrate that you were, and still are, a very careful student of history: Whenever your boss wound up with, "Have you got all that straight?" you responded with a final, "Yes, m'am!" and hung up.

You turned in desperation to your secretary and growled, "A day shot to hell, a week in a handbasket and a month all fouled up. She's done it again…!"

But you could get revenge: You called one of your subordinates and after the initial good morning you said, "Joe, yesterday afternoon I was sitting in my living room with the TV turned on, and I got to thinking." Joe burped. He complained about his aching back and exclaimed, "You, too?" With that you launched into the same lecture given you but ten minutes before, and Joe took out his pencil....

When you were through, Joe vented his frustration on an innocent colleague who shared his office and ended up with, "She's done it again...."

Joe, too, decided to get revenge. He dialed Jane, one of his own subordinates. But this time it didn't work, because Jane belonged to a union and didn't have to put up with this sort of thing. Although Joe had the right to tell Jane what to do, Jane had the right to tell Joe where to go.

There will always be some who see in this brief situation comedy confirmation of "the ruthlessness with which the profit-hungry leaders of our industrial society seek to achieve their oft-quoted aim to give ulcers, not to get them." An articulate few have a trendy, pejorative stereotype for this kind of management style. They call it *Theory X*.

A Little Light on Theory X

There is no doubt that this sort of thing can be very disruptive. Surely a day does not go by without the president of at least one of the *Fortune* 500 companies, with a few well-timed and well-placed telephone calls, putting significant segments of his company in administrative turmoil for days, if not for weeks, to come. And should he be derelict in his duty, one or more of his vice presidents will step in the breach and start it at their level. If they fail, general managers will initiate it at theirs and so on. If all else fails, foremen will perpetrate it on their workers.

It would seem that people who perpetrate this sort of thing must be either knaves or fools. The amateur manager is firmly convinced that they are. But that they are neither I can prove by using you, my reader, as my case in point.

Recall the last time you dialed one of your own immediate subordinates: While you were dialing his or her number, you saw him— in your mind's eye—sitting behind his desk, staring at the wall, wondering what to do next. You hoped your call would be just in time to rescue that person from his or her predicament. Your call was benignly motivated; its intent was to help. That's how it looked at *your* end.

This little "sitcom" illustrates what I prefer to call *the paradoxical conflict of roles,* a conflict peculiar to the process of management. When your boss initiates this process by calling you, he or she is playing the role of managER, for he is attempting to get something done through you. Simultaneously, you are playing the role of managEE, the one through whom he or she is attempting to get it done. The skill required to be an effective managEE is quite different from the skill required to be an effective managER. That can explain what has been noted by many competent observers: Few managers are equally effective at both. The professional manager will cultivate his or her skill in both roles, but if he or she desires eventually to reach the top, his or her skill in managEEship will be the decisive one. One of the career-fatal misconceptions of the amateur is that, in order to succeed in management career-wise, it is sufficient just to excel as a managER. This misconception is abetted by two strong influences:

1. The influence of academia whose curricula in management stress the managER role to the virtual exclusion of the managEE role;
2. The influence of this academic perspective on management, which can result in a manager saying to his subordinate managers: "Don't worry about your next raise, your next promotion or your next bonus; just do a good job, and all these things will take care of themselves."

ManagER and ManagEE

The amateur will wake up to the truth one day when he or she loses out on a promotion to a colleague whose track record as managER was far less impressive than his or her own, but whose performance as a managEE—in the eyes of his or her superiors—was more impressive by far.

The professional in management knows that since the conflict between his or her two roles is inherent in their very nature he or she cannot excel in both at the same time in any given circumstance. One will have to yield to the other, and the professional is prepared to make that judgment call when the moment of truth arrives. Fortunately, each role has its day: When you interface with your boss, your role is exclusively that of managEE; when you interface with your subordinates, you are their managER. But in formal company management meetings where managers from several management levels are present, all but one is in the presence of his or her own boss, and all except the lowest ranking are in the presence of their subordinates. This inhibits the "honesty" and "openness" characteristic of informal egalitarian conclaves because each individual is preoccupied with maintaining simultaneously the integrity of both his roles. (The management theorist perceives them as trying to talk out of both sides of their mouths at once!) But both roles are equally essential to the effectiveness of the management process; so the resulting inhibitions are inevitable. Although the amateur is defeated by these inhibitions, the professional deals effectively with them. And, predictably, the utopian management theorist would wish to *eliminate* them! For this purpose he has resorted to a technique that places psychotherapy at the service of social engineering: It is called "sensitivity training." Intruding upon the privacy of the individual consciousness and denying organizational reality, it serves only to break down managER/managEE relationships that have already been resolved to their own satisfaction and to provide "research data" for his arsenal for social change. He persists, however, because he needs to publish his "findings." Since he must publish or perish, we may expect that sensitivity training will continue to nibble at the periphery of corporate life for some time to come.

The "Nut" and "Bolt" of It

Because these two roles are inherently in conflict, neither can prevail without appropriate accommodation by the other. An analogy between the nut and bolt should help here: A bolt cannot achieve the ultimate in self-actualization until it connects with a nut. A nut cannot fully realize its own potential until it connects with a bolt. Now, therefore, if your boss is a lefthand-threaded "bolt" and you are a righthand-threaded "nut," which one of you will get rethreaded? For the amateur this is an experience to be avoided. For the professional it is a necessary means to a desirable end.

The horror story depicted in the "sitcom" on which this discussion is based is admittedly extreme. But we will nevertheless return to it later to show that, although some advocate eliminating such holocausts by bringing its perpetrators (top management) to book through social engineering techniques, history and experience show that the way each manager chooses to play his or her managEE role can have a decisive influence on how the boss chooses to play his or her managER role. (The reverse is also true.) Which role, then, must initiate the process of reducing the disruption? It is the role that is likely to benefit most immediately and directly from reducing it, namely, the managEE role.

Our horror story will have a happy ending only when its victims undertake to change their style of managEEship to one that will elicit an appropriate change in the managER style of its perpetrators. Some may object that this presumes a much higher level of maturity than most people in middle management possess. We don't know; but we do know that without that presumption there would be little challenge.

The ManagEE's Initiative

The initiative for resolving the role conflicts between you and your boss must be yours. The view that it *should* or *ought* to be your boss's initiative may make you wait forever for him or her to take it. This should come as no surprise: Your boss has much less personally riding on his or her relationship with you than you have personally riding on your relationship with your boss.

The art of managEEship will be the subject of a later chapter. Meanwhile, we must move on to the second objective source of your time management problems and the next element of your management molecule—your peers.

YOUR PEERS

Figure 1 on page 47 depicts your management molecule (this term will be defined later) as it will look when completed. We have just positioned your boss as its principal member. Next come your peers.

These we classify as (1) external and (2) internal peers. *Peer* in this context does not necessarily mean equal in status, salary, authority or position; it means only that they do not exercise line authority over you nor you over them. No managER/managEE conflict is inherent, therefore, in your relationships with them. Nevertheless, their initiatives toward you can be just as disruptive of your time.

Your External Peers

If you are a salaried manager in the private sector of the economy, your *external peers* are located in one or more of the following six elements of our society:

1. Customers   4. Labor
2. Investors   5. Government
3. Suppliers   6. Public

If you are a sales manager, most of your external peers are in the customer element; if you are a purchasing agent, most of these are in the supplier segment; if you are a manager of industrial relations, most of them are in the labor element, and so on. But if you are your company's president, all of your external peers are in all six of these elements, but limited to a level comparable to your own. Just as a fish is created for its medium—the sea—and depends upon it absolutely for its survival and growth, so the private corporation is created for this six-part socioeconomic medium and is equally dependent upon it for its survival and growth. Just as your boss's power base in relation to you derives from management's Golden Rule, so the power base from which these six elements influence your company derives from their *sovereignty* in their areas of legitimate concern.

The customer's right to choose what and from whom to buy is the source of his or her sovereignty over the supplier in matters of price, quality and delivery. This sovereignty is not fixed: An adverse economic cycle can create a shortage of suppliers, and the customer's sovereignty will be weakened as a result.

The investor's right to choose among a wide range of investment opportunities makes him or her sovereign over the securities marketplace in matters of quality, yield and performance. Here again an economic upcycle can result in a weakening of the investor's sovereignty through speculative excesses in the securities markets.

The supplier's sovereignty in a competitive economy lies in his or her legal right to enforce purchase agreements. When an adverse turn in the economic cycle "shakes out" the weak suppliers, the survivors enjoy—for a time—a sovereignty over the customer that monopolies normally enjoy.

The labor element derives its sovereignty from the strike weapon and the protection of labor law, although this sovereignty has historically been temporarily weakened from time to time by adverse turns in the economic cycle.

Government derives its sovereignty from its power to tax, regulate and enforce. Its *effective* sovereignty can be significantly affected by the government's budget process, e.g., it can be weakened when there are insufficient funds to carry out these functions adequately.

Finally, the public, through special-interest groups, derive their sovereignty from certain constitutional guarantees (such as freedom of speech, of assembly, etc.) that give them access to the media, access to legislators via organized lobbies, and so on. Their effective sovereignty can be weakened by shortages of funds, competition from other special interests and inscrutable shifts in public opinion. But that American business has learned to respect their sovereignty is by now well established.

Sovereign Power

Sovereign power is why, for instance, a well-timed telephone call from the purchasing agent of a key industrial customer to the cognizant sales manager of its industrial supplier can freeze the latter organization into a state of administrative paralysis for some time before the next thaw sets in. Meanwhile, one can only imagine what will happen to the aphorisms still affixed to the office walls: "Plan Your Work, Then Work Your Plan." They will be fed to the shredder.

How each manager deals with these power bases when he or she is on the receiving end distinguishes the professional from the amateur. For example:

Two area sales managers working for the same company in different parts of the country finished the same working day the same way: Neither had found time to do what he or she had planned to do that day because they had both been interrupted by twenty important, but unanticipated, telephone calls. Manager A, upon returning home for dinner, greeted his or her spouse with, "It was just another one of those days. I did more things today but I still got nothing done. Once that phone started ringing, it was just one interruption after another. One more day like this, and I'm throwing in the towel. Since my boss thinks my job is so important, I'll give it back to him on a platter." Manager B, on arriving home, said, "Honey, this was one of the best days in my career. I received twenty unexpected telephone calls. I wish I could put in a hundred more days in a row like this!"

The difference? You've guessed it. Each one of Manager A's calls was from an irate customer demanding immediate satisfaction or else. Each one of Manager B's calls was from a satisfied (but far from satiated) customer placing a repeat order larger than the last one.

An interruption is not an interruption when it's a *welcome* interruption. And you can tell the amateur sales manager from the professional by what he does between these interruptions, because that will determine the proportion of welcome to unwelcome calls. So who was to blame for Manager A's exhausting and frustrating day? Manager A, of course. And who will get the credit for Manager B's excitingly profitable day? The customer, of course. (Life is not fair, remember?)

With this we will temporarily interrupt our discussion of the external peer element of your molecule until the remaining two elements are in place—your internal peers and your immediate subordinates.

We turn now to the third objective source of your time management problems, your internal peers. *Internal* peers, as opposed to the external peers previously discussed, work within the same overall corporate (or institutional) complex as you do and play a significant role in supporting (and, failing that, in frustrating) your legitimate goal-oriented plans, programs and activities. The term *peer,* as before, connotes not equality but the absence of any managER/managEE "contract" overhanging your relationship with them. Many of them are, of course, your equals by one or more of the criteria we mentioned earlier.

Your Internal Peers

Organizations of any significant size characteristically consist of two complementary parts: (1) The *line* organizations, such as Production and Sales, are responsible for serving directly the purposes for which the enterprise exists; (2) the *support* organizations, such as Property Maintenance, Personnel, Purchasing, Accounting, etc., provide to the line organizations such services and support that would be inefficient or uneconomical for them to provide for themselves. But it is not all that black and white. When the accounting department depends on the personnel department for recruiting, it is in that instance acting in a "line" capacity; the personnel department is acting in a "line" capacity when it depends upon the maintenance department to keep its air conditioning at peak performance.

In what follows, I shall develop an *economic* model of organizational behavior, as opposed to the countless sociological models attempted by behavioral scientists during the past fifty years. I shall do so because (1) behavioral scientists are currently locked in ideological warfare among themselves, the end of which seems nowhere in sight; (2) their preoccupation with "who's right?" is diverting attention from "what's necessary?"; (3) management theoreticians are hovering over the conflict hoping to pull some ideological chestnuts out of the fire; and (4) though no scholar, I understand economics a lot better than I do sociology.

For the sake of the argument that follows, assume that you are the head of one division of your company's Manufacturing Department and that each such division has complete responsibility for and control over its product while it is in production. Your job title is "Manufacturing Superintendent," your boss is "Manager of Manufacturing," and his boss is "Operations Vice President."

Your *internal peers,* located outside your division but within the company, are, but are not limited to, these:

Purchasing	Administrative Services
Personnel	Finance and Accounting
Building Maintenance	Sales
Quality Control	Safety Engineering and Inspection

That's as far as I care to extend the list lest I get into grey areas that might needlessly divert our attention later on. For example, "machine maintenance" does not belong on this list if each division is responsible for maintaining its own equipment; otherwise it does. The list is, in any event, long enough and diverse enough to serve our immediate purpose, because it identifies the sources of most if not all of your internal *system-imposed time.*

The job descriptions of the management positions in the support organizations all contain a statement to this effect: "This organization is responsible for the *supply* of such appropriate and timely support to the using organizations as they may legitimately *demand* from us." Although this statement is about as exciting as your average out-worn platitude, the word "legitimately," requiring as it will countless individual judgment calls every day, will surely liven things up in practice. Nevertheless, when you see those two italicized words in close juxtaposition, you will be reminded at once of a field of vocational endeavor, in which one must have a Ph.D. to qualify, whose practitioners devote their careers to tracking supply and demand. Economics, you say! And those who track these things for the benefit of interested parties are, of course, economists. Most of what follows I have learned from them, although I am about to apply it in a context that they will surely greet with astonishment. If they, in turn, learn something from it, they make take it as partial payment of my indebtedness to them.

Supply and Demand

The administrative process in your company may, therefore, be seen as the *intracompany economic system* through which the organizational resources of the company are allocated and reallocated according to the highly volatile changes in the need for and the availability of those resources. There are similarities and differences between the intracompany economic system and the private sector economic system of which it is my intended analogy. So first to the similarities:

They both require legal tender, e.g., some kind of form properly filled out and authenticated, which legitimizes the transaction. Although in the private sector economy this is usually a coin or greenback of some denomination, in the intracompany economy it is something else. In either case, possession is a boon—and nonpossession is a frustration—to those in desperate need. Let's see how it works:

Your secretary eloped without notice and you ask Personnel to recruit a replacement. Instead, they give you a form called a Personnel Action Request to fill out.

Your chair is broken down beyond repair and there are no replacements in stock. You ask Purchasing to buy another. Instead, they'll give you a form to fill out, called a Purchase Request.

It's August in Houston and your air conditioning has broken down. You ask Building Maintenance to fix it. Instead they give you a Maintenance Service Request to fill out.

The Intracompany Economic System

The Bible asks, "If a man asks you for a loaf, will you give him a stone?" The answer is yes, if your job is in Personnel, Purchasing or Maintenance! Not only that, but the forms, printed in pad form on $8\frac{1}{2}'' \times 11''$ stock, must be made out in triplicate, with nineteen numbered spaces to be filled in, and at least three authorizing signatures in addition to your own.

By contrast in the private economy you can satisfy your need for an aspirin by going to the drug store, where such things are in supply. You ask the clerk for a bottle of aspirin. There will be a slight pause until you have handed over the required form, properly filled out and complete with all authorizing signatures. The form is called a "greenback" and is supplied in fully executed form by the U.S. Bureau of Printing and Engraving. It is small enough to be conveniently carried in a wallet, purse or billclip, and only one copy per transaction is required. So you get your aspirin *almost* as soon as you ask for it.

This is because the private sector cannot survive the kinds of delays in legitimizing transactions that are endemic to intracompany economics. If the legal tender printed by the Bureau of Printing and Engraving even approximated the counterparts furnished to intracompany economic systems by their internal "support" organizations, it would create such a drag on the private sector economy that the effect on the Gross National Product (GNP) would be disastrous. Since corporations do not track the Gross Management Product (GMP) of their intracompany economic systems, the stern warning of an ancient adage cries out: "The trend that is not being watched will not be acted upon...."

Now to the differences. There are two that are relevant to our purpose: monopolization and undercapitalization. Both are explained below.

1. The first difference is that whereas the private sector economy is competitive, the intracompany economy is monopolistic. In the former, suppliers are competing with each other for customers' patronage, using as their legitimate weapons price, quality and delivery, and as their scorecard, share of market. In the latter, the "user" organizations are competing with each other for the resources "cornered" by the administrative monopolies, using as their legitimate weapons their company's centrally controlled priority schedules and budgets, and as their scorecard their share of the monopolized supply. Your Personnel Department does indeed have a corner on the intracompany market for personnel services: Just try in any well-managed company to exercise your free market choice and circumvent Personnel by hiring directly off the street better-qualified people than they could find (such as your nephews, nieces, brothers-in-law, etc.) and see what happens to you!

What share, then, of the intracompany personnel services market do your personnel administrators already enjoy before they even go to work each morning? One hundred percent. And if you can get 100 percent enjoyment out of your job before going to work, why bother to go?

Administrative Monopolies

That applies equally to the other administrative monopolies as well and helps explain why they appear not to be motivated by the high sense of urgency more characteristic of the using organizations, particularly Production and Sales. If one's share of market is not affected by anything one does or doesn't do, the only motivation left is to keep from losing all of it in one fell swoop, which is what happens when one is fired. But as of this writing, no personnel person has to my knowledge ever been fired solely for incompetence. There is too much security in monopoly for that to happen.

This puts the burden on the users to compete vigorously among themselves for their "fair share" of the resources controlled by the monopoly suppliers. Since what is one's "fair share" depends upon whom you ask, some will be accused of ending up with more, and others will complain of ending up with less, than their fair share. This competition results in the misallocation of resources in spite of the company's centrally promulgated priority systems and alloction policies which are designed to prevent that. But those systems and policies cannot respond swiftly and flexibly enough. Historically such monopolistic systems in *national* economies have relied on corruption to do their work for them. That kind of corruption involves the illegal use of free market economics to keep the official system from paralyzing itself. The state-monopolized economies of the so-called iron-curtain countries are modern examples of the vital role that corruption plays in maintaining their day-to-day viability.

"Corruption" plays the same indispensable role in your own *intracompany* monopolistic economic system. It is the "you scratch my back, and I'll scratch yours" technique familiar to us all. Without it, the quick shifts in the allocation of organizational resources necessitated by the sudden and tentative shifts in priorities and urgencies could not be effected. Centralized allocation mechanisms cannot respond with the required alacrity and precision. Fortunately, the intracompany equivalent of corruption is neither illegal nor proscribed; indeed, it is encouraged by noncommital company policy, and it is never made a moral issue, except occasionally by those who habitually end up in the "have not" column. But that is to be expected. "You scratch my back, and I'll scratch yours" will continue to be both a legitimate and an indispensable form of corruption as long as intracompany economic systems continue in their present monopolistic form.

But consider the alternative, the hypothetical scenario in which the monopolistic system is dismantled. This could be done by converting the present system of administrative resource allocation into a free-market, competitive, intracompany economic system. The first step would be to hire a brand-new MBA, and appoint him or her as a special assistant to the president with the following title: Intracompany Department of Justice. Armed with an administrative meat cleaver, he or she would hack apart the monopolies of Personnel, Accounting, Maintenance, Purchasing and so on so as to force them to compete. It would not be enough to break them up into two of each; it would have to be at least three of each. Two would surely collude, thus defeating the purpose of the break-up. But a third could not resist the opportunity to divide and conquer the other two, so competition would be assured. Soon a stable system of three or more competitors would be established in each "market."

The Alternative to Administrative Monopolies

A reward system would then be established that would provide the necessary motivation to compete. The tried-and-true system for this market share, which would be computed—say weekly—for each identified market. This would be quite feasible with the ability of modern computer technology to track, compute and display the supply-demand transactions as they are executed and documented within each market. The weekly "market share" of each of the three or more competitors plotted as a trend would replace the current performance appraisal system so far as the support organizations were concerned. The using organizations would be free to choose which Accounting Department, for example, they wanted to deal with and would make this choice on the basis of their own organizational self-interest as they saw it at the time. The particular Accounting Department that, at year-end, had the largest "share" of the accounting services "market" would be undeniably the one that best met the users' needs as they saw it, and it would be justly rewarded with a whopping bonus from the corporate treasury. I'll let your imagination extend this scenario into the "markets" serviced by Personnel, Maintenance, Administrative Services, Purchasing and so on. The effect of such an economic system on your company's Gross Management Product (GMP) would be dramatic.

Whereas in former days of monopoly you would call Accounting for some figures and get this reply, "We're short-handed, so we only compute those figures once a week; call us Friday," now in the new competitive environment, you would get those figures at once even if Accounting had to turn the department inside out to find them. After all, you would now have a choice; two or more other Accounting Departments would already be making proposals to get your business.

Hard to imagine? Sadly, yes. Accountants are not trained to be of service; they are trained to get the goods on whomever they can. Any company that switched over to an intracompany market economy of this description would be faced with a wholesale exodus of its CPAs in search of the *job security* provided by monopoly. A few would remain, namely, those who would be challenged by the *career security* available to those who could successfully compete. Thus would be born the accounting profession of the future. Will we have to wait for this until hell freezes over? That depends on whom you ask. Any CPA will answer with a hopeful "Yes."

I leave it to you to think through the changes that would thus be wrought in the other intracompany service markets and the impact these changes would have upon the affected careers. Most important, imagine by what factor the Gross Management Product (GMP) would rise. My own imagination fails me; it is soon paralyzed in the awesome contemplation of the infinite.

During my years as a management consultant, I have never overlooked an opportunity to try to sell this concept to presidents of companies large and small, but without success. They have rationalized their disinterest by pointing to the unacceptable overhead cost of my proposed competitive system. On a three-for-one break-up basis, the overhead payroll would have to triple, floor space would triple, office furniture and equipment would triple and so on, but the markets to be served would still be the same size. When I emphasized that the incalculable factor by which the GMP would rise would make even the increased costs a bargain of a lifetime, they repeated "Ridiculous!" I could not understand their blindness to the greatest breakthrough of the century in management technique, until my wife opened my eyes: "Greatness," she said, "is rarely recognized *during* a man's lifetime."

For your own career-planning purposes you must, therefore, without anger or resentment, learn how to make the most of the system you are going to have to live with for the rest of your management career—the monopolistic intracompany economic system—which is the internal source of your system-imposed time. So let us proceed now to the second of the two differences between the private sector economy and the intracompany economic system.

2. The second difference is that the intracompany system is characteristically and uniformly undercapitalized, e.g., the support organizations are normally understaffed and underbudgeted in relation to the legitimate demands for their services that the using organizations press upon them if they are to meet their goals.

Undercapitalized Monopolies

Every business school textbook on organizational structure deals with the principal of *organizational balance*, which simply states the obvious—that the support organizations must be staffed and budgeted at a level adequate to the legitimate demands of the line (and other "using") organizations. Ratios are adduced as rules of thumb, such as the "personnel ratio," which for manufacturing industry is about 120:1. Other ratios have been researched that vary from industry to industry, and within an industry from support function to support function. Thus, it is possible for an MBA on his first job to calculate easily the "ideal" staffing ratios for his own company. It follows that lack of knowledge cannot be the reason that most companies are content to live with staffing ratios far below their scientifically validated ideals. There is, as you may expect, a very sound reason why they do, especially if they have to sell in unregulated, competitive markets. For example:

Five companies are selling similar products in the same markets. Their products are price competitive. For argument's sake, assume that their organizational structures are almost identical since they follow the industry pattern, and that they all budget and staff their internal support organizations at the ideal ratios furnished them by their industry association. From a competitive standpoint they are now even with each other so far as their administrative overhead costs are concerned. One of them suddenly decides to increase its share of the existing market (at the expense, naturally, of its four competitors) by significantly cutting prices. Since it is a high volume, low mark-up product line, any meaningful price cut will have to be paid for by cutting budgets elsewhere in the company. Some maintenance can be deferred, value engineering programs in Purchasing can be shelved and so on, with no short-term adverse consequences. But manufacturing and sales budgets will be untouched because that is where the *near-term* profits are to be made. The four competitors will react to this by doing likewise and the customers will start having a field day. But the new MBA will shake his head in discouragement. He had done a great piece of work for top management in arriving at the ideal staffing ratios only to see the results of his labor hauled away with the trash.

It is quite a different story, however, in private companies enjoying local or regional monopolies, such as telephone companies and electric utilities, whose prices are not controlled by classic market forces. Instead, they must be controlled by appropriate government regulatory agencies. Since such agencies are awed by "studies" by competent "authorities," they accept the recommended ideal staffing and budget ratios as the basis for establishing the allowable cost of administrative overhead. Nevertheless, the regulatory agencies rarely grant utilities price levels adequate to the reasonable requirements of their intermediate and long-term plans, so to raise the cash differential, utilities tend to abandon ideal staffing and budgeting patterns until the next rate hearings.

Government agencies, too, are forced to understaff and under-budget their internal support units, but for a reason peculiar to the nature of government itself. Congress, for whatever reason, follows a legislative process that has two parts separated in time. The first is authorization for the agency to carry out certain policies, projects and programs, and the other is authorization for it to spend a specified amount of money in carrying them out. Typically, the money voted in the second part is inadequate to the tasks mandated in the first part. So here we go again!

There is a third aspect of staff or support departments besides their being monopolistic and undercapitalized. That is their need for self-preservation. It is common among the advice-giving departments like Personnel, Marketing-communications, Staff-development, and Finance that they exist only to deliver advice to the Line; they are typically "ways-of-doing-it-better" departments. Because they don't hold the key to physical inventory like, say, the store's department, they must either sell their advice or create a monopoly for it through intracompany legislation. It is common for these departments to seek protection through legislation. If you are in the business of giving advice to the Line about, say, advertising, your self-preservation need will be better served if you hold the right to approve the business manager's program. If you are in the business of advising on hiring decisions, you will be much more secure if the Line is forced through an administrative procedure that requires your involvement. The fact that these departments exist makes them want to do something. The net result is often control and interference with the Line, more administrivia. The Line lacks the authority to proceed without them.

The origins of this phenomenon lie with the misplaced delegation of authority on the part of the CEO to the Staff departments. Because they act with the authority of the CEO, they can build their empires and conduct their guerrilla raids into the Line at all levels under the protection of "HE wants it this way." There is a solution; instead of creating a staff department to act with the authority of the CEO, the CEO instead builds Staff advice into his policies set for the Line. Then instead of the business manager sending his suggested ad campaign to the Advertising department for approval, he interprets the Company advertising policy and acts within or without it according to his judgment and career orientation. The Advertising department would then advise the CEO on how well the Business Manager is doing. The net result is that the Business Manager actively seeks Advertising's help—*if* he gets quality advice. The correct role of "how-to-do-it-better" departments is to so influence the CEO that he builds appropriate goals for the Line out of their advice. These departments no longer try to give advice to the Line as their primary objective but, rather, help the CEO in measuring the Line in the activity. In days of old, military generals employed Staff for exactly that purpose—to give advice to the general so that he could better measure his commanders.

This chapter is equally applicable to managers in the private sector and in government agencies.

To summarize briefly:

Comparisons	Private Sector	Intracompany
Medium of Exchange	Legal Tender	Official Red Tape
Structure	Competitive	Monopolistic
Viability	Adequately Capitalized	Undercapitalized

Doing Business, Intracompany

With this summary in mind, let us return to you in your position as Superintendent of Production. You suddenly develop a requirement for six Type "Y" castings to be delivered to the receiving dock outside your shop by 9:00 A.M. Monday morning. You fill out the proper Purchase Request in the prescribed number of copies, obtain the required additional authorizing signatures and hand-carry it over to the Purchasing Department. For this transaction to have been worth the cost to you in time and effort, those castings will have to be (1) *what* you want (not Type "X" or "Z"), (2) *where* you want it (*not* at your sister plant 150 miles to the east of you) and (3) *when* you want it (*not* at 9:00 A.M. Thursday morning). This all-or-nothing requirement we'll call, for short, a "three-point landing." And it *is* an all-or-nothing requirement. A two-point landing (e.g., where you want it, when you want it but not *what* you want) is no better than nothing. The same can be said for the two other two-point landing combinations. One-point landings (what you want but delivered to the wrong plant three days late) are worse than nothing. And what abut "flyovers"? Words fail! One of the mottos on your office wall is apropos: "Better to do something than to make something into nothing" (from an old Chinese proverb). So what are the odds that you will get a three-point landing on this transaction? In what follows we will examine just what creates those odds.

The people working in all the internal support organizations are as proud of their work, as jealous of their reputations and as concerned about being effective as anyone else is, including those working in Production and Sales. Since they are undercapitalized, the demands placed upon them by user organizations far exceed their capacity to respond with three-point landings *every time*. Since they are a monopoly, they cannot rely on competition to absorb the excess demand. They accept as inevitable a performance standard of something less than perfection, e.g., a ratio of the number of "three-point landings" to the total number of "take-offs" within, say, any thirty-day period. They can influence that ratio by (1) influencing the number of such requests actually logged in any thirty-day period, and (2) influencing the type of request logged in. As to the first, the fewer they log in, the more time and attention they can give to the ones they do log in, thus raising the odds that each one will deliver a three-point landing to the user. As to the second, the less prone the Purchasing Request is to a *less*-than-three-point landing the better the odds in the user's favor; it follows that discouraging those Purchase Requests that smell like "lemons" will raise the odds in the user's favor. In other words, when demand for administrative support exceeds its supply, something has to give. In the competitive private sector economy, when supply and demand get out of balance, there is a mechanism inherent in the free marketplace that restores the balance. It is the pricing function of the marketplace to maintain that balance. So, too, in the intracompany economy. In that context "price" is the nature, number, complexity and denominations of the administrative transactions (e.g., red tape) required that constitutes the "cost" to the user. All these things translate into time and "hassle" that has to be expended by the user before the support department will commit itself to starting the ball rolling. (By "denomination" we mean the organizational level from which authorization must be obtained.) This cost to the user can be rapidly increased by adding complexity to the red tape, increasing the required number of transactions and tacking on bits of time- and energy-consuming administrivia. As the cost thus increases, marginal demand begins to disappear. As demand continues to fall off, a level of demand is reached that the support organization can service with an acceptably high performance standard for three-point landings. But what about the demand that was discouraged to the point that it was not serviced at all? Was not the company damaged thereby? Absolutely not. The users in question decided that the value of the requested support service in those specific instances would not be sufficient to justify the cost in time and hassle, so they made do with "bailing wire and twine" instead. This is managerial innovation at its best. Don't knock it.

The Cost of Doing Business, Intracompany

The actual mechanism of administrative price raising is sometimes so subtle as to elude all but the most experienced and sophisticated eyes. For example, fifteen minutes before closing time the phone rings in the Purchasing Department and the voice at the other end calls in a verbal purchase request. The purchasing employee, hearing what's being ordered, senses a possible "lemon" (e.g., a potential "flyover") that she would have to analyze before deciding to officially log it in. That would take at least thirty more minutes and her car pool leaves in twenty minutes. So the response is, "I'll have to have that in writing." Did you see the price go up? The following Monday the request did arrive—in writing. The employee noting again that the request was flyover prone went over it with a fine-toothed comb. Face brightening up, the puchasing employee mailed the request back to the originator with a handwritten note: "Box 18 on Form 4269A contains the wrong authorization number." On Tuesday morning the originator of the request, immediately upon reading this, calls the purchasing employee and asks, "What *is* the right authorization number?" To which the employee responds, "Our job is to spot the *wrong* ones; your job is to find the *right* ones." The price is soaring! The originator will soon find some other, more innovative way to do what he or she wants to do; the company will benefit; and Purchasing will have avoided a commitment that undoubtedly would have hurt its three-point landing record.

In all fairness to the Purchasing managers who read this and to those managers of Personnel, Maintenance, Accounting, etc., who also will read this, let me say that it is not my intention in any way to demean your role in the eyes of the line organizations. If they, by a quirk of fate had made their careers alongside you in the support functions of business, they would be doing the same things you do and for the same overriding reason, namely, career survival. My purpose has been to get them to understand why you must do many of things you do, which to them may often have appeared wastefully bureaucratic if not wantonly obstructive.

Nor do I imply that the price-raising mechanism I have described is done *consciously* by the support organizations in order to discourage demand. Normally when demand becomes excessive, it has a disorganizing effect on the support organization; this results in a campaign to "create order out of chaos" and to "police up" the administrative procedures. The effect is nevertheless the same: to raise the cost to the user and thereby discourage the demand. The pricing mechanism I have described is valid; it matters little what human motives impel it to perform its appointed function.

Intracompany Regulation

There is, however, a limit to how high prices can safely go. The limit has been reached when the using organizations go over the head of an offending support organization and complain to top management about "that smug, inertia-ridden fiefdom that acts as if the rest of the company owes it a living." Top management will now act to control prices just as the federal government does in dealing with monopolies: regulation. Top management's way of doing this is to institute a work-simplification program within the offending support organization and thus to get prices down once again to an affordable level. When the program is completed, demand will rise again to meet the lowered price. Sooner or later prices will rise again to meet the higher demand, but this time not quite high enough to invite another work-simplification program!

A substantial portion of your internal system-imposed time is your "cost of doing business" in the intracompany economic system. But it is good only for cash-in-advance transactions (i.e., pay now, fly later). What with the limitation of the pro-forma forty-hour work week, few line managers have anything like enough "cash" to set in motion even the minimum support they require from the intracompany economy. The professionals know what to do about this, the amateurs do not: It is to maximize one's intracompany credit rating (i.e., fly now, pay later). We will expand upon this in a later chapter.

Doing the Impossible

Meanwhile, a ray of sunshine in this discussion of the "dismal science" (an appellation once attached to classical economics by the ideological ancestors of today's social theorists): The support organization *can* do the impossible for the using organizations any time they want to. The trick is to get them to want to. And by the "impossible" I mean anything that would be impossible for them to do for you but which they could do for themselves with little effort. Two examples should suffice:

1. During a summer heatwave your office air conditioning breaks down. You put in a formal Maintenance Service Request. Four days later with nothing happening you call Maintenance and ask them, "How about it?" They reply that they put in the work order as soon as they received your request but, the weather being what it is, there are thirty-eight requests ahead of yours. You then ask them for an estimate. "Three weeks at the earliest," is the reply. You counter with, "Let's compromise: How abut twenty-four hours?" "Impossible!" they answer, hanging up. Impossible, indeed! At that very moment the room air conditioner in the office of the head of Maintenance Department broke down. I will leave you to estimate for yourself how long it took *that* work order to produce its intended result!

2. A manager entered the recruiting section of the company's Personnel Department with a Personnel Action Request for the recruitment of a replacement for her secretary, who had recently quit to take another job. Getting little response to her sense of urgency, she went over the recruiter's head into the Personnel Director's office asking for top priority handling of the request. Trying to be accommodating, the Personnel Director asked what the qualifications requirements were. "The same as for the one I am replacing, but with one important difference. This time the candidate must be a stunning beauty to meet the added job requirement that she represent us to the public." Throwing up his hands, the Personnel Director exclaimed, "That's impossible. Women who meet that requirement are in such demand that there are none left in the labor market." The manager threw in the towel and on her way out passed three Personnel Department employees, each of whom was a stunning beauty. Running back into the Personnel Director's office, she shouted, pointing to the three employees, "What about *them*?" The Personnel Director replied, "They just prove my point: they were the last three on the labor market."

So they *can* do the impossible—for themselves. They would do it for you, too, but The School of Hard Knocks has taught them that they will regret it if they do. In the past when they did it for the amateur manager, he or she had taken it for granted. "That's what you get paid for," they were told. Subsequently, the amateur would cite it as a binding precedent for repeated "impossible" tasks until they finally had to drop the amateur's intracompany credit rating to a level at which even the "possible" wouldn't be worth the hassle.

So the next time you, as a professional, are able to get a support element of your molecule to do the impossible for you, don't let the secret get out; if it does some other manager will pounce on the opportunity to demand *equal treatment* and your credit rating as well as his will plummet. "There are times," said Benjamin Franklin's grandfather, "when the less said, the better." He had it *almost* right!

YOUR SUBORDINATES

The fourth and final objective source of your time management problems is your subordinates. They have as much power to turn your day into "just one damned thing after another" as do your boss, your external peers or your internal peers. They do not derive their power from the Golden Rule of Management as your boss does, for nowhere does it say in their job descriptions that they are responsible for recruiting and hiring your eventual successor, or for executing your annual performance reviews, or for recommending you for a termination or for a raise. Those are strictly Golden Rule prerogatives. Nor do they have access to the power of an external sovereign force in our society—the labor movement—for as managers they had long since exchanged the job security associated with an honest day's work for a fair day's pay for the career security associated with their own managerial judgment and influence. Nor do any of them enjoy a monopoly on judgment and influence. Any one of your subordinates who feels that he or she is irreplaceable is, at least on that score, an amateur sorely lacking in humility. It would be in that person's enlightened self-interest to visit during next lunch hour the nearest graveyard to study the epitaphs of those who deemed themselves irreplaceable shortly before they expired. What is, then, the power base they possess that enables them—intentionally or not—to throw your day out of control?

They have the *ball* and are running with it right now. How they run with it and where they take it could do you credit or could do you in. You and they both know this, and this mutual awareness is an important ingredient of the managER/managEE role conflict discussed earlier. It is how they play their managEE role that determines how much of your day will be consumed in subordinate-imposed time. Those who practice amateur managEEship will create an excessive drain on your time because the "needle" will be pointing up; those who practice it professionally will create for you virtually no subordinate-imposed time; the "needle" will be pointing down, as it should be. The extreme form of the upward-pointing needle is, of coure, the wanton act of insubordination; however, most up-needle situations are well within the bounds imposed by the conventional norms of compliance and conformity and are, therefore, both morally and ethically correct.

Their subtly lies in the fact that there is no theoretical organizational model that legitimizes the upward-pointing needle. To illustrate this source of subordinate-imposed time I shall give two examples, both involving subtle amateurish manag*EE* behavior.

Suppose that one of your subordinates, Ruth, has never during the five years since you hired her done anything you wanted her to do that she did not want to do. This has been a source of acute frustration to you. Moreover, she has successfully thwarted all your attempts to fire her by avoiding any overt act of insubordination. Your company policy does permit firings for cause, but only with complete and accurate documentation of the supporting facts. So she has had you over a barrel. (It should be added that anything you have wanted her to do that she wanted to do she did superbly; but that, obviously, is not what you have wanted to fire her for.)

She has been, moreover, a more thorough student of your strengths and weaknesses than you have been of hers, which puts you at a disadvantage in dealing with her. But never mind; all managERs suffer this disadvantage vis á vis their managEEs since each managEE has only one boss to study, but the boss has many managEEs to study. As you might therefore expect, she has found your Achilles' heel, and you are still looking for hers.

The ManagER's Achilles' Heel

Your Achilles' heel is that you delegate very broadly and are generally unfamiliar with your subordinates' day-to-day workloads. This does not *have* to be a managER's Achilles' heel, but since you are an amateur, you have allowed it to become yours. Let us watch her take advantage of it:

You call her into your office and say, "Ruth, here is an important responsibility I want you to take over. You are just the person to handle it." She replies, "I am gratified by the confidence in me that this implies. Since I'm putting in full time keeping my present show on the road, something will have to give. Just tell me what you want me to stop doing, and I'll take it on."

Since you haven't the faintest notion of what she is doing, she has you stymied. You would be embarrassed to admit to her openly that you, her managER, are unable to answer. So you mentally debate the use of one of two possible dodges: (1) You might say to her, "I'm so glad you asked that. I could tell you, of course, but I think it would be better if I got some input from you first. Draw up a chair and let's list on a pad what you are involved in." But this could take hours, time you don't have. Or (2) you could say to her, "How should I know? It's your job. You figure it out. But it had better be right." But this would be in violation of what you were taught in the company's management-training course, where it was drilled into you that it is the supervisor's responsibility to define for each subordinate his or her duties, responsibilities, authorities and priorities as well as exactly what is expected of him or her, so that come the annual performance evaluation, fairness and justice will prevail.

Just as she knew you would, you replied, "On second thought, forget it; I'll handle it myself."

As she triumphantly leaves your office, you murmur to yourself, "There goes the most compliant subordinate I have ever had. She obeys my every command. And she will obey to the letter the one I just gave her, namely, *forget it.*"

And where does that leave you? The victim of an up-needle with an untold number of hours of subordinate-imposed time you had not planned on. Your plan for that week has been shot.

When Is Insubordination Not Insubordination?

This story with Ruth would have been quite different had you been a different kind of person. But that would not have cramped Ruth's style. It would only have meant to her that your Achilles' heel would have been a different one, calling for an appropriately different tactic on her part. But the outcome—the up-needle—would have been the same.

For my second example I'll replay the encounter between you and Ruth, but this time your Achilles' heel is that you keep yourself constantly abreast of everything that is going on, even to the smallest details of your subordinates' jobs. Once again this would not *necessarily* be a manager's Achilles' heel, but amateur that you are, you have allowed it to become yours. After calling her into your office and announcing that you are giving her the added responsibility and after she responds with, "So what do you want me to stop doing so I can take this on?" you reply, "I'm so glad you asked. Take this down: I want you to stop doing the following three things." When you have finished a detailed description of them, she looks up at you and says, "How bad do you want me to stop doing these things?" You reply, "I want you to stop doing them real bad—the new responsibility I am giving you has the highest urgency." "That's all I wanted to know," she replies as she leaves your office.

When she gets back to her desk, she calls an emergency meeting of her five subordinates and announces, "The Chief has decided that we are going to stop at once doing the following three things—get your pencils out and take this down." When she finishes, her five one-feather Indians ask in chorus, "How bad does the Chief want us to stop doing these things?" "Real bad," she replies. And five lusty voices shout back, "Whenever the Chief wants something real bad, that's exactly how he is bound to get it." And it isn't long before you start getting it—real bad. You begin receiving phone calls from peers who are complaining that your organization is no longer responsive to them, that your people are putting them off with disclaimers such as, "The Chief has discontinued that," or "Our priorities have been changed on us; call back in a couple of weeks," or "You'll have to clear that with the Chief—there is nothing we can do," etc. Poison pen memoranda are arriving via the interoffice mail from peers telling you of the havoc being caused by your policy and priority changes. And by the third day your office looks and sounds like the information counter at a busy airport all of whose out-bound flights have just been cancelled. The administrative structure you have spent years building, nurturing and fine-tuning is now rocking on its foundation, and within a week it collapses before your very eyes.

After the smoke clears away the five one-feather Indians poke their heads gingerly up through the debris and, like little weather vanes, survey the landscape. "My, my," they exclaim. "What a way to run a railroad. But don't look at us—we only work here. It was the Chief's doing: This is what he wanted and this is what he got. But if he had asked us ahead of time, we could have told him that this is what would have happened!" And that would not have been a prediction, but a promise, because they made it happen that way.

If you want to teach your boss never again to order you to do anything you don't want to do, just carry out his next order to the letter, deviating not an iota, suspending both your judgment and your influence. This technique is known as "vicious compliance," and can be practiced with the highest order of career impunity.

This is another dramatic instance of the up-needle phenomenon, the principal source of subordinate-imposed time. The professional manager knows how to stay clear of it; the amateur allows himself to be engulfed by it.

THE MANAGEMENT MOLECULE
AS ASSET OR LIABILITY

Figure 1 shows a circle drawn through the four objective sources of your time management problems. If you spend most of your management time *reacting* to these sources, you will lose control of the timing and content of most of what you do. Their judgment and influence— and not your own—will be shaping your career; for no matter how competent your job performance in other respects, you will inevitably join the company of the also-rans in management whose annual performance reviews carry this typical comment: "John Doe is doing a good job, but..." What is said after the "but" is bound to carry more weight with top management than what is said before the "but," especially when promotions and raises are being decided upon.

The four elements on the periphery of the circle are your managerial *resources.* They have, in return, the prerogative of making certain legitimate claims upon your time. It is in their role as *claimants* that they create your principal time management problems. We will refer to Figure 1 as your *management molecule,* after its familiar chemical analogy.

MOLECULE OF MANAGEMENT

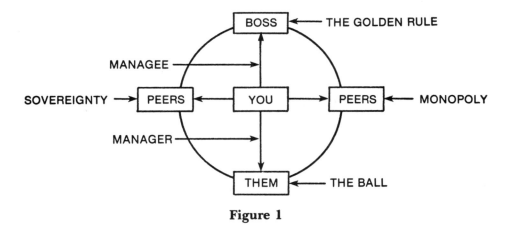

Figure 1

Chemists define the molecule as the "smallest chemical unit of a substance that is capable of stable independent existence." For example take water: It is wet. The smallest possible piece of water is one that, if you divide it further, is no longer wet but becomes instead two dry gases—hydrogen and oxygen. The piece of water that preceded this result is called a *molecule.*

The management molecule is likewise "the smallest piece into which management can be divided that still possesses all the properties of the parent substance." Let's see if it meets the molecular test by dividing it further: If you chop your boss off, you are now in business for yourself and must arrange for your own financing. The property of *accountability* has been lost, so you are no longer *in* management. If you cut off your subordinates—both direct and indirect—you lose your line and/or staff *authority* with no hope of gaining leverage. So again, you are not in management. If you cut off your internal peers you will be like a lone quarterback trying to play football on a vacant field. Since you are not part of a team, there is no allocation and coordination of *responsibility* and so you are not in management. And if the external peers are lopped off, they can "lop" you off in response and the game will be over! (Their sovereignty is not to be trifled with, remember?)

Now look at Figure 2. Your boss is shown to be in the middle of his own molecule just as you are in the middle of your own and just as your subordinates are in the middle of theirs. Those in the middle are known as "nuclei." Your boss is the principal member of your molecule, just as you are the principal member of your subordinates' molecules. You are at the bottom of your boss's molecule just as your subordinates are at the bottom of yours. Some of your peers work directly for some of your boss's peers and/or supervise directly some of your subordinates' peers. Your peers, likewise, are nuclei of molecules of their own, and you occupy a peer position on many of those molecules as well. The internal dynamics of each and every molecule at all organizational levels is governed by exactly the same laws, except the one at the top, which does not have the internal peer element, and the many at the very bottom, which do not have the subordinate element. But the other three elements in each case are nevertheless very much intact. This, then, is a representation of the *molecular* structure of your company's organization. It is not intended to replace or to be an alternative to the formal organization chart. What the human skeleton is to the human organism, the organization chart is to the management organism. What we are describing, then, is the molecular structure of the management organism.

This means that the proper point of departure in the study of the practice of management is the molecule, and it must begin with the nucleus—not just with any nucleus, but the nucleus of your own molecule, namely you. For your subordinates it must begin with each of

MOLECULES OF MANAGEMENT

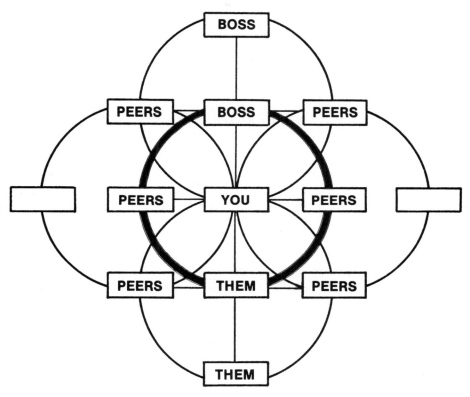

Figure 2

them. Likewise for the president of your company. What all of this means, finally, is that to succeed in the professional practice of management one must accept full responsibility for one's own managerial career, and be of whatever assistance one can to others who accept full responsibility for theirs. It is the mark of the amateurs in management that they hold their company responsible—in whole or in part—for the development of their careers; or worse still, for the adverse career consequences of their own failures in judgment or influence. The professional knows that although opportunities may abound, they carry no guarantees.

Your present molecule can be either the principal liability or the principal asset to your management career. Whichever it turns out to be depends wholly upon the kinds of initiatives you take (or fail to take) with respect to it.

Your Molecule as a Liability

Public opinion today accepts as legitimate at least the following three reasons for dismissing an employee or manager: (1) illegal, immoral or unethical behavior, (2) economic necessity (i.e., the layoff) and (3) failure to perform up to expectations. The individual can control the first but not the second. But what about the third? The answer to that is different for the manager from what it is for the worker.

To illustrate, suppose that your boss has decided, for whatever reason, to fire you. Since your behavior has been morally and legally impeccable he cannot use reason (1); the company is prospering, so he cannot use reason (2); you are performing well above expectation so he cannot use reason (3). But he also knows that your performance is critically dependent on two things: (1) your competence and (2) the support you get from the members of your molecule. The loss of either one would be fatal to your job performance. Since he can do nothing to weaken your competence, he is left only with the possibility of weakening your molecular support.

He therefore calls a meeting at his home on a Friday evening (it would not be prudent to hold such a meeting at the office during regular hours, as we shall see) to which he invites your subordinates, a half dozen of your internal peers on whom you depend for 80 percent of the internal support you value most, and eight or nine key purchasing agents of the companies who give you, your company's regional sales manager, 80 percent of the business you value most. He opens the meeting: "I have called you together to help me achieve an objective, which is to fire John Doe (you). As John is an honest, clean, upstanding citizen, his job will be budgeted for as far ahead as I can see, and his performance is exceeding our expectations. If I were not a man of high moral and ethical standards, I would invent some plausible pretext for firing him, but it would be a dishonorable act and bring discredit upon the company. I am therefore asking you to assist me in bringing about a state of affairs that would make the dismissal of John morally and ethically beyond reproach." Here follows the response:

Internal Peers: "We'll be happy to help, but we will not compromise our performance standards for such a purpose. Shorthanded as we are, we are still meeting our standard of more than 40 percent three-point landings and less than 20 percent fly-overs and plan to continue to meet it. However, we have much discretion as to how that 20 percent is distributed among the using organizations. So, until we hear from you to the contrary, the fly-overs and as many one-point and two-points as may be necessary will be concentrated in John Doe's area."

External Peers: "We will cancel all orders outstanding and place a stop on all repeat orders. Your competitors will close the gap."

Subordinates: "We'd be glad to help, too, but not if we have to compromise our own performance standards. No one bats a thousand, but we do bat better than 500 in carrying out John's orders, meaning that half the time we execute them precisely and half the time we screw them up in execution. We won't change that. But from now on whenever he makes a bad decision, we will execute it with precision, and whenever he makes a good one (which is half the time) we will screw it up in execution."

How long would it take for your performance record, which your company documents weekly, to go into a steep dive? Neither the credentials listed on your résumé, nor your enviable past track record, nor your high score on the Sales Management Aptitude Test, could save you now. They will be of value only for getting your next job, not for keeping this one.

Perhaps some of my readers are beginning now to suspect why their own managerial performance may recently have been slipping. A possible molecular conspiracy, no less?

Relax. This can never happen to *you*. Since the beginning of the Industrial Revolution, the people who populate individual molecular orbits have never been able to get together on anything! And that's what saves you. But no doubt there are a few paranoids in your company who are egotistical enough to believe that there exist many responsible and mature managers who would consider them worth the time, the effort and the cost of such a conspiracy! And there will always be a cynical also-ran lurking in the shadows to whisper in their ears that "corporate greed and jealousy" make such conspiracies both plausible and probable.

All of this is to remind you—if you need reminding—that a manager bereft of molecular support is dead in the water. Should this ever happen to you, you need only go to the center of your own molecule to locate the cause—and the remedy.

Your Molecule as an Asset

Improbable as molecular conspiracies may be, it is sometimes useful to postulate them, as we did in our previous illustration, in order to bring out in bold relief organizational realities that would otherwise go unnoticed. What, then, would be the consequences to your job performance and ultimately to your career if you were the beneficiary of a molecular conspiracy to make you an outstanding *success*?

Suppose that your boss has decided, for whatever reason, to get you a whopping bonus. This will take some doing on her part because your job performance is marginal on all counts and your company does not authorize whopping bonuses to any but stellar performers. Your boss also knows that your performance is critically dependent upon (1) your competence, which she can do little about, and (2) your molecular support, which she can do a great deal about. A dramatic rise in either one alone would have a spectacular positive impact on your job performance, so she knows what she can and must do. She calls a meeting for a Friday evening at her home of the make-or-break members of your molecule (as in our previous illustration) and opens the meeting: "I have called you together to help me achieve an objective, which is to get John Doe, one of my regional sales managers, a whopping bonus. As you know, this can only be done in recognition of outstanding performance, and John is now on the company's marginal list. I am therefore asking you to assist me by bringing about a state of affairs that will make a whopping bonus for John morally and ethically justifiable." Here follow the responses:

> *Internal Peers:* "Until we hear otherwise from you, we'll concentrate our 40 percent three-point landings in John's area to whatever extent necessary. But we will not raise our performance standards on the service we render him, for that would not be fair to the other using organizations. We won't play favorites."

> *External Peers:* "Until further notice, we will—at the expense of your competitors—give John increasingly profitable repeat business."

> *Subordinates:* "Whenever he makes a good decision, we will carry it out with precision. Whenever he makes a bad one, we will screw it up in execution so as to make John come out smelling like a rose. But our overall batting average will not change, not even for John."

It would not be long before your weekly performance record as regional sales manager would make a sharp turn to the upside. Within six months you would be the talk of the region. Within the year your boss would have no difficulty getting you your bonus. Eighteen months later you would be named by the corporation as Regional Sales Manager of the Year. Two years later the editor of your company's house organ would interview you for the monthly career profile he or she writes on emerging fast-track managers the company is trying to keep an eye on. And, of course, you have been enjoying it all with the bliss that results from your unawareness of the conspiracy that is at the root of your success.

The editor would ask you, "To what do you attribute your meteoric rise in the ranks of high-performing managers?" You would reply that you believe that although some folks just have what it takes, some don't. Sales managers are born, not made. You would remind him of your father's words, "You can do almost anything you set your mind to," and that unless you are gifted with that undefinable ingredient, you don't have a chance. It is a fact that you just happen to have what it takes.

Ungrateful wretch! Prime evidence of the "arrogance of the sales mentality!"

No manager is an island. Other than your job competence, the support of your molecule is your greatest single asset. So the next time you are recognized or rewarded for superior performance, check to make sure you haven't been taking this asset for granted. When you can succeed without knowing why, there is no incentive to find out; when you fail without knowing why, it is too late to find out. Although the amateur is noisily celebrating his successes, the pro is quietly arranging to repeat his.

CONSTRUCTING YOUR OWN MANAGEMENT MOLECULE

If there is anything that disenchants people on the rim of your molecule, it is to be taken for granted. Most of the people who occupy a peer-support position on your molecule occupy like positions on many other "user" molecules, too; their support must be spread adequately over them all. Undercapitalized as they are, this support is at times spread very thinly indeed. When any of them feels that you have been taking him or her for granted, he or she may shift support from you to others who, in their opinion, place greater value on, and make better use of, such support. This will be purely a judgment call on his or her part, and may therefore be in error. Even if it is, you cannot afford too many such errors by too many people in a peer-support role to you. By the same token most of the people who occupy a peer-user position on your molecule occupy like positions on many other "support" molecules as well; their cost of doing business (time and hassle) and their cost of less-than-three-point landings must be spread adequately over them all. When their costs of dealing with you rise out of proportion to comparable costs of dealing with other support-role personnel, they may feel that you are taking them too much for granted and may go over your head to higher authority to redress their complaint. This, too, may be an error in judgment on their part, but you cannot afford too many in any given period of time, or it will subject you to a top-management inspired audit of your operations and work-simplification program to boot.

The amateur believes that his assigned duties and responsibilities automatically confer upon him an unquestioned right to the active support of his superiors, peers (in both user and support roles) and subordinates; the professional takes nothing for granted so he assiduously cultivates all three and, failing that, he or she makes a career decision.

Molecular Support—
A Right or a Condition?

As for the amateur, this belief, though erroneous, is arrived at quite legitimately. Both company organizational manuals and college texts on organization behavior employ rhetoric to the effect that "support systems must be designed to assure adequate administrative and organizational resources to the Line." The word "assure" is what does the damage. Systems, as such, can assure nothing; only the people using them can. As Benjamin Franklin's grandfather once put it: "It is better to strike a straight blow with a crooked stick than to spend the rest of your life trying to straighten the damned thing out."

In view of the foregoing, the conventional definition of management that we have thus far been using must be expanded to read: "Management is getting things done through the active support of others," where:

1. The added phrase is "the active support of"; and
2. The meaning of the word "others" is no longer limited to one's immediate subordinates, but now includes everyone else on your molecule as well.

Since such support is not automatic, it must be generated; and the only person in a position to generate the support you need is, of course, you.

Your career survival depends on your doing so. If, in the eyes of your superiors, you are more effective in this than most other managers with whom you are being compared, you have career viability. Your job may be eliminated but if you are career competitive, you will have a much better than even chance of surviving the job. A less competitive colleague will be let go instead. A molecule can thus be a career asset or a career liability to the person who is its nucleus, as we saw earlier.

Compatibility, the Prerequisite to Rapport

But it does not necessarily follow that, other things being equal, a person who "just goes about it in the right way" will succeed in turning his or her molecule into a career asset. Every professional manager can expect that, sometime during his or her career, he or she—through the vicissitudes of personnel administration—will find himself at the nucleus of a management molecule where he or she simply does not belong. Given who he or she is and who the people on his or her molecule are, an incompatibility can exist that technique and skill alone cannot overcome. Without compatibility confidence, rapport and re-spect cannot take root; until they do, support will not be forthcoming. For example:

Suppose that you, whom we shall call Helen, had recently re-signed a management position in Salt Lake City to take a similar but a far more attractive position with another company in New York City. As a professional manager you began at once to take stock of your new molecule. Within a few months you became convinced that the difference in "culture" between your former molecule and your pres-ent one was as night is from day, because the managerial values, philosophies, outlooks and priorities that you brought with you were incompatible with those entertained as a matter of course by the people on your new molecule. You were not yet prepared to judge them as better or worse, but as just *different*; so different that you were making unsatisfactory progress in developing rapport with them. This is taking its toll on the rate at which you are breaking into your job, and it looks improbable that you'll get your job off the ground any time soon. What to do? You are a pro, so it should not take many words for me to describe what you would do. But let me first digress briefly to speculate what you, if you were an *amateur*, would likely do in this situation:

1. You might try to convince the forty-odd people on your molecule to "the way we did things in the last company I worked for in Utah." Meanwhile, since you are a key figure on many of *their*

molecules, they will also be trying to get you to see things *their* way. So here we have a one-sided contest of values, forty against one. Regardless of whose values are "right," the odds are overwhelmingly against yours.

2. You may decide, nevertheless, not to give ground. You tell yourself that it is a matter of principle, not a matter of consensus. The issue must be decided on its merits, you insist, and not by majority vote. Your molecule is now becoming a liability and this makes your boss increasingly nervous.

3. Meanwhile, an old friend who has been working for this same company for years calls you saying that he has an opening on his staff that you would fit like a hand in a glove. "We are your kind of people," he says. "Let me arrange for your transfer." You reply sternly, "I cannot leave here now. My mother admonished me, as a child, never to run away from a problem; that people who do so are cop-outs, lacking in character. She often reminded me of the motto, 'If at first you don't succeed, try, try again.' If it hadn't been for that motto on his laboratory wall, Thomas Edison would never have invented the electric light bulb and we'd still be watching TV by candlelight!"

How on earth could running away from *this* problem possibly be a cop-out? If you accept the transfer, you would be doing (1) your old friend a favor, (2) your present boss a favor (since you are driving him up the wall), (3) one of the candidates for your job (whom your boss has already lined up) a favor and (4) yourself a favor by giving yourself a fresh start with a more compatible molecule. That motto on Thomas Edison's wall is indeed valid for vocational work, as Edison proved; but in management work it can lead to disaster. I am not rejecting the motto out of hand, however; instead I will restate it in a form applicable to the practice of management:

> If at first you don't succeed,
> Suck another seed;
> But don't suck the same damned seed,
> For it makes people nervous.

But since you are a professional, Helen, you would have left that molecule long before matters had gotten this far out of hand.

When a Career Decision Is the Crucial Decision

Some time ago I ran into an acquaintance who had left his company six months before. To satisfy my curiosity I asked him if he quit or was fired. "No one will ever know," he replied, "It was a photo finish." I thought that was cutting it a bit too fine. For what is normally attributed to stubbornness when found in children is most often attributed to strength of character when found in adults. If every employed man and woman in America knew that it is to his or her career advantage to quit before being fired, American business would never have to fire anyone for incompatibility again.

We come now to listing the current members of your molecule by *name*. The smaller the list, the more opportunity for you to engage in rifle-shot human relations; if the list is too large, the shotgun may be necessary. However, it is better to have the active support of the vital few than the friendly indifference of the well-wishing many—if you have to choose. This idea is expressed in the well-known "80/20 rule" widely used among salespeople for managing their sales time. It goes this way: "Since 80 percent of my business is produced by 20 percent of my customers, I put 80 percent of my selling time on that 20 percent of my customers and 20 percent of my selling time on the remaining 80 percent."

With that in mind, take a clean sheet of paper and caption it at the top with these words: MY MOLECULE. First write down the names of your immediate subordinates and of your boss. (That was easy!) Next write down the names, if any, of not more than three managers at or above your boss's level who have the greatest influence with him. They could be decisive allies on issues you may in the future be pressing on him; they could also be liabilities if you just take them for granted.

Identifying Your Own Management Molecule

Now for the difficult part, the internal peer elements. Write down the names only of those internal peers who are in a position, either in a peer-support or peer-user role, to make you or break you in a key part of your job two, three or more times in a year. If you compromise the make-or-break requirement, your list could get too large. The fact that an individual has been of real help or hindrance in the past doesn't count; it must be make-or-break. Or the fact that a person's support has on more than one occasion been crucial doesn't count, either, if that person was not in an authorized position to render that support. This may at first strike you strangely, but an illustration from baseball may help: If a first baseman, deciding that the next opposing batter must be struck out, pitches one across the plate and the batter swings and misses it, the play obviously doesn't count; the first baseman was not in an authorized position to take that initiative (see Appendix A).

As your list grows, bear in mind that a list in excess of fifty names is too large for rifle-shot human relations. So make sure that you are not including on your list people who are in fact (or should be) on your subordinates' molecules, because that is usually where many of your excess names are likely to come from. There is a second criterion that must be applied to the names before being listed. The prospective candidate must have a regular interface with you to qualify for a place on your molecule, otherwise there would be no practical need to be listed. This criterion will also keep your list from becoming too long. (There will be some "political" exceptions to this that will be suggested three paragraphs below.) When your list is complete enough to be useful, remember that its purpose is to identify specifically by name the persons included in *your* "others." It is not an elitist list nor a black-ball list, a fair-haired boy list or a persona-non-grata list, a hit-list or a payoff list, or any other productivity-irrelevant list. It is your *constituent* list, the names of the people whose support you must have when the chips are down. The public politican provides an excellent analogy: His constituents comprise but a fraction of the voters who are in a position to support him; nevertheless it is *the* fraction that can make or break him at the polls. Although he would want to kiss every baby in his district, he at least makes certain to kiss the vital few. That's why in politics it's not what you know, but who you know that counts; and why, in management, what you know doesn't count until you have the support of who you know.

Whom You Know vs. What You Know

Next list your external peers, but once again on a make-or-break basis only. If your job is in corporate public relations, then the media are the locus of some members of your molecule. Put down the names of *individuals;* organizational titles alone will not do. You cannot influence a title on an organization chart, only the person occupying it. When the incumbent changes, the name on your list must also change, even though the position title does not. Sales managers will list the names of those whose buying decisions carry the greatest weight within their customer organizations—not just their position titles. Tax accountants and attorneys will make it their business, likewise, to replace government bureaucratic titles with individual names, for as Benjamin Franklin's grandfather put it: "It's hell to work with a nervous IRS examiner, especially when you are the one who is making him nervous!" And those of my readers in Purchasing, in Personnel, in Corporate General Counsel, in Shareholder Relations, etc., will do likewise.

Don't trouble yourself about that 80 percent you have to omit from your list; you are not giving them the cold shoulder even though some of them may be closer to you than a brother and sister; whatever time you owe them must be taken out of the time you spend pursuing your own personal values and finance with the time you spend at work. You will need all the working hours you can spare for the people who do qualify for inclusion on your molecule.

Some individuals will pose difficult decisions. For instance, you may be considering the name of a manager whose position would not qualify him for a place on your molecule; however, he just happens to be the board chairman's son-in-law. To a management theorist this would be an irrelevant consideration; nevertheless, would it not be prudent to grant him at least an honorary membership? No harm would be done in any case. Other similarly ambiguous choices will have to be confronted where prudence may have to outweigh reason. Surely there's no point in starting off on the wrong foot with a person who, although not qualifying for a place on your molecule, has a better than even chance of becoming your boss in the foreseeable future.

Your own personal philosophy of human relations will now be coming to the fore. It does not really matter what your philosophy is as long as you succeed in getting and holding the support you need. For instance, suppose your philosophy is that "people are just no damned good, and that goes for all the 40 billion that populate this earth." This attitude will be no handicap to you if you can make an exception of just the 40 on your molecule. That exception would be so insignificant (0.000000001) that you would not have to compromise your convictions at all!

Meet Your Sole Supporters

Those of my readers who are heads of households may wish to take their lists home and level with their families. I can picture one of you calling a family conclave, showing them your list and saying, "I am about to make a long overdue confession: I am not, as I have been chauvinistically insisting for so many years, your sole support. Instead, it is the people on that list who are; if they don't support me, I cannot support you; I am merely a middleman. Therefore, meet your sole supporters."

I can hear your youngsters replying: "Most of these names we recognize from having been at company picnics: But some of these are names of people who are just not our kinds of folks, people whose friendship we wouldn't especially seek out. Why did you pick *them* for your molecule?" And I can hear you reply, "I did not pick any of them; I was not even consulted. They were tossed at me by cruel fate. But I agree: Had the choice been mine, half these people would not be on this list." "Then stroke these people carefully for our sake," is what I hear them say. Not for the customers' sake; not for the company's sake; not even for the country's sake; but surely for the sake of your "ideals."

Granted, half the people on your molecule are no bargain. But neither are you all that big a bargain on someone else's molecule. It is often our lot, as human beings, to be stuck with each other. Molecular lists are *constituent* lists and, as such constitute the manager's—or politician's, if you will—power base.

A politician who is successful at the polls is said to have an effective following. Only then is he or she said to be an effective leader. A manager who has the support he needs from the members of his molecule is said to have a following within the company. Only then can he be said to be effective in managerial leadership. Since his following is located above him (his boss), beside him (his peers) and below him (his subordinates), his own leadership position is always in the middle. The amateur, however, believes that "leadership begins at the top" and is exercised downwards; but the pro knows that managerial leadership begins concurrently at the center of each molecule in the corporation and is exercised radially.

Where Managerial Leadership Begins

Textbooks on organizational development consistently declare that management leadership begins at the top, but they just as consistently don't specify exactly where the top is. The impression is therefore conveyed, whether intentionally or not, that effective managerial leadership is not possible at lower organizational levels if it is not already being practiced at the higher levels. This would be true if the practice of management were not to be regarded as a professional activity to the same degree as the practice of law, medicine or engineering. If it is *not* to be so regarded, then this textbook-conveyed impression would give the amateurs at lower management levels a legitimate excuse for one-orangemanship or two-orangemanship.

A parallel from the medical profession may suffice: Picture yourself on an operating table about to have your appendix removed under a local anesthetic. Just after the doctor has opened your abdomen and located the inflamed organ, the electricity goes off and the room is plunged into darkness. You hear the doctor say through the darkness to the nurse, "Well, that does it! If top management does not do *its* job, we can't do *ours*. Guess we'll just have to leave the patient as he is while we sit it out in the coffee shop until the lights come on. Let's go." Before they could leave, you would be screaming, "Is there a *pro* in the house?"

What is a pro? A doctor who knows what to do if and when the lights go out—no matter whose job it was to see that they didn't. In management you often do not find out who the pros are *until* the lights go out. Management, at your level, begins with *you*, regardless.

The Sources of Your Managerial Influence

Let us now turn to the basis of your managerial influence, the kind of influence that will get and hold an organizational following: We have already used, without defining them, the terms *competence*, *personality* and *character*, and we have no need to define them now, either; for others are influenced (1) not by your competence, but by their *confidence* in your competence, (2) not by your personality, but by their *rapport* with your personality, and (3) not by your character, but by their *respect* for your character. So it is not your traits, per se, but others' experiences with them over time that determines the amount of their confidence, rapport and respect. This allows you to be yourself, while paying attention to others' experiences with you. Thus:

1. Your *competence*, as a source of your managerial influence, is the degree to which others are confident that you know what you are doing and that you know what you are talking about.

2. Your *personality*, as a source of your managerial influence, is the degree to which others enjoy rapport with you, that is, find you easy or difficult to listen to, to talk to or to do business with.

3. Your *character*, as a source of your managerial influence, is the degree to which others respect your personal commitment not to

allow them to wind up with the short end of the stick if they take you at your word. If they do not see such a personal commitment as *characteristic* of you, then to that extent your influence will be weakened.

Although it is possible for the clever to deceive others on any one of these (the con artist, the phony, etc.), the other two provide necessary checks. Caveat emptor! (See Appendix B for more on this.)

As noted previously, the internal dynamics of each and every molecule is identical to that of every other molecule making up the organization. The principles governing their operation are also identical, very much like baseball at the little league, bush league, minor league and major league levels is the same except for the sizes of the bats and mitts. The differences are in degree, not in kind. This leads us to a principle that I first heard stated nearly thirty years ago by Lawrence Apply, the president of the American Management Association, which he called the Unit President Concept: "Every manager from supervisor through CEO is the president of that part of the enterprise over which he or she exercises stewardship and must be held accountable in the same way."

The Unit President Concept

Let's check this concept out with the following illustration: Imagine that two of your immediate subordinates, Pat and Otto, are chronically locked in interpersonal conflicts. Pat feels that Otto is pigheaded and Otto likewise believes that Pat is stubborn. They each "know" that no one can work with the other. Otto is a peer-support member of Pat's molecule, but Pat does not qualify as a member of Otto's molecule. Thus Pat's job performance is seriously handicapped as a result of this continuing interpersonal conflict. He finally comes to you and says, "It says in Otto's job description that he is to provide service to me. He isn't doing it. Believe me, I've tried everything. But you are Otto's boss, I'm not; it's your job to tell him to shape up or else."

What would you do? Never mind what you might have done in the past; what would you do, now that you are halfway through this book?

Let's play this one according to the molecular principles. Here are the relevant facts:

1. Pat is at the center of his own molecule and is therefore responsible to you for getting Otto's support.

2. Otto is responsible to you for performing the duties in his job description.

3. Both Pat and Otto are supervisors.

Here follows the dialogue:

YOU: *(Smiling warmly as you lean back putting your feet up on the desk.)* So you've got a molecular problem, Pat. Welcome to the club! I am up to my neck with molecular problems of my own. I always get a lot of help hearing how others solve theirs!

PAT: I know this is my problem, but I need your support. If I were in business for myself I'd solve it by dropping Otto, but I'm in business for you so I can't do that. You are as much Otto's boss as you are mine. Since it takes "two to tango," I'd like you to call Otto in here.

YOU: *(Dialing Otto's number.)* Hello? Otto? Please get in here right away.

OTTO: *(Entering.)* What can I do for you?

YOU: I am not interested in knowing who's at fault here. But I am intensely interested in finding out whether two grown men in supervisory jobs can get along together during working hours if their jobs depend on it—which they do. So be back here together first thing tomorrow morning to tell me that you both understand that keeping your interpersonal problems out of my hair is a condition of your continuing employment here, and that you agree to joint accountability to me on this matter. If you cannot give me that assurance tomorrow by 9:00 A.M., don't come at all. What happens after that will be my decision.

The power of such situations to lure managers into trying to play the interventionist role of amateur psychiatrist, or county judge, or shepherd, or priest, or parent, or scoutmaster is enormous. Yet experience tells us that:

1. If the manager does hear them out and judges the issue between them, one of them will nevertheless regard himself as the loser even if he accedes to the judgment. Losers aren't interested in making peace, only in getting even; it is he who wins the last battle who wins the war. Therefore, if the manager assumes a judicial role, he will only keep the conflict alive. Peace, to be lasting, must be made by the warring parties on their own terms. Third parties

can and often do provide the necessary incentive, but they cannot make the peace.

2. Managers are in a sound moral, ethical and legal position to require, as a condition of continuing employment, behavior acceptable to the boss during working hours. The school, the church and the home are the proper institutions for fitting people for a world of responsibility. It is neither desirable nor obligatory for employers to mop up after them.

So much for the management molecule and *interpersonal* conflict. Had the focus instead been on an *issue* conflict related to work, you as their manager would have had both the right and the obligation to intervene if and as you saw fit. Managerial life becomes complex when you confuse roles. If you do, you will need courses in counseling and human intervention. But the professional manager knows that intervention in personality-related issues involves judgment calls he or she is neither required nor competent to make. This makes Pat and Otto as responsible for the management of their molecules as you are for the management of yours—and as your president is for the management of his. That's the Unit President Concept in action and constitutes the *democratic* element in professional management.

First Things First

Once your molecular list is as complete as you need it to be, opportunities to use it for time management purposes will abound at every phone call, every hallway encounter, every organizational meeting and every interoffice memo you get in your in-basket. Just one example:

Down the hall from you is the office of an old colleague who, every Monday morning at nine, has been dropping into your office to describe in lengthy detail his Sunday afternoon on the golf course. Because you are a nice person and have made a great effort to be accommodating, it has cost you more than an hour of working time on each occasion. You would have liked somehow to discourage this habit of his, but you have not yet found a way that would not make you feel guilty of insensitivity. So you have continued stoically to endure his impositions on your time.

But now it will be different. Next Monday when he starts his story, you will open your desk drawer and pull out your molecular list to see if his name is on it. If not, you'll say to him: "I don't have to listen to this. Your name is not on my molecule. See for yourself." With that you thrust the list under his nose, and motion him toward the door. His feelings, since he is an obvious amateur, will no doubt be hurt. But guilt feelings will no longer afflict you: Your molecular list gives you solid moral justification for insisting upon *first things first*!

But suppose, on the other hand, his name *is* on your molecular list; what then? You will patiently hear him out, of course. And the time lost in so doing you will charge off to the administrative overhead cost of molecular maintenance.

3

Principal *Subjective* Sources of the Manager's Time Management Problems

A third source of wheel spinning time is an ambivalence, endemic to our industrial culture, between two apparently contradictory sets of values: (1) The so-called *Work Ethic* epitomized in the familiar "an honest day's work for a fair day's pay" and what I prefer to call the *Management Ethic* which, however stated, reaffirms the fact that judgment and influence command a higher price than time and effort. Choosing the set of values (e.g., between "what you know" and "whom you know") appropriate to his or her career aims is the third precondition for effective time management.

GETTING THE SUBJECT
SQUARED AWAY

Efficiency vs. Content

A hardworking, harried and distraught manager strode in desperation into his boss's office and in a fit of emotion blurted out, "I'm ready to quit. I'm overworked. Right now I'm doing the work of two men."

"Tell me who they are," replied his boss, "and I'll have them fired."

It would be a disservice to this manager to help him make more efficient use of his time. Why help a manager become more efficient at doing what he or she should not be doing in the first place?

Many books and articles are available to help managers make more efficient use of their time. They deal with priority systems, control systems, physical systems and so on. In so doing they are, we believe, begging the real question. Before addressing the efficient use of *management* time, we must understand clearly what it is.

There are, of course, many kinds of time other than management time. There is seed time and harvest time, breakfast time and dinner time, Christmas time and Easter time, concert time and rehearsal time, to name a few. No one normally confuses breakfast time with what he or she would normally be doing during dinner time or doing during harvest time what ordinarily is done during seed time, and so on. Each adjective modifies the noun "time" in terms of an activity that is widely known and understood as being different (i.e., the difference can be recognized on sight) from the activities connoted by the other adjectives. So it is with two kinds of time a farmer, for example, puts in each year, seed time and harvest time. A book on time management entitled *Managing Seed Time* would be of primary interest only to people who farm for a living. If the book sold well, another time management book entitled *Managing Harvest Time* would be a sure winner. Although both books would be about time management, there would be no duplica-

68

tion or overlapping of content between them. Any farmer who was subsequently seen doing during seed time what must only be done during harvest time would either become the laughing stock of his neighbors or the object of compassionate concern, for he would clearly have had the contents of two different books on time management mixed up!

Comedy and Tragedy

This phenomenon, which can provoke both amusement and compassion, is defined by professional story tellers as "the incongruous juxtaposition of two incompatibles." It also happens to be the scholarly definition of comedy and tragedy. The difference, however, is significant: If it is happening to someone else, it is comical; if it is happening to you, it is pathetic.

And so it is, too, with the two kinds of time that managers put in almost every day, namely, *vocational* time and *management* time. Management time comprises only a portion of the entire time a manager spends on his job. The remainder (excluding coffee breaks, time out for trivia and for social amenities) is vocational time. And, as we shall soon demonstrate, it is the incongruous juxtaposition of these two incompatible kinds of time that is a source of every manager's time management problems. It is also the basis of most of the humor and pathos in management, which makes the writing of this book a fascinating adventure for me and the reading of it, I trust, a profitable and entertaining experience for you.

Management Time vs. Vocational Time

Vocational time is the time spent doing things. Management time is the time spent seeing to it that things get done. These two kinds of time are incompatible: The more time you spend personally doing things, the less time you have for seeing to it that other things get done; and the more time you spend seeing to it that things get done, the less time you have for personally doing any of these things. If you insist on doing both, you'll wind up with an eighty-hour work week—a terminal state of affairs that can only end in a career crisis.

Entry-level jobs at the bottom of every organization chart are, with a few exceptions to be noted later, 100 percent vocational in content. As we move higher in the chain, the proportion of management time required increases until, at the top of the overall organization, nearly all of it must be managerial.

The less professional you are as a manager, the more time you must spend practicing the vocations of the people who work under you. If you are totally incompetent as a manager, then, in order to survive in your job, you must spend all your time in the vocations of the people under your supervision. This means that the management component of your time will shrink to almost zero. By the same token, the pro in management spends little or no time practicing any of the vocations under his or her direction.

It follows from this that a good manager is able to work through others successfully regardless of the business, its product, its market or its technology. In practice, however, we rarely find managers who are that good. But those who are that good are rewarded by being able to "write their own tickets" career-wise. To become that good is an attainable goal for any manager who takes as professional an approach to managing his or her management time as—in the past—he has taken to managing his vocational time. However, it doesn't come naturally, no more than the practice of surgery or engineering comes naturally to anyone.

The manager who is doing the work of two or more people cannot succeed in *management*. He or she hasn't the time.

This book will not deal with the techniques of managing the vocational portion of the time managers must put in every week, however considerable it may be in many instances. It will only deal with those characteristics of vocational time that must be recognized and understood if we are to appreciate their influence on how managers manage their management time.

How to Recognize Vocational Time

To illuminate these characteristics, let me first make clear just how you can recognize vocational time when you see it. Through the examples that follow there runs a common thread. When you see it, you will recognize it whenever and wherever you encounter vocational time again.

Vocational time is spent by:

- a company president proofreading the final draft of the annual report for typographical errors;

- an electrical foreman splicing two wires to make a reliable electrical connection;
- a sales vice-president taking a repeat order on the telephone from a regular customer;
- a supervisor of the typing pool in corporate headquarters typing a routine interoffice memo;
- a manager of a downtown retail department store on a ladder taking inventory.

In all of the above examples managers are putting in vocational time. They are all doing things that must be done—by someone. As managers they have the right and the duty to decide who will do them. How they make this decision determines whether they are amateurs or professionals in the practice of management.

If in each case they were adequately staffed with competent personnel (competent, that is, by personnel department standards, which might well be damning them with faint praise) and were not imposed upon by tight personal deadlines beyond their immediate control, their decisions to do what they were doing must have been purely a matter of *personal preference*.

If, on the other hand, they were each shorthanded, or the competence available to them was not adequate to these tasks, or if they were under severe external time pressures, their decisions were a reflection of circumstances beyond their immediate control. You cannot distinguish the professional from the amateur in management simply by *what* he or she is doing; you must also know *why* he or she is doing it. If these managers were limited by circumstances that allowed them no other choice, they were no less professional for having done these things; if they were not limited by such circumstances, they revealed themselves as amateurs precisely for having done these very same things as a matter of personal choice.

As we will show later on, managers have discretionary use of only a small portion of the time they put in on the job. Most of their decisions are governed by circumstances over which they have little *immediate* control. What distinguishes the professional from the amateur is what he or she does with what little discretionary time he or she has. The professional use of discretionary time will tend also to multiply it, thereby giving the manager the additional discretionary time necessary to influence that which he cannot otherwise control.

Explaining vs. Rationalizing

Let's assume that the above five word pictures reflect amateurs rather than professionals at work. Highly visible to other persons in the vicinity, they know they are running the risk of being teased about how they are spending their time. You may expect them to be armed to the teeth with rationalizations for what they are doing. (A rationalization in this context is a reasonable but self-serving explanation for doing what no reasonable person would do.) They have become stock-in-trade for amateurs caught-in-the-act for so long that they are easy to catalogue. What are some of these rationalizations?

1. "If you want it done right, do it yourself." This has to be a rationalization, not a reason. What the amateur really means is that when anything goes wrong, as it surely will, he wants to be there when it happens. But that would require that he be everywhere at once.

2. "I want my subordinates to see that I am able and willing to do anything I expect them to do." If this were a valid reason, every chicken farmer would have to lay at least one egg a day to maintain the respect and admiration of his hens.

3. "I do it to keep my hand in." If this reason were a valid one, then the amateur has his hand in the wrong job. The ordinary reason for keeping your hand in someone else's job is to make sure you are qualified for it in case you should lose your own. But in each of the above five vignettes the manager had his hand in a lower-paying job. He should instead have been keeping his hand in a higher-paying job, his boss's, so that when, for whatever reason, his boss vacated the job, the manager would automatically be promoted into it as the most qualified candidate available.

4. "I owe it to my subordinates to give them frequent examples of how something looks when it's been done right." Does this manager want us to believe that his subordinates will never "catch on" for good? Or that they need frequent opportunities for watching genius at work? If so, he had better correct that situation.

If, then, one can elicit only rationalizations from such obvious amateurs, to whom must we look for the reasons why managers, not forced by circumstances to do these things, still do them as a matter of personal choice? To psychologists, of course!

Psychologists have, for the past fifty years at least, studied managerial behavior almost to death. As we shall see, they have put their finger on the real reason why managers choose to behave in this way.

Deviant vs. Normal Managerial Behavior

Psychologists attribute the managerial behavior in our five illustrations to a strong tendency, normal to most human adults, to retreat to the familiar. They state the principal involved as a variation of the more familiar pleasure-pain principle:

When a normal human being (by "normal" is meant anyone whom a psychiatrist would trust loose on the streets for an hour) has a choice between doing what he or she does well and likes to do and doing what he or she does not do well and has not yet learned to like to do, will always—other things being equal—choose rather to do those things he or she does best and likes to do most.

Applying this principle, we note that these five managers were doing things that they had learned to do well and learned to like to do in earlier jobs in their careers, that is, in their *past*. But what they were not doing—managing—was, for some of them, still largely in their *future* and therefore they had not yet learned to do it very well nor learned to get much satisfaction from it. Each, including the president, had "made it" (their last promotion was evidence of that), but, judging by what they were doing, they didn't yet "have it made." They were therefore journeying through their careers facing the past and backing into the future. Along the way they encountered many obstacles, all of them by surprise. These are called lessons in the School of Hard Knocks. Not looking where they are headed, they encounter many lessons that their career objectives could have told them they did not need and so should have avoided; they also missed many lessons that their career objectives could have told them they needed and should, therefore, have been included in the journey. This is a wasteful way to go through any school. Henry Ford may have had this in mind when he said, "The School of Hard Knocks teaches its lessons well, but when you graduate you are too old to go to work." Most of us keep facing the things we do best and love to do most.

What, then, is the remedy? Why, *about-face and forward march*, of course. But that would not be normal human behavior. It is not normal to look forward eagerly to doing things you do not yet do well and have not yet learned to like to do, with your back toward the things you do best and love to do most. If this is not normal, then what is it? Deviant from normal, of course.

Professional vs. Amateur in Management

Psychologists have identified many kinds of deviant human behavior and the most widely talked about is insanity. But the kind of deviant behavior we are talking about here is professionalism in management. The professional manager is as different from the normal manager as is the insane from the normal human being. Although the insane can be, for his or her own good and the public comfort and convenience, segregated from the rest of society, the professional manager is allowed to run freely among his peers. Even though professional managers constitute only a small minority within the managerial class, they serve as a standard of comparison that makes them objects of envy and resentment on the part of many in the majority.

To illustrate how different professional behavior is from normal (amateur) behavior in the field of endeavor, I shall take an example from the medical profession, because it stands at the apex of the hierarchy of standards of professional practice. It, too, has its amateurs, who act as foils against whom disciplined professionals stand out in bold relief.

Example from the Medical Profession

Imagine yourself lying on your back in a hospital operating room about to have your appendix removed. You have opted to have the operation perfomed with a local anesthetic so that, wide awake, you could, with the aid of a forty-five-degree mirror suspended from the ceiling, watch the wonders of medical science emerge from your abdomen. The doctor, deftly wielding his scalpel, unzippers your abdomen and searches for the inflamed organ. It persistently eludes him because, owing to your age, it has migrated to a position beneath organs that are now in the doctor's way. He carefully unpacks your abdominal cavity, laying these obstructing organs alongside your body, securing them to the operating table with pins to which have been attached numbered flags. With bulging eyes and mouth agape at the surgeon's amazing skill, you ask him, "Doctor, to what do you owe your astonishing skill in performing appendectomies?" To which he pauses to reply, "When it comes to pulling appendixes, either you have it or you don't. Appendix-pullers are born, not made. Unless you are a natural-born appendix-puller, you will never do well at it. It has to be in your blood. My father was one of the greatest appendix-pullers of all time, and his father before him pulled a mean appendix. I'd like to show you a chart of my annual kill/cure ratio over the past twenty years, a performance record that few other doctors can match. Unless appendix-pulling comes naturally to you, you'll never rack up a record like that."

Will that answer comfort you? You will likely be up off that operating table in a second and start running down the hospital corridor shouting, "Is there a deviant in the house?" By a deviant, of course, you mean a doctor who, if appendix pulling had ever come naturally to him or her, had been packed off to a medical school where for four to six years its faculty had systematically taken out of him or her every "natural-born" tendency for performing surgery and replaced them with deviant methods, namely, the methods of professional surgery. The professional practice of medicine—or of law or engineering or accounting—does not come naturally. It is an acquired discipline. So is management.

MANAGEMENT—AN ACQUIRED DISCIPLINE

It does not come naturally to manage professionally. Management is an acquired discipline. The practice of management can be professional to the same degree as the practice of law, engineering or medicine, but not in the same sense. The vocational professions are rooted in specific academic disciplines while the practice of management is rooted in the disciplines administered by the School of Experience (see Appendix C). The School of Experience and the School of Hard Knocks differ only in the student's orientation. The amateur faces the past, backs into the future and gets lessons knocked into him whether he needs them or not. That is the School of Hard Knocks. The professional faces forward selecting some lessons and avoiding others in accordance with his or her career aims. That is the School of Experience. Both schools occupy the same turf—the forty-hour work week on the job. Therefore, the same diagram, Figure 3a, will serve as a schematic for both.

The Lures of Vocational Work

The job from which you were promoted (or hired, as the case may be) into your first management position is represented by the baseline

A–B of the diagram. All of your forty-hour work week was taken up by vocational time. During this period in your career, you discovered the satisfaction available in being *identified* with a recognized line of work, in *pride* in a job well done and in using *instant feedback* for staying on top of the job. The more successful you became, the more you associated these satisfactions with your success, and the more resourceful and self-reliant you became. It was your resourcefulness and self-reliance, no doubt, that gave you the edge to win that promotion. These two qualities are indispensable in any candidate for a beginning-level management job.

What you could not have known at the time was that these three sources of job satisfaction are simply not available in the practice of management (at levels C–E and higher). Not knowing this, your early experience in your first management job (at level C–E) was no doubt confusing, frustrating and disappointing. The three satisfactions that you had previously taken for granted were just not there. (Why this is so will be dealt with later.) This void had to be filled. Having little or no experience with the kind of satisfaction uniquely available in management, you found yourself reaching for any vocational work you could lay your hands on.

In what follows, I shall elaborate on this phenomenon by reference to three vocational lures that pull managers back from their professional status to the security of their vocational past. I shall do this in considerable detail in order to help those readers who have not yet discovered the legitimate sources of managerial satisfaction. Although most such are still in the early stages of their managerial careers, a surprising number in upper management have still not made this discovery and are putting in an excessive amount of vocational time in pursuit of the only source of job satisfaction they still know and understand. And they do this at great cost to their own managerial effectiveness.

Identity:
The First Lure

Let's say that you are now at the first level of supervision represented by the lowest dotted line at level C–E in Figure 3a. Your School of Experience will last your entire career and most of it still lies ahead of you. When someone asks you what you do for a living, you reply, "I am a manager." The questioner gives you a suspicious look as if you were trying to hold something back: "Manager? of *what*!" You now

SCHOOL OF EXPERIENCE
THE MANAGEMENT RECTANGLE

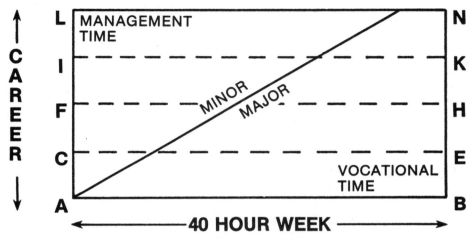

Figure 3a

know that a nonvocational identity is not satisfying in a society that places a high value on "an honest day's work for a fair day's pay." Yet managers are paid not for their time and labor but for their judgment and influence. Although managers may of necessity often labor long and hard, that is neither what they are being paid for nor what they are identified with. To call oneself just a manager is tantamount to accepting, at least socially, the status of a nonidentity. Even politicians fare better than managers do in this respect. It is natural, therefore, that managers look to their vocational origins to satisfy their needs for identity fulfillment.

How they do it first came to my notice twenty-five years ago when I was in the headquarters building of one of the largest electrical equipment manufacturers in the nation. On the top floor (level L–N) was what employees dubbed "executive row" where eight vice presidents sat cheek-by-jowl in wall-to-wall carpeted, mahogany-paneled "foxholes" out of which they fought the company's battles. Occasionally, they took potshots at each other just to adjust their sights. They would walk the corridors dressed in expensive, but subdued, business suits cut to Madison Avenue's specifications. From the breast pocket of each one there protruded by a half-inch a white linen monogrammed handkerchief. From each, that is, except from the pocket of the vice-president of Engineering. From *his* pocket there protruded instead, by a half-inch, also white, a slide rule.

Other things being equal, one would suppose that if a white handkerchief could do the job for seven vice-presidents, it should do it for the eighth as well. But in this case other things were *not* equal, a statement that the engineering vice-president was symbolically trying to make. He did not wish to be mistaken for your run-of-the-mill vice-president who got to the top through *who* he knew instead of *what* he knew. With a master's degree from M.I.T. in engineering, a Sigma XI key and dozens of patents to his credit, he had reached the top floor competently, honestly and legitimately.

The thread of this story reached its knot every Monday morning at ten when the eight vice-presidents trooped into the president's office for his regular weekly staff meeting. He usually kicked things off by tossing a challenging problem on the table for the conferees to get their teeth into. The engineering vice-president would promptly whip out his slide rule and come up with the solution five minutes after everyone else had worked it out in their heads. But at least his method was legitimate, whatever else might be said about theirs. Above all, he was loyal to the long and honorable tradition of his vocation by identifying with it at every appropriate opportunity.

There is both humor and pathos in this example of the incongrous juxtaposition of management time and vocational time. When it happens to someone else, it is funny, but when it happens to you, it is pathetic—remember?

I call this slide rule his *vocational vestigial organ.* Just as our physical appendixes are vestiges of an organ once indispensable to the progenitor species of the human race, so too that slide rule was indispensable to the earlier stages in the development of the vice-president's career. But that which made it possible for us to become what we are will, if we do not remove it, prevent us from becoming what we hope and deserve to be. That is why vestigial organs, whether they be physical or vocational, must submit to the knife before they start infecting an otherwise healthy body, or an otherwise promising managerial career.

Most of my readers have their vocational vestigial organs still intact, as I have mine. Preventive surgery seems so postponable. And except for the vice-president and his portable computer, the tool superintendent and his tools, the hospital administrator and his stethoscope and a few others we could name, most vocational vestigial organs are not associated with prominently displayed symbols. This makes their presence all the more insidious, their identification all the more difficult and their removal all the more unlikely.

Let us turn now to a second source of satisfaction in vocational work that is not available in the practice of management, namely, pride of craft.

Pride of Craft:
The Second Lure

Upon graduation in 1934 from Princeton with a bachelor's degree in physics, I accepted a job with a geophysical subsidiary of the Amerada Petroleum Company in Tulsa, Oklahoma, as a laboratory assistant. (That was at the bottom of the Great Depression. What few job openings there were went to the best students; the rest went on to graduate school.) When I signed in, my boss took me down the hall to meet the "gang" with whom I would spend the better part of the year learning the ropes. Some were just-hired college graduates like myself, some were in their second or third year with the company, and two were high-school graduates who had been with the company so long that their careers had become stuck to the woodwork. There were seven of us. We sat on stools about four feet apart in a row along a workbench that ran the length of the room. Before us were set up the jigs and fixtures we used for winding the galvanometer coils it was our job to produce. (If you don't know what a galvanometer coil is, you haven't missed a thing. But because of the pride of craft available to the talented winder, it is germane to the purpose of this book to dwell on it for more than a few minutes.) The galvanometer coil, when wound to Amerada's specification, consisted of thirty turns of number 40 enamel coated wire, three-quarters of an inch long, a quarter-inch wide. It went into an oil-damped vibration galvanometer, held by elastic suspensions between the poles of a permanent magnet. Attached to one face of the coil at its middle was a tiny mirror. Six such galvanometers were then mounted in an oscillograph that trained six light beams on these mirrors, which in turn reflected them onto sensitized paper that, when the camera was operating, rolled past these beams much as a movie film rolls today. This technology was then used by field parties for seismological prospecting for oil.

Because of the miniature size of these coils, we had to use a jeweler's magnifying eyepiece, jeweler's soldering iron, jeweler's tweezers and needle and thread.

Why, you may ask, did they use college graduates for what ordinarily would be "blue collar" work? Simply because of how the specifications were written. None of us got credit for winding a coil until it had passed inspection, which included a specified frequency response curve, a specified sensitivity (degrees per milliampere) and a specified damping constant. Unless the individual winding the coil is at home with the physics of what he is doing, involving as it does such things as torque, elasticity, moments of inertia, damped simple harmonic motion and coefficients of viscosity—as well as the second-order differential equation relating these things to each other—he would have little chance of ever being able to wind a coil to specification. (Years later these coils were wound by machine. This obviated the need for anyone other than the designer of the machine to know anything about the physics of the galvanometer coil. It is humbling to even think about it.)

It so happened that I took to coil winding like the proverbial duck to water, but it wasn't easy. My boss was too busy to give me any instruction. When I asked a fellow worker to show me how, he replied, "Figure it out yourself. Nobody showed *me* how." (This was called "on-the-job-training.") I decided it would not be useful to try asking any of the others. But I had to learn. My job depended on it. So I stayed late one evening and raided the inventory for three finished coils that had passed inspection and tried, by tracing backward from finished product to raw wire on a spool, just what I would have to do to reverse the process. I drew heavily on techniques of inference and deduction I had encountered in Sir Conan Doyle's detective novels and was handsomely rewarded.

My coils were now passing inspection, albeit only after three or four resubmissions. As time went on, the number of coils I was daily adding to inventory was trending upward. When it reached eight coils in the same day, the rest of the gang hinted that eight per day was the maximum. Naively, I thought they were challenging me. I found out otherwise when, the next day, I added nine coils to inventory. When they saw that, they asked me to meet them behind the warehouse after work as they had something of a very personal nature to explain to me.

I spent the next day on sick leave.

Thereafter, the quality inspection record of my coil output rapidly improved until it exceeded the records of any of the other six men. Moreover, although I never again delivered more than eight coils to inventory in any one day, I often *completed* more than eight and secreted the overage in a change wallet I purchased for just that purpose. I kept a clandestine cache of sixteen coils in that wallet at all times so that in case I inadvertently fell among evil companions on a weekday evening and had to spend the next day at work recovering my faculties, I could dip into my wallet for the eight coils I owed the inventory and clear my record for the day.

Then something really wonderful happened. During a game of two-handed poker at lunch, the inventory clerk told me that some of the field party chiefs had begun ordering replacement coils—not by stock item number as was usual—but by name, *my* name. They claimed that an Oncken coil was no run-of-the-mill coil. Although it performed like any other coil they said it was a pleasure to work with something that carried a master's touch. He added that he would have to limit this privilege just to party chiefs having the highest seniority.

What Stradivarius had become to the violin, what Rembrandt had become to the portrait and what Shakespeare had become to the sonnet, *I* had become to the galvanometer coil! And we four had made our marks with the humblest of materials: wood, canvas, paper and wire.

I then began to lose myself in my art. I walked, talked, drank, ate and dreamt galvanometer coils. One day I was walking down the hall toward the water cooler when suddenly my shoulders began oscillating with a rhythmic regularity not unlike the shoulder shimmie of the striptease dancer in a burlesque show. One of the gang saw it and rushed up to me offering to help me in any way he could. He must have thought I was suffering a nervous attack. I waved him off with, "There's nothing the matter. I'm okay. I just got to wondering what it would be like to be a galvanometer coil in a four-cycle field."

There you have it. Unless the artist can lose himself in his creation and be at one with it, he will never reach those heights of self-fulfillment reserved for those who are willing to sacrifice everything save life itself for the joy of dwelling even for a brief moment at the pinnacle of the state of the art.

Pride of craft, essential as it is at the vocational level, can be a serious detriment at management levels. Let me interrupt my mini-autobiography (there is more to come) to illustrate:

The manager I am about to describe is of a type so generic that most of my readers will conclude that I have been reading their mail. I am referring to the individual for whom many of my readers have worked at some stage in their careers. He is a division manager, which makes you and four of your colleagues his section managers. Each of you has the responsibility to prepare replies, for his signature, to incoming correspondence that relates primarily to the duties of your respective section. He has delegated this to the section heads in order to ensure that the specialized knowledge and technical accuracy expected by the correspondent is evident in the reply.

However, he has long considered himself to be God's greatest gift to the English language since Shakespeare. He feels morally obligated, therefore, to share the blessings of that gift with his fellow man at every opportunity.

When he comes to work in the morning, several letters are already on his desk for his signature. He will rewrite them, regardless. His pride of craft will not allow him to place his signature on anything but an authentic version. This takes time, so the replies are often held up. You and the other section heads often have to call the correspondents asking them to be patient. Sometimes the passage of time makes the replies moot. The five of you have learned not to try to draft workmanlike letters; the boss will only rewrite them anyway so why waste time trying? This only makes his rewriting job more time-consuming and confirms his long-held opinion that American educational institutions have failed their students miserably, especially in the art of English composition. Meanwhile, you and your colleagues have nicknamed him "Old Bottleneck," the classic example of the manager who is hamstrung by a self-inflicted, up-needle condition.

When others suggest to him that this predilection of his is frustrating his subordinates, hurting the company and extending his workday unduly, he takes umbrage in the self-serving rationalization, "If you want it done right, do it yourself," which he supplements with a brief homily on the *pursuit of excellence*.

Apropos of this is one of Peter Drucker's well-known observations: "Managers often spend so much time trying to do things right, they rarely get around to doing the right things." The "right thing" for this division manager to be doing was to manage, which in this instance would include letter-writing sessions for his subordinates; alas, he had little time to do this, owing to his hopeless addiction to *pride of craft*.

Instant Feedback:
The Third Lure

And now back to my mini-autobiography at the point where I left off.

One day my boss's boss called me into his office to announce my promotion to succeed my boss; he had been transferred to the field (in those days promotions were so rare it would have been a cruel joke to ask the candidate if he wanted it). I asked when I started, and he replied, "At once." I asked him for thirty minutes' delay so I could gather up my jigs, fixtures, jeweler's glass, soldering iron and tweezers and set them up in my new office. He said, "Those things go with the job and not with the man, so that's where they'll stay." "Then what am I supposed to do in my new job?" He replied, "The things that go with that job." "And what are they?" I asked. "You'll find out a lot faster after you take over the job than you will by listening to me. *Take over!*"

Those were the days before company training programs were even heard of, before behavioral scientists had introduced trendy catch phrases like "human resources development." I would not, in any case, have thought of myself as a resource, although I did think of myself as human. With or without training programs, it is simply astonishing how much and how fast a person can learn once he or she decides that there is no alternative. I learned at the outset that as a reward for excellence in coil winding the company terminated my coil-winding career and held me accountable instead for the quality of coils that would be wound by six other men who weren't good enough at it even to get promoted. And I was soon to learn that this promotion would turn out to be not a reward but cruel, sadistic punishment administered without letup, hour after hour, day after day. (Referring to Figure 3a, I am now at level C–E.)

As I walked into my new office to "take over," the phone was ringing. Our accounting section was on the line wanting to know why our unit cost had risen 15 percent in the last month. If this trend continued for another three months, they said, we could buy galvanometer coils from Westinghouse cheaper than we would be making them. We could then abolish the coil-winding section and let the gang go. While I was mulling this prospect over in my mind, the other line rang. I picked it up, asking accounting to "hold." A field party chief was calling from Sapulpa, Oklahoma, saying that the galvanometer coil suspensions of Lot 5947 tended to snap at high-decibel impulses and told me to segregate the ribbonstock that was used on that lot. I said I would, and picked up the other phone only to find that accounting had left the wire without hanging up so I couldn't call back. Then came the morning interoffice mail (the office boy doubled as mailroom clerk), some of it from downtown headquarters with "urgent" stamped on the envelopes. From this point on, it was just one more thing after another until 4:30 P.M. when I left for home.

My boardinghouse landlady greeted me at the door with, "What kind of a day did you have?" Wearily, I replied, "I did more things today, but I still got nothing done." She had greeted me many times before with the same question, but this time my answer was unexpected. Formerly my answer had been something like this: "I delivered eight coils to inventory today. At a unit cost of $1.75 per coil (my labor plus material plus distributed overhead), it is way under the $3.00 per coil the company would have to pay for a Westinghouse coil. Amerada can't afford to do without me!" She mused, "Sounds like an honest day's work for a fair day's pay, Bill." She was right.

This illustrates the third source of satisfaction in vocational work: *instant feedback*. As a coil winder I was always *where* it was happening, *while* it was happening because I was *making* it happen. If anything went wrong, I was the first to know it went wrong, and could correct it before anyone else knew it went wrong. And what no one else knew went wrong didn't really go wrong!

Instant feedback gives one an exhilarating sense of total control. To be sure, total control involves the oft-maligned technique of cover-up. But this is different. *This* is the kind of open, honest, straightforward cover-up for which the eraser on the end of a lead pencil is the classic symbol. The eraser is the instrument with which every American citizen can exercise his constitutional right to make a fool of himself in private!

In management, feedback from below is always delayed. Since you can rarely be where it's happening while it's happening, you have little *during-the-fact* control over anything that's happening. After-the-fact control controls nothing either; the water is already over the dam. So when anything goes wrong within your jurisdiction you are never the first one to know. The person who made it go wrong will be the first. When you are the last, the news will no doubt come from your boss, which is hardly a preferred way to get it. At this late stage there will be little left for you to do but to hose down the ashes, for what went wrong is past the point of no return.

To avoid such outcomes, and to regain the satisfactions formerly enjoyed in their prior vocational jobs, managers go to great lengths to be everywhere at once. This is physically impossible, of course, so they develop tactics that will at least reduce the feedback lag. To the many examples of this that are doubtless coming to your mind, I will add one of my own.

The amateur manager who insists on opening, reading and routing all incoming correspondence, who must sign all outgoing correspondence, who must personally check all expense accounts, approve all requisitions, etc., etc., is often criticized for his or her lack of trust in subordinates. This criticism is off the mark. It is not his or her lack of trust but the lack of satisfaction in knowing what is going on soon enough to be able personally to intervene. Only the "expulsive power of a new affection" can terminate his or her love affair with omnipresence. Short of that he or she has little to look forward to but a truncated career; it is certain that upper management, aware of this daily scenario, has written him or her off as a candidate for advancement.

SCHOOL OF EXPERIENCE/HARD KNOCKS

Let us now resume tracing a manager's path through the school represented in Figure 3a. Pursuing an analogy with the four-year traditional high school or college curriculum, the vertical dimension represents the curriculum's traditional time span, which we will set at the pro-forma thirty-year career. The horizontal dimension represents the hourly units in which credit is given, which we will set at the pro-forma forty-hour work week. I realize that for many a forty-hour work week is a utopian dream. So let me define the *pro-forma* forty-hour work week: It is the work week that hourly personnel avoid working as much as, and that management personnel dare not work as little as. That is why it has never been actually worked by anyone, ever. It is merely a formal abstraction necessary to the negotiation of union contracts and to making my own point with Figure 3a. As the manager moves up through successive levels of greater responsibility, a larger portion of his or her time is managerial in content and—if he or she maintains a constant forty-hour work week—a declining portion of his or her time is vocational. Nevertheless, if his original vocation was, say, engineering, he will regard his *major* as engineering and his minor as *management*, for the greater part of his time may well be vocationally occupied. But most of us fail to recognize the managerial component for what it is, especially when we first encountered it at level C–E. We got used to describing it merely as "just one damned thing after another" because that was how we experienced it. It began to crowd out the things we did best and loved to do most. We evidenced our aversion to it by giving it a name not found in management textbooks. We called it "crap." "I'm up to my armpits in crap" is a familiar rejoinder in coffee-break vernacular. The derivation of the term may be of interest: It is an acronym for *C*ompany *R*esponsibility *A*fter *P*romotion. (If you had thought it stood for something else, your mind was wandering!)

Doing Battle with Administrivia

Our initial response to the "crap" (which incidently includes a significant amount of "administrivia") was to fight it, lest we became engulfed by it. We were fighting the wrong problem, of course, but you can get promoted in spite of not recognizing what your problem is. (For proof of this take yourself as a case in point. Why were you promoted to your present job? Surely not because you were much good as a manager. You were promoted because you were the least worst of all the known candidates when the job opened up. Had there been anyone better in the running, you would not have made it. Moral: You don't have to be a perfect performer to succeed in management; you need only be a little better than the others with whom higher management is comparing you. Now take one more look at your competition and relax!)

So you are eventually promoted. Your immediate reward for fighting "crap" at level C–E is now even more crap at level F–H. Your next promotion rewards you with even more crap until at level I–K you are spending more time fighting "crap" than you are on the things you do best and love to do most—the vocational. When a junior in college, for example, finds that he or she is spending much more time on his minor subjects than on his major, he or she knows it is time to switch. After all, many of his classmates are now majoring in one of his minors and minoring in his major.

Will managers switch? Not on your life! To do that, they would have to turn their backs on their three principal sources of job satisfaction with little or no experience with the satisfactions of management that are available to replace them. So what do amateurs do to extricate themselves? They redefine the problem!

They decide that "crap" is not the problem and therefore fighting it is not the solution. The problem as they now see it is that whereas their first job on the ladder (level A–B) was 100 percent vocational, it is now, say, but 20 percent vocational. Since the angle of the diagonal line is anchored in organizational reality, it can't be pushed back to the left. So the solution is instead to maintain a constant forty-hour *vocational* work week while still giving the management component its due. Referring to the parallelogram A–M–R–B in Figure 3b, they do this by taking work home nights and going to the office weekends so that they can maintain a *constant forty-hour vocational work week*. Since the management component enlarges along the diagonal as they move up the career ladder, the *total* work week increases in duration until at level

SCHOOL OF HARD KNOCKS
THE TRAPEZOIDAL SUBTERFUGE

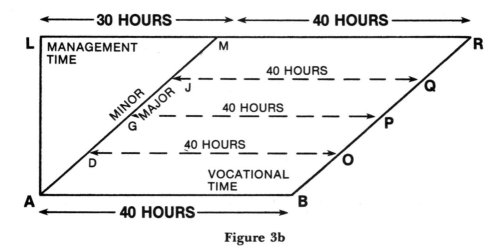

Figure 3b

L–R the manager is putting in a seventy-hour work week consisting of thirty hours managerial (L–M) plus forty hours vocational (M–R). He rationalizes this to his wife, as she complains about his living his job at the expense of his duty to his family, with the words, "Honey, you have it all wrong: It's all for you and the kids."

Nonsense, it's *not* for her and the kids. It's all for *him;* he just won't give it up: His identity, his pride of craft, his instant feedback. This is the biggest fraud perpetrated upon women and children in the last one hundred years. Women executives perpetrate this fraud with equal skill. And if the spouses of you married readers see this, it will become a different ballgame all at once.

The Trapezoidal Subterfuge

We call the quadrilateral A–L–R–B the "trapezoidal subterfuge" because not only does it solve nothing, it also creates problems far more serious than the problem that gives rise to it and which it purports to solve. The trapezoid is the inevitable consequence of an assumption, held unconsciously by most amateurs, that there is a positive straight-line relationship between the weight of organizational responsibility one carries and the amount of personal time necessary to make good on it. The truth, as will be demonstrated below, is that there is little if any correlation between the two. Sometimes it can even work the other way: A heavier load of responsibility can be effectively discharged with a lesser commitment of personal time. This follows at once from our statement made earlier that managers are paid primarily for their judgment and influence and not for their time and labor, however long and hard they may have to work from time to time.

This unconscious assumption has deep roots in every manager's past. Earlier in his working career when most of his time was legitimately vocational, this assumption was an effective time management tool. In vocational work it *is* true that the more you have to do the more time it will take in which to do it. The valid measure of the productivity of vocational time is units per man hour. If you have eighty hours of work to do and only forty hours to do it in, you'll have to split it between yourself and someone else who is as productive as you are. This is the industrial-engineering approach to time management. It is valid exclusively in managing vocational time; but when applied to managing management time, it will result in the time management trapezoid.

Thus referring to Figure 3b, the amateur manager at level L–R is putting in a seventy-hour work week. If he or she now acquires substantially heavier responsibility, either by delegation or by promotion, he or she will continue unconciously to assume that this will require a proportionately greater personal time commitment on his part to make good on it. Limited as he is by the fixed rate at which the earth revolves on its axis, he is now already close to the absolute limit of the time he can devote to his job each day without precipitating a personal crisis. His unconscious assumption tells him that there is, therefore, an absolute limit to the weight of responsibility he can carry, and at a seventy-hour work week he is now at that limit. Since there is no more, that's *it* for him. He has had it. He can kiss his future goodbye for it is now all behind him.

The Truncated Career

If you are a trapezoidal manager, it can be "it" for you at twenty-five, thirty-five, forty-five years old or more. It can be "it" for you at any age, at any organizational level, in any kind of business. "It" doesn't respect persons, ages, status or business. "It" is responsible for the many promising careers that were prematurely truncated, responsible for the many "also-rans" and for the many superannuated and overworked middle managers who have spent years counting the days to their retirement. And it is an inexhaustible source of material for novelists, playwrights, business journalists and management theorists who like to dramatize both the humor and pathos in organizational life.

If you are locked into a seventy-hour trapezoidal work week, theorizers have nothing for you. Their remedies—and they have them—will at best create employment for social engineers and nothing more. But I have better news for you. Since you and you alone got yourself into this fix, you and you alone can get yourself out of it. Life doesn't begin at forty any longer; it begins the moment you discover what life is all about. And—take my word for it—it's never too late to discover this for yourself and benefit from it. (I speak from experience. I was forty-eight years old, married with children aged seven, eleven and fourteen when I made a career decision by leaving a secure management job to become an independent consultant. What I am about to suggest you do may not be as risky or dramatic, but the rewards will surely be there.)

Where Professional Management Begins

The first step is to commit yourself to the time-tested working assumption that there is no *inherent* relationship between the weight of organizational responsibility that a manager carries and the amount of personal time he or she must put in to make good on it. Repeat over and over to yourself until you have internalized it to the point where you act on it daily without giving it conscious thought.

The second step is to understand that there is no theoretical limit to the organizational responsibility you can handle provided you increase the value of each hour you put in proportionately to the increase in responsibility. Management time has two properties: duration and value. The first has a definite limit that can be quickly reached. But as you acquire additional responsibility either by delegation or promotion, the value of each hour you put in must increase proportionately. If it does not, then duration will have to increase to make up for it. As duration increases, so does the length of the work week and the trapezoid will once again overtake you.

I want you to turn a corner now; to make the first of a number of deviations from the conventional "wisdom" of conventional management theory. This is the first corner to turn to become a professional (more will come later in the book), and it will require practice to shed the pervasive influence of your Business School Education. It will be important to repeat over and over again the first of several new truths (actually old truths) to make the transition.

However, merely to repeat over and over a time-tested truth is not, in and of itself, sufficient for internalization. It has to have a valid principle going for it. Coué, the early twentieth-century Frenchman, became famous for his success formula, namely, to repeat before one's bathroom mirror daily, "Every day in every way I'm getting better and better." This turned out to be more than a mere exercise in auto-suggestion; it was a straightforward application of the self-fulfilling prophecy, a phenomenon recognized as valid by most psychologists. What I am asking you to repeat over and over has something just as valid going for it, namely, the principle of leverage, first enunciated more than 2500 years ago by the Greek mathematician Archimedes, without which the Industrial Revolution could not have happened. Without it, I would have been unable to use its managerial analogy in describing how the *value* of the output from management time can be multiplied without increasing the *duration* of the input.

But first let me illustrate that this process of internalization has to contend with (1) continuous and persistent counter-propaganda from others in your organization about the sacredness of the Protestant Work Ethic at *your* organizational level, and (2) abundant evidence that many of the most successful managers at or above your level in your organization have long since taken full advantage of this managerial principle of leverage but nevertheless are putting in a seventy-hour work week. Because their application of the principle is unconscious, intuitive and nonverbal, they lead others—and themselves—to the false conclusion that their success as managers is due primarily to the fact that they labor long and hard at their jobs. I hope that by reading this book they will find that they are succeeding in spite of that fact.

Resisting Deceptive Counter-Propaganda

Let me illuminate these two deceptive influences with two illustrations:

Assume that I am a district sales manager of a company with national distribution. I report to a corporate vice president, sales, located in another city. Reporting to me are eight regional sales managers and reporting to them, in turn, are eight area sales supervisors. To each of them report eight "pocket-picking" street salesmen gathering in the sheaves of greenbacks (pardon the mixed metaphors). There are thus within my district 500 salesmen whose time is 100 percent vocational. It is to them that most run-of-the-mill books on time management are applicable.

Shortly after the end of the last fiscal year, the corporate office came out with the year's sales results, showing that our district had grossed $40 million, or $80,000 per salesman on an average. Considering that our MBO* had targeted $38 million, we felt that Corporate owed us at least a Brownie Point. My vice-president called me to voice his personal congratulations. But he added that he was nevertheless very troubled about my personal performance as a district sales manager and that he was taking the next plane to talk with me personally about it.

When he arrived, the conversation went like this:

V.P.: How many hours a week do you regularly put into your job?

ME: Exactly forty, no more and no less.

V.P.: And what was your gross sales this year?

ME: You know what it was: $40 million.

V.P.: Do you realize that you could double your sales volume if you personally put in an honest week's work like our president and I do?

ME: You mean eighty hours?

V.P.: That would be an honest week's work considering that you are being paid twice what you're worth right now.

ME: I am a professional manager, and I know that there is no relationship between the length of time I personally put in on the job and the value of the final result.

V.P.: Yes, there is.

ME: No, there isn't.

V.P.: Yes, there is.

ME: No, there isn't.

At this point my boss reached across my desk for that color picture of my wife and family, held it up to me, and suggested I carefully study the caption I had written across it before saying another word. (The caption read, "My ideals.")

ME: You're absolutely right. Funny, I hadn't seen it just that way before.

I had lost a small argument and secured my family's well-being. You see I am not a yes-man. I am a principled idealist. The primary value of an honest job is its ability to finance your ideals. I will never

---

*This is an acronym for Management by Objectives.

compromise them. I had no choice, therefore, but to subordinate my
convictions to my ideals and so I began putting in an eighty-hour work
week.

Then came a turn of events that would be a bonanza for the
corporation but a disaster for me. The rumor mill had carried to the
lowest recesses of my district a complete and accurate account of the
argument I had just lost. Most of the street salesmen had been waiting
to get even with me about a series of imagined grievances that I had
sensibly ignored, and they pounced at once on this opportunity. They
conspired to double the district's sales volume to $80 million next year,
which would place my boss in a solid moral position to continue to
require an eighty-hour work week from me indefinitely, thereby
doubling the time I would be available to hear them out. They did this,
as you might well suspect, not by working longer and harder every day,
but by reordering their priorities and revising their sales tactics to
match.

After that year's results were in, my boss called me on the phone:

V.P.: You see. I was right.

ME: If you say so.

V.P.: I want to make sure you get the point. Your forty-hour work week
resulted in $40 million in sales, and your subsequent eighty-hour
work week resulted in $80 million. There is a formula there, isn't
there?

ME: Yes, sir.

V.P.: Get out your pencil. Now that you have the formula, I'm going to
give you your sales goal for the upcoming year.

ME: Just a minute, sir. If you're about to say what I think you're going
to say, you will be charged with being an uncaring person
unmindful of your human obligation to enhance the quality of
life of those who, owing to fateful circumstance, are subject to
your arbitrary beck and call. I plead with you not to offend the
sensibilities of right-thinking people.

V.P.: You have me all wrong. I am not one to be careless of human
values. I am the soul of empathy and compassion. I will, therefore, be satisfied if you just repeat last year's performance. You
doubled your volume last year; double it again!

He hung up.

I was caught between a rock and a hard place. I called my wife
about it. She said that this problem was bigger than the both of us, and
that help was now needed from a cosmic source.

I knew where I could get that help—from the district guru. (In every company location at least one such guru can be found within easy walking distance.) A guru, in this context, is a manager who many, many years ago got caught between a rock and a hard place with his boss and failed to extricate himself. Since that time his career has gone absolutely nowhere. He had, in effect, been fired, so he just stayed on the job. This gave him plenty of time to reflect upon his demise as well as upon the why-fors and the might-have-beens. This long period of cogitation turned him into a very wise man. He now spent most of his time counseling with younger, fast-track managers by placing his hindsight at the disposal of their foresight.

Caught Between a Rock and a Hard Place

I ran down the two flights of stairs to the guru's office, where I found him sitting cross-legged atop his desk, draped Ghandi-fashion in a tattered bedsheet, contemplating his navel. One hand held an extra-dry martini, and the other held a stylus with which he was about to carve in his desk top, in Sanskrit, his latest cosmic insight.

I interrupted the guru (he moved not a muscle) with a life-or-death plea for counsel. After he heard me out, he laid down his alcoholic stimulus and his steel stylus and said, "Your boss was only trying to get your attention. I see he has it at last. When you beat the company's $38 million sales target by $2 million, he also knew about Market Research's data proving that, what with inflation, the demise of one of our competitors and the product modifications we are coming out with, $80 million the following year was well within your grasp. But you were so Brownie-point hungry over your $2 million overshoot, he was sure you thought that you had it made. It's next to impossible to challenge a man who thinks he has it made."

"How do you know all this, oh Guru," I asked worshipfully.

"I haven't been chiseling sanskrit in this desk top for twenty years for nothing," he replied. "And I know a lot more: Your boss found out long ago about the salesmen's conspiracy to get even with you by doubling their sales volume. He made his own analysis of how they did it. And something else you don't know: The sales force is now getting its second wind, and no matter how many or how few hours *you* put in, they are going for the $160 million."

"But my boss still expects me to put in an 'honest week's work' as he and our president do," I demurred.

"He told you that in a desperate attempt to get your attention. Putting in an eighty-hour work week is one way you can convince him he has it. But that is all it will do. Find a more productive way to convince him. Then it won't matter to him what hours you keep."

And thus I learned that the duration of the input to my time had more to do with others' perceptions of me than with the value of its output. But more of this later.

In my second illustration, I shall play the role of president of a local manufacturing company having six plants situated within the greater metropolitan area. A self-made man, I took twenty-five years to rise from hourly worker to company president. As a journeyman mechanic in the Maintenance Department, my job had been to perform routine maintenance on the air conditioning and heating equipment in those plants. For this purpose the company capitalized my job with $40 worth of tools (including tool belt and holster) on which I was to earn an adequate return. The applicable R.O.I. formula was down time as a percent of total scheduled up time, which both I and my foreman kept track of daily on the equipment for which I was responsible. I was also allocated a weekly allowance of $40, which I was free to budget as I saw fit for transportation and meals as I traveled between plants. It had the true characteristic of a management budget: By running like mad and not eating, I could pocket all of it. My third resource, time, was allocated to me in the forty-hour work week units guaranteed in the union contract. That was far and away the most satisfying job in my twenty-five year career—the identity, pride of craft and instant feedback were all there.

Are Boards of Directors Fair-Minded?

Today I am sitting atop a $40 million capital investment on which the shareholders expect an adequate return, and I am trying to make do with a $40 million annual operating budget. During these twenty-five years, two of my three management resources have thus risen by a factor of very nearly a million. In all *fairness* by what factor should my third resource, time, have gone up? My board of directors is as fair-minded as life permits them to be, but as J.F.K. once observed, "Life is not fair." So, like many other CEO's similarly put upon, I settle for what life allows me, a factor of two, resulting in an eighty-hour work week. In all reasonableness (fairness aside), when the required factor is of the order of a million, how significant is a factor of two toward meeting it? It would take too many zeros after the decimal to reach a definitive answer to that question; at the CEO level there is no significant difference in impact between a forty- and an eighty-hour work week.

This brings us to the concept of leverage once again, and the role Archimedes played in focusing our attention upon it.

History, alleged by historians in the following instance to be apocryphal, has it that Archimedes walked into his class in Physics 305 one Monday morning and announced that he had just had an insight. At this his students heaved a sigh of relief, for they had learned that whenever their beloved professor had an insight there would be no quiz that day. Going up to the blackboard, he drew this diagram, familiar today to every high school student of physics:

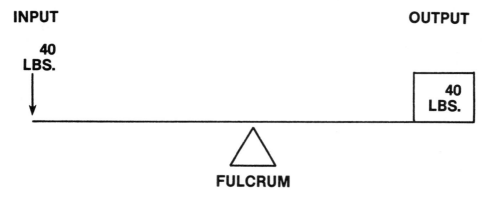

Archimedes' Insight

"Pay close attention," he continued, "for this insight will kick off the Industrial Revolution two thousand years from now. By that time you will have long since been dead, but at least you will have a leg up on the future, which is what a university education is all about. Assume that you want to lift a forty-pound weight and you have no more than forty pounds of muscle power to lift it with. Watch closely: By balancing a plank at the middle and placing the rock on one end, you can lift the rock by pressing down on the plank at a point equidistant at the other end."

The students weren't impressed. "Professor, this gives you no advantage over lifting the rock with your bare hands and only adds mechanical red tape between the effort and the result," ventured a student in the back row.

"A gold star for you, Junior," beamed the professor. "I started out that way to find out how alert you all were this morning. So now to my insight: If the requirement (weight) rises from 40 pounds to 40 million pounds, what do you do with the input?"

"You move the fulcrum over," shouted the class in unison.

The Art of Fulcrum-Moving-Overmanship

"Right," responded the professor. "But you will be dismayed when I tell you what I learned last weekend. On my way back from my fishing lodge, I stopped off at the Delphic Oracle to edit its weekly economic forecast." He continued, "As you know, the letter always ends with the "sooth of the week" that the soothsayers had just finished saying. You will see it in this morning's edition: 'As we peer down the corridors of time, we see arising upon the face of this earth a species of humanity that will be called supervisors, foremen, managers, executives, administrators, captains of industry and industrial statesmen, who, when faced with requirements that have gone up by a factor of a million, will respond by pressing twice as hard.'"

As he spoke, he completed his diagram thus:

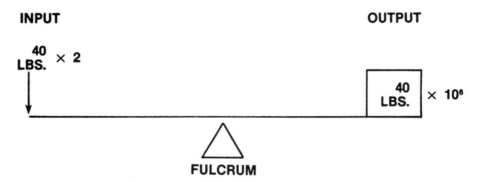

His students were dismayed. "No wonder," one of them said, "that we consider our era to be the golden age of civilization; for if that is how the cream of humanity will respond to so simple a problem, the history of civilization henceforth will be on a downward spiral back to where it started." With that the class bowed their heads for a minute of silence. This was Archimedes *real* insight, swept under the rug by historians to this very day. After all, they have a vested interest in historical progress, which is why they keep insisting that the story is a fabrication.

Moving your managerial fulcrum over in order to leverage the value of your time is an art, which we will henceforth refer to as the art of fulcrum-moving-overmanship. When the amateur is faced with additional responsibility, he or she reacts by working longer and harder at what he or she has been doing all along; the professional responds by moving his or her fulcrum over to the new point of balance dictated by the additional responsibility.

But fulcrum-moving-over takes additional time, as we shall see as we compare the amateur and the pro:

When a boss approaches one of his or her amateur subordinate managers with an additional load of responsibility, the amateur will typically react with words to this effect: "I am gratified by your confidence in me. However, I am already carrying a full load of responsibility to the limit of my working week. What do you want me to stop doing so I can take this on?" If the boss is also an amateur, he or she will be frustrated and antagonized by the sharp end of the needle turned upward by the response. If the person is a professional, he or she will typically reply, "I am delegating to you the solution to that problem along with the additional responsibility. Keep me posted on the progress you are making with both."

If the subordinate is an amateur, he or she will either become trapezoidal or will quit, whichever is deemed to be the lesser of the two evils. But if he is a pro, he will reply, "I am gratified by your confidence in me and am glad to take this on. Please permit me to take off a couple of hours early today so I can make the necessary personal arrangements," thus keeping the needle in the down position.

The Professional Moves His Fulcrum Over

Arriving home early that afternoon, the pro greets his wife with, "The boss just threw another chunk of responsibility at me. Therefore, you will not be seeing me for a season, for I shall be temporarily absenting myself while moving my fulcrum over. But when it is at the new point of balance required by that responsibility—which may take several weeks—I shall return." She throws her arms around him and says, "I'll be here waiting for you. You've always made it back before. You'll do it again. Let's go out on the town tonight and celebrate."

Back at work, he continues to put in forty hours a week keeping his *present* show on the road (he knows better than to hope his boss would relieve him of any of that) plus an *additional* forty hours per week moving his fulcrum over, to get the additional leverage for a total of eighty hours. But that additional forty hours is only temporary and will disappear when the fulcrum is at the new point of balance. He will then be able to carry the new total responsibility on the regular forty-hour work week.

This will be made abundantly clear as we continue with our illustration. On the Saturday morning after our pro and his wife spent the evening out celebrating, his children were playing in their backyard sandbox with their neighbor's children. The latter asked, "Where is your daddy this morning? He's always playing with us on Saturday mornings. What's wrong?" "Nothing is wrong," replied his children. "He has absented himself temporarily to move his fulcrum over. But he'll be back. He has always made it back before, and he'll make it back again."

Four weeks later our pro, fulcrum in balance, made it back to the sandbox. His boss, who lived several houses up the street, passed by on his regular Saturday morning stroll and spotted our pro getting delivery—in the sandbox—of what he went to work for, and made a careful mental note of it.

The following Monday he called our pro into his office and greeted him with these words: "Sam, I see that you have time to squander on your family, church and social interests. What a waste of managerial talent! Get out your pencil. I have a fresh load of responsibility for you."

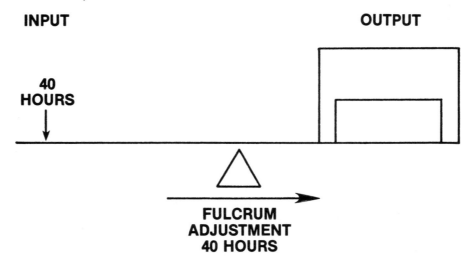

The Name of the Game

Once again our pro will go through the temporary eighty-hours-a-week cycle, only for his boss in due time to load him up with even more. This cycle is inescapable for those who aim to maximize their upward organizational mobility. Its unquestioned acceptance is essential to career success in management. It is incompatible with the vocational work ethic implied in "an honest day's work for a fair day's pay." That is why a career in management is not for everyone. It is only for those to whom the ends are worth the means. Even so, the means carry no guarantee. There is only one top job in any organizational hierarchy. The pro accepts this, too. That is why he or she is mentally and emotionally prepared to settle for the joy of the chase should the quarry become too elusive. It is of the essence of good sportsmanship and sound mental health to be prepared to be a good loser. But no one is a failure who fails to bat a thousand as long as there is a next time up at bat—as there always is for those who are able and willing to stay with the game.

This temporary eighty-hour work week is trapezoidal, to be sure, but trapezoidal to the *left* as in Figure 3c because fulcrum-moving-overmanship involves *managerial,* not vocational, activity. The dotted line A–S–L in Figure 3c will eventually disappear so that the manager can plow the forty hours thus released into the other roles he or she plays in life.

SCHOOL OF EXPERIENCE
THE LEFT-LEANING TRAPEZOID

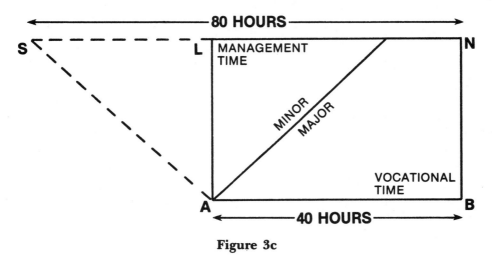

Figure 3c

The Left-Leaning Trapezoid

You play not only the role of manager, but possibly also the role of spouse, parent, neighbor, citizen, church member, political activist, stamp and coin collector, mountain climber—you name it. These roles are what you get up for every morning. Anything worth getting up for must be adequately financed. This has been true without letup ever since the Garden of Eden was shut down. Since its gate has been barred against reentry, you must assume it will continue to be true at least during your lifetime! *That's* why you go to work!

I stress this because, when asked why we get up each morning, we often unthinkingly reply, "In order to go to work." Upon sober thought, most of us will agree that we go to work in order to finance what we get up for. But the amateur, being permanently trapezoidal to the right, never has the time to get delivery on what he or she is spending all his or her waking hours trying to finance. The pro, being only occasionally trapezoidal to the left, does have the time to collect on his or her regular forty-hour weekly investment of time. And that is what management life in its simplest terms is all about.

Archimedes' enunciation of the Law of the Lever opened up a separate branch of physics, called mechanics, thus making high school physics more difficult than it would otherwise have been. It was not only applicable to the lever, but also to the inclined plane, to pulley systems, to the jack-and-screw and to gear trains. It is this last application that has direct relevance to managerial leverage.

The Mechanical Gear Train Analogy

Figure 4a depicts a conventional organization chart. Although I would have preferred otherwise, I have depicted the various positions as equilateral rectangles as a concession to usual custom. I would rather depict them as circles, so that you could be the "big wheel" rather than the "biggest square." If we represent them thus as in Figure 4b and if the wheels at any level are smaller than the wheels above them, and if, moreover, we notch the rims of the wheels thus converting them into gears, we will have the makings of a gear train. If we finally adjust the gear levels until each row of gears engages the row above it, then all *you* have to do is turn through a very small angle to set the bottom gears whirling! That is how you can multiply the value of the output of your time without increasing the duration of your input. The secret is in the gear ratios. But two objections will inevitably be raised to this illustration:

1. Those who are managerially handicapped by having had engineering educations will spot at once that this gear ratio analogy is fatally flawed. (But this book is not for those who will, for that reason

LEVERAGE

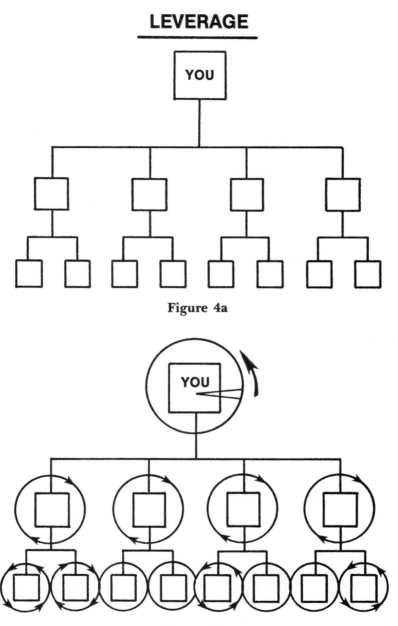

Figure 4a

Figure 4b

alone, miss my point.) Analogies characteristically break down somewhere, and it will be especially instructive to examine the breakdown in
this case: Since the gears on each level will also engage each other

laterally, the torques in adjacent gear trains will be in opposite directions, thus freezing the entire mechanism into a locked position. This is an illuminating analogy to the well-known "bureaucratic bind" through which individual ends are thwarted by organizational means, a phenomenon to which I have already referred.

2. Others who have learned to view organizational behavior from a more theoretical perspective may react to this gear train analogy with moral trepidation: "What about 'quality of life' at the level of the lowest spinnee? This analogy implies an uncaring attitude on the part of the top spinner—a cold disregard of human values, a transparent attempt to whitewash the exploitation of man (spinnee) by man (spinner)." Such concern is clearly misplaced because it overlooks four decisive facts: (1) except for the bottom row every wheel plays or has played both roles, of spinner and spinnee; (2) every wheel is a participant by choice in this arrangement; (3) the opportunities, incentives and role models are clearly visible to those on the bottom row who want to make a career of the game at higher levels; and (4) for those who do not, surely there are other rewarding games in town.

The Three Constraints on Managerial Leverage

Up to this point I have made it clear that fulcrum-moving-overmanship is the key to managing management time, but I have not yet described in detail exactly how it is accomplished. Before I can get to that, I will have to explore with you in greater detail the *objective* sources of the manager's time management problems, namely, (1) the gears above, which are the source of boss-imposed time, (2) the gears on either side, which are the source of his or her system-imposed time and (3) the gears below, which are the source of subordinate-imposed time. These are the three objective constraints on the fulcrum-moving-over process; and the newborn professional manager, having turned the corner, will, in his naiveté and enthusiasm, not understanding the laws governing their operation, run roughshod over them in his determination to increase his organizational leverage. This will result in wholesale gear-stripping with the entire system ending up "spinning its wheels." With each gear thus spinning freely, activity will be high with organizational productivity reduced to zero. To forestall that outcome I shall in the next chapter bring the management molecule back to center stage for a thorough examination of these constraints and the laws by which they operate. When that is behind us, we will resume our course toward fulcrum-moving-overmanship.

4

Building Molecular Support

The most significant attribute contributing to a manager's *upward career mobility* is his or her constructive influence with the boss and with higher management; the one contributing most of his or her *personal productivity* is the ability to get the system working for him or her rather than vice-versa; the one contributing most to his or her *managerial leverage* is to be accessible to subordinates while leaving adequate time to him- or herself. Formulating the three corresponding strategies is the fourth precondition for managing the manager's time.

YOUR BOSS

As pointed out earlier, the role conflict inherent in the managER/ managEE interface must be resolved on the managEE's initiative; although both have much at stake in the relationship the manager, in the managEE role, has far more to gain or lose from it than the boss does in the managER role. And as we are about to show, the professional practice of managEEship by the subordinate manager significantly lessens his or her boss's burden of leadership and supervision, and correspondingly increases the subordinate's scope for exercising judgment and exerting influence. In sum, the boss benefits by having more time to devote to his own managEE role, and the subordinate benefits by having greater discretion in the exercise of his managER role. They both benefit by being able also to devote more time to maximizing, each at his or her own level, their respective intracompany credit ratings. And all this is the precondition for the effective practice of fulcrum-moving-overmanship, the detailed discussion of which is still to come.

But now to the art of managEEship:

Suppose that you have certain duties, responsibilities, roles or functions (hereinafter referred to as "activities") about which your boss's anxiety level is very, very low. This is because he has acquired a high degree of confidence in your competence, rapport with your personality and respect for your character in relation to these activities. As a result he is able to sleep like a baby at night not knowing what you are doing. You have noticed this in his behavior and have accommodated your own to it. Consequently, when anything comes up in this part of your job, you *act on your own, reporting only routinely*, if at all.

But there are other activities of yours about which your boss is somewhat anxious because—for whatever reason—he has acquired less confidence in your competence, and/or less rapport with your personality and/or less respect for your character in your performance of them. He therefore cannot rest easily at night without knowing what you are doing. You have taken note of his behavior in this regard and have accommodated yourself to it. So when anything comes up in this area of your job, you *act, but advise him at once.* You then seek immediate confirmation, in his behavior, of your judgment in choosing this tactic.

There are still other activities over which your boss is plainly nervous, because certain things have happened in this area of your responsibility in the past that have given him much less confidence in your competence, and/or rapport with your personality and/or respect for your character to the extent that, so far as these activities are concerned, he could not sleep soundly at night knowing that you could be taking an initiative without clearing it with him first. You have likewise observed this in his behavior and modified your tactic accordingly: When anything comes up in this part of your job, you first *recommend to him what is to be done and then take the resulting action.* As before, you look for confirmation, in his behavior, of your choice of this tactic.

Your Boss's Anxiety Index

Over still another area of your activity your boss has become rather neurotic, because past events in this area have caused him sufficient anguish (who or what was at fault is irrelevant—only his anguish matters here) to seriously undermine his confidence in your competence, and/or his rapport with your personality and/or his respect for your character. His neurosis triggers an allergy: In this part of your job he is allergic to your ideas (with his own, however, he is quite comfortable); so when he encounters one of yours, he suffers an uncontrollable asthmatic attack. You have noted this in his behavior and have accommodated yourself to it. Therefore, when anything comes up in this part of your job, you go to your boss, state the problem, and *ask him what to do.* Now he need encounter no one's ideas but his own and he is thus spared, through your thoughtfulness, the agony of an asthmatic attack.

There is a final, residual part of your job over which your boss is psychotic. Words fail me to describe what he has suffered over it. Suffice it to say that—for whatever reason, it matters not—he has lost all confidence in your competence in the activities related to it, has lost all rapport with you with regard to them, and considering that he has consistently wound up with the short end of the stick, his respect for your character is describable only with four-letter words. His psychosis triggers a different allergy, for in this part of your job he is allergic to any and all ideas—including his own. You discovered this one day when you were walking down the hall toward the water cooler and spotted him fifteen feet ahead of you going the same way. Suddenly, as if out of the blue, he suffered an abdominal pain that dropped him to the floor. You ran up to him offering assistance, but he waved you away with, "I'm all right. I was just walking along and suddenly I got to thinking about that part of your job. But the thought went away and I'm all right again. Thanks, anyway." This incident duly noted, you then resolved that if ever again your boss encounters one of his own ideas about that part of your job, you would surely not be the one who made him think of it. So whenever anything comes up in this part of your job, you just *wait until he tells you* what to do, however long that may be. (This is called the *taboo* area in the manag*ee* role of every manager's job.)

Let us now summarize these levels of action for easy reference:

5. Act on own; routine reporting only

4. Act, but advise at once

3. Recommend, then take resulting action

2. Ask what to do

1. Wait until told

The Managerial Freedom Scale

This scale is a measure of the degrees of freedom the manager may enjoy in his manag*EE* role insofar as his boss's constraining influence is concerned. (The numbers are reversed to serve a purpose to be made clear in a later chapter.) We will now show that as one progresses from level 1 to level 5 the manager increases his freedom to use his judgment and influence at his own discretion.

Imagine, first, that your boss sees you as a "wait until told" type of manager in your manag*EE* role. That's because every time your name comes up he sees you that way in one of his typical encounters with you. Now, he may have you all wrong; you may not really be a "wait until told" type at all. But if that is nevertheless his spontaneous image of you, he will respond to that image rather than to the reality, which he does not see. As your manager he will have no choice but to tell you what to do and when to do it. This places you at the bottom (level 1 spot) on your freedom scale where you surrender control over both the *timing* and *content* of what you do with your boss-imposed time. I prefer to call it the "prison house of management." And it imposes on your boss the burden of having to do your thinking for you, thus making him a victim of an up-needle situation. You and he are therefore both losers in this, and it's all because of the image he has of you. If he has the wrong image of you, surely it could not be by malice aforethought. Someone must be misleading him, and you are the prime suspect. And if you are misleading him, surely you are not conscious of it. So if your boss's image does not correspond to the *real* you, your responsibility is clear: To behave in a way that will enable him to see the reality rather than the image he has mistaken for you. But don't try to correct his image of you by talking him out of it, because that will only create another image of you in his mind—that of a person who would rather talk than act. You don't want that image to add to his mounting misperceptions of you!

Image or Reality?

Imagine, second, that your boss perceives you instead as an "ask what to do" type of managEE. That's because every time your name comes up, an image pops into his head of a typical chance encounter with you in the parking lot, the cafeteria line, or the washroom where you greet him with, "By the way, that problem I mentioned yesterday has come to a head. What do you want me to do about it?" He has always been able to give an on-the-spot, clear-cut answer. Now in this situation you controlled the *timing* (it was on your initiative, not his) but not the *content* (it was his decision, not yours) of what you do with your boss-imposed time. You do not even begin to resolve the managER/ managEE role conflict between your boss and you until you cross the barrier from level 2 to level 3. Note that the word "act" appears in each of levels 3, 4, and 5, but is absent below the line in levels 1 and 2, where one can only re*act*.

It follows that the professional manager in his managEE role will avoid dealing with his boss from levels 1 and 2. And in his own managER role he will discourage his subordinate managers from using levels 1 and 2 in their dealings with him, although this may take some doing if up until now he has tolerated excessive use on their part of freedom levels 1 and 2. The following two examples may therefore be of help at this point:

Suppose that you had just called a special policy session with your five subordinate managers (in their managEE roles) and began, to their surprise, with these remarks: "Ladies and gentlemen, it has finally dawned upon me that although I have delegated to each of you a great deal of responsibility, I have not granted any of you nearly enough freedom of action to discharge those responsibilities successfully." Pausing a moment to take in the approving glances your people are exchanging over these opening words, you continue, "Now, I have up here on this flip chart something I shall call your freedom scale, on which five levels of managerial freedom of action are defined." You then define for them, much as I have done on these pages for you, what this scale and its individual levels mean. "I have concluded that I can greatly expand your freedom by limiting your authority. You see, up until now I have given you carte blanche authority to decide, on any and all matters, from which of these five freedom levels to lead in your dealings with me. I am, therefore, as of this date, hereby rescinding from each and every one of you until further notice the authority to lead from freedoms 1 and 2. This will raise your average freedom substantially to a level more nearly commensurate with the amount of responsibility you are carrying." You pause. You hear only silence. "Did you all get this?" They nod in stunned wonderment. "Fine. Meeting is over. Good luck. Enjoy your freedom!"

Authority vs. Freedom

Of course, they don't get it. Although they had up until now been complaining among themselves about how little freedom they had, they now agree that *this* is not the kind of freedom they have been longing for. You get a hint of this only two hours later when you encounter one of them by chance in the washroom. He greets you with, "By the way, what do you want me to do about the accounts receivable problem your boss brought up the other day?" You reply, "Now just wait a minute! Were you at our meeting a couple of hours ago? You were? And did you hear my withdrawal of your authority to lead from freedom 2 in dealing with me? You did? Then I hereby charge you with an act of insubordination—of knowingly and without just cause taking an action (Freedom 2) from a position of authority that you did not have. See that this does not happen again!" He has now three authorized alternative levels to choose from, namely, levels 3, 4 and 5. And since the only difference between level 2 and level 3 is a little skull work that in the past you have been lured into doing for him, he should not find the burden unbearable. And for you a needle that had been persistently in the up position has been rotated 180 degrees, thus (1) reducing your subordinate-imposed time and (2) increasing his control over the timing and content of what he does with his boss-imposed time.

But how do you get people to stop leading from freedom level 1? Here is where job descriptions are useful regardless what other purposes they may have been designed to serve. The majority of my readers have some kind of job description covering their duties, responsibilities, roles and functions. If so, your companies no doubt enforce a policy of regularly reviewing them and updating them. Imagine that you and one of your subordinates, Jane, are crouched over your desk reviewing in her job description the section entitled "Duties and Responsibilities." You say, "Now that we've read section 1 together, tell me briefly what you've got going in that area." She does, and to your satisfaction. Section 1 is thus current. So you proceed with, "Now read section 2 and tell me what you've got going there." Here again you are satisfied that she is in fact discharging the stated duties. As you continue in this fashion, you come to the inevitable: "Now read section 7 and tell me what you've got going there." She replies, "I have given that a great deal of thought." "I'm sure you have, but that is not what I asked," you respond. And then this:

SHE: I have put an awful lot of time on this.

YOU: I don't doubt it. But my question is, what have you got going there?

SHE: Burp.

YOU: Let me explain: Can you produce some footprints in the administrative sands of time that would tell me that something went by section 7 recently?

SHE: What *is* this?

YOU: Please don't misunderstand me. I am not trying to evaluate your performance; I am just trying to locate it.

SHE: All right then. There is nothing to show you yet.

YOU: I take it that there is no visible evidence that you have anything going here. Why isn't there?

SHE: You haven't yet told me exactly what you expect of me in this area.

YOU: You mean you have been waiting all this time for me to tell you?

SHE: The management-training course taught us that it is the supervisor's duty to make clear to his subordinates exactly what is expected of them. I was waiting for you to do your duty.

YOU: Were you at that meeting several days ago where I withdrew your authority to lead from freedom 1 in dealing with me?

SHE: Yes.

YOU: I hereby charge you with an act of insubordination, of know-ingly and without just cause taking an action (freedom 1) from a position of authority that you did not have. See that this does not happen again.

Although this may be a rather forceful way to get her attention, it won't be difficult for her to redress your grievance. At the very least a memorandum on your desk with a thoughtful and factual recommen-dation as to what performance you might expect from her in section 7 will get her off the hook.

The way to get people to take initiatives they have been habitually avoiding is simple: *Block all other alternatives.* When the option of doing nothing is no longer available, most people will opt for doing some-thing. That's what happened to her, and with that another upward-pointing needle was rotated 180 degrees and locked into the down position, where it should have been from the very beginning.

And the few people in management who will still not break their habit of seeking the comfort and safety of freedom levels 1 and 2 should be encouraged to transfer to better-paying jobs on the payrolls of your competitors. This will not only put a drag on your competitors' operations, but also enable you to promote replacements who have a more professional attitude toward managing their management time, thus giving you a double benefit. But this must be done as soon as the symptoms show up. The longer you put it off, the harder it will be to pull it off. If you want to give a person a second chance, let it be at your competitors' expense, not at yours.

Climbing the Freedom Ladder

This brings us to our discussion of freedom levels 3, 4 and 5, which, in that order, give the manager, in his or her managEE role, progressively greater control over the timing and content of his or her boss-imposed time. For this purpose I shall use a parable in which I shall play the role of vice-president of a hundred-year-old manufactur-ing firm. We are the dominant producer of mouse traps in the world and, because mice have not changed their habits in one hundred years neither has our basic product design. We have no research and development expense and our tooling costs are the lowest in the industry. In short, we have it made.

Recently, however, our company was acquired by a conglomerate, which installed one of its own as president, who immediately hired an outside consulting firm to study our operations and make recommend-ations. One year and $1 million later their report emerged, a copy of which was given to each vice-president.

The leading and principal recommendation was that our com-pany go in-house to meet all its information-processing needs. Esti-mates as to capital and staffing requirements were given, and recommendations were made as to the recruiting of key personnel having the requisite technological expertise to manage the resulting data-processing operation. No recommendation was made, however, as to where, organizationally, the operation should be berthed, although a job description had been written for the top job. Our new president called a meeting to decide this matter, but none of the vice-presidents was anxious to have a "whiz kid" organization destabilize *his* depart-ment. Indeed, none had agreed that we should accept any of the consultant's recommendations, although we did agree that at a cost of $1 million we could not afford not to. Sensing the ambivalence that dominated the meeting, our president decided that this new operation would be the responsibility of my department. He reasoned that since my retirement was only eighteen months away, I would probably be gone before anything of significance happened. His logic was unas-sailable and confirmed by the concurring glances of the other vice-presidents in my direction. So I resigned myself to taking responsibility for the successful implementation of the recommendation. That I needed at once to recruit the best data-processing manager in the country was obvious.

The consulting firm, which also had a "headhunting" service, volunteered to find him. Within a month I was notified that they had located him and that he was ready to be interviewed. I decided instead to take their word for it and made him the offer at once. Three days later he accepted and five days later he reported for duty. At twenty-eight years old, he had a Ph.D. in computer technology, had read several widely quoted papers at international conclaves of the profes-sional society to which he belonged and—as the consultant told me—had an I.Q. of 175 and sported a Sigma Xi key. Having never made it past eighth grade myself, I was relying on this man to get me off the hook.

When the Pro Works for the Amateur

In our initial meeting together I asked him what he planned to do. "Research," he replied. I asked him how one would go about doing that. He said that if I had known how, I would not have needed him.

Relieved, I told him he was free to go and do it, but how, I asked, would I know it when I saw it? "It will be a report," he replied. "When will it be ready?" I asked. He replied that I could expect it within three months. This jolted me; I had rather hoped that my retirement date would have preceded it. We shook hands and I didn't see him again for about two months.

What I did not know was that in addition to being a top professional in his vocational field he was also a true professional in management—especially in its managEE aspects. So watch how I discovered this as I continue my story.

It was now 4:30 P.M. Friday, nine weeks after the young man signed in, and I was behind my desk elbow-deep in paperwork at the end of the hardest working week of my career. My head was splitting, my temples thumping. There was nothing the matter with me that a double martini and a dancing girl wouldn't fix. I had already arranged for them both to be ready for me at the club at 5:15 P.M. Only forty-five minutes stood between me and instant rehabilitation when our young man presented himself in my office doorway and said, "Sir, do you have a minute?"

Seeing what looked like the dreaded report in a ring binder under his arm I growled, "Can't you see I am up to my armpits in crap?" He replied, "Sir, I sensed before I came in that you were working under great pressure and should not be disturbed. But I just couldn't hold back, considering that I have under my arm what could easily become the biggest Brownie points of your career." "Then don't just stand there; I've been short of those things for years. Sit down. Show me what you've got!"

Seated side by side at my conference table he began giving me a "walk through" of his report. The first chapter listed the sequential steps to install the necessary hardware, with the capital cost of each. As the total mounted, my anxiety mounted, too. At the half-million-dollar mark I began to perspire. "That's a lot of money!" I exclaimed. "It ain't peanuts," he agreed. "But suppose something goes wrong?" I asked. "A half million down the tubes," he said. "Then I've just run out of time," I replied, getting up. He beckoned me back down. "But in the next section I get to my failsafes, based on the inevitability of Murphy's three Laws." "Murphy's what?" I asked. "Never mind, I have researched the experiences of many projects like this one and have catalogued all of the things that have gone wrong, which are therefore the things that can go wrong here too. Also, I have interviewed eight other companies who have been through what we are about to go through and asked them all the same question, namely, if you had it to do over, what would you do differently? I took down what they said on tape and analyzed it all. From this I developed my failsafes as insurance on each step of the way." "Show me them," I said, forgetting that I had just run out of time.

Now if fear of the unknown is truly one of the sources of our anxieties, then this young man was on the right track! Replacing my unknowns with knowns, I had less to fear, and I showed my relief by closing the report and saying, "It's five o'clock and I have to leave for a 5:15 P.M. appointment. I'm taking this report with me so I can get deeper into it. When I've finished I'll let you have my decision."

The young man as a professional in his managEE role had to think fast. If he acceded to this he would be glued to the 1 position on his freedom scale (i.e., wait until told) where he would have surrendered to me control of the timing and content of our managER/managEE relationship, perhaps indefinitely. As a pro his instinct was urgently to avoid this possibility. "I am gratified that you think so well of this report," he said, "and I would be glad to leave it with you but I just noticed something in this report that would insult your intelligence if I left it as it is. Let me have it back, and if you will give me an appointment at 10:00 A.M. Monday, I'll be here with a revision that will blow your mind."

By now I was just putty in this young man's hands. He got my last half-hour of the week by dangling a Brownie point before my eyes, he got an appointment with me for 10:00 A.M. on Monday with his mind-blower and left me with nothing to burden my time except that appointment. As Benjamin Franklin's grandfather once observed, "He who has the working papers has control." A down-needle, if ever I saw one. And I didn't have to lift a finger.

He Who Has the Working Papers Has Control

Monday morning at 10:02 A.M. he showed up. "You're late," I chided. "Let's see that mind-blowing revision." He opened the report, pointed to the middle of a paragraph, and said, "I revised that semicolon to a comma." Surprised, I asked, "Could it have made all that difference?" "Read it yourself and find out," he chuckled.

So now he had me reading it! Had he acceded to my desire to keep that report over the weekend, I would not have read a word of it by 10 o'clock on Monday. I was reading it now, all right, and under his direct supervision to boot. One of the principles of professional managEEship is not to let your boss read anything you write him except under your immediate supervision (if you can possibly help it), simply because he is not competent to do so alone. There is no telling what strange extraneous thoughts might enter his head to divert his attention from what you are earnestly trying to say. Moreover, when you leave, you can take the paper with you, thus leaving the needle in the down position—the position that keeps you out of freedom levels 1 and 2 and frees your boss of any additional subordinate-imposed time in connection with this matter.

As we continued together section after section of the report, unknowns that I didn't even know about were being replaced by knowns I didn't even know existed. Anxiety was being slowly trans-formed into familiarity, but at 11:00 A.M. my secretary interrupted us for a meeting I had to attend. I grabbed the report saying, "Young man, I'll finish going through the rest of it before the week is out and I'll let you have my decision. I have to go now."

The young man was thinking fast. Just as professional house-to-house salespeople memorize every ploy and objection customers are known to use to avoid making a buying decision, so he had mastered the devices amateur managERs are known to use to deflect the initiatives of their professional managEEs. He then quickly said, "Sir, I am embarrassed—*two* shoddy jobs back to back! It's never happened to me before. But I cannot insult your intelligence by leaving with you a report with a missing enclosure." I leafed through it and said, "I don't see any missing enclosure." "No wonder," he replied. "It's missing! But if you'll let me have it back and give me another appointment at 10:00 A.M. tomorrow, I'll have an enclosure that will make your eyes pop."

This pattern continued on a daily-appointment basis in which his ingenuity in holding on to the initiative was sorely tested, for I was the ultimate in amateur managERship. This validates the principle stated earlier, that in resolving the role conflict inherent in managER/managEE relationships the initiative must be taken by the one playing the managEE role if there is to be any chance of success.

On the following Monday morning (the sixth such appointment in a row) I sensed in myself a touch of boredom as he walked in at 9:59 A.M. My emotional tone over this period had evolved from anxiety through familiarity but not yet to anticipation. Putting in still another hour on this—by now—familiar matter had little appeal for me. I said to him, "All we've done on this project for more than a week is just talk, nothing but talk. This company was not built on talk. Action is what made us what we are today. When, young man, are we going to start seeing some action on this project?" "Right now," he answered as he left my office as if propelled by a rocket. Suddenly I wondered what had happened. I wondered whether he thought I had just authorized him to go ahead with the project. My anxieties mounted. I called to my secretary, "Have that young man come back." When he returned, I said, "Did you get the idea that I just authorized you to go ahead with that project?" "I got that loud and clear," he answered. "You are right, of course," I shot back. "But how much latitude do you expect to use in carrying it out?"

The Break for Freedom

Remember, now, this man was a pro in his vocation, yielding to no one in the data-processing field. Predictably, nothing but level 5 on his freedom scale would satisfy his professional pride. "Carte blanche, with only routine reports, of course," he answered. "That's what I was afraid of," I countered. "Instead you are to keep me abreast of what you're up to on a current basis." But he was not about to accept freedom level 4 without a struggle worthy of his self-esteem. "Don't you have confidence in my competence, rapport with my personality and respect for my character in managing this project?" he asked. "I am extremely high on you in all these respects," I said warmly, "but it would nevertheless make me very nervous if you exercised the latitude implied in carte blanche." "But why would that make you nervous, if you are as high on me as you say you are?" he asked plaintively. "I would like to answer that," I replied, "but there is a federal law prohibiting the practice of psychiatry without a license. Still, you are entitled to an answer. I have for years been retaining a psychiatrist for the sole purpose of answering questions my subordinates have been asking me about the workings of the innermost depths of my psyche. He is an expert at 'unscrewing the inscrutable.' You should be enlightened by his report, which, considering his case backlog, will be ready in a couple of months. Then you'll have your answer. But between now and then, keep me informed on a current basis."

He had just been rethreaded, a necessary means to a desirable end, which was to wrest freedom level 5 from me in due time. Meanwhile, he wondered, at freedom level 4 what constituted keeping me informed on a "current" basis? Three times a day? Every twenty-four hours? He didn't know.

The Bolt Rethreads the Nut

As he shuffled down the hall, he knew he had to have that question answered. The simplest way would have been to return and ask me. But that would be typical amateur managEEship; he would have been leading from freedom level 2: What if he received an answer he didn't want? As Benjamin Franklin's grandfather observed so well, "If you don't want to do what your boss tells you to do then for heaven's sake don't ask him; but once having asked him, then go do it, but don't hang back and gripe, for it shows you as a poor sport."

So he decided to use the scientific method of hypothesizing. Having studied my strengths and weaknesses for more than two months he decided that my emotional stamina was such that I could tolerate my fear of the unknown for an accumulation of up to twenty-four hours of unknowns, but beyond that he'd run the risk of losing even his number 4 level of freedom. He decided to test it.

Twenty-four hours later he called—just three seconds before I was about to call *him*. I answered his ring. "Good morning, sir," he began, "I am calling to keep you informed on a current basis." I shot back, "It was a photo finish. I was just starting to call you. It seems forever since I've heard from you. Fill me in." As he filled me in, replacing my twenty-four-hour accumulation of unknowns with one known after another, my anxieties steadily subsided. At the end of exactly eight minutes I indulged in a hearty yawn. Hearing that, he brought his call to a prompt conclusion. When the boss is bored, he is no longer anxious, mused the young man to himself, so to extend the call any longer might have made him anxious again. Quitting while I'm ahead has always served me well. (I did not know all this at the time, of course; only now as an author is my muse serving me so well.)

At exactly the same time the next day he called me again. This time it was close, but no photo finish. And finally I yawned again, but this time after only seven minutes. The following day my yawn came after only six minutes. He spotted a trend! In his mind's eye he extrapolated it, saying to himself. "If this rate keeps up, on the eighth day the boss will be bored *before* I call him." And that is just what happened, as we are about to see.

The Trend Toward Ultimate Freedom

On the eighth day I answered his ring, and when he was one minute into his report I interrupted. "Young man, you seem to be having a problem of some sort with your self-confidence. Every day you've been calling me about what you're up to. Did you have a mother-dependency problem as a child? You seem to have a deep-seated need for stroking, or comfort, like a youngster running to the teacher with 'See what I did.' I believe in you—so square your shoulders, head up! Carry the ball."

If the young man had been an amateur instead of a professional he would have been outraged by this and rightly so. The unfairness of it! He had been doing exactly what I had told him to do, and now he was being cut down for it in a most demeaning way. An amateur would surely have insisted upon his right to fair and just treatment.

But that he was a professional became immediately obvious. Although I was wrongfully cutting him down, he sat grinning from ear to ear with deep satisfaction, exclaiming to himself, "Hot damn! My extrapolation came out on the button! Who needs fairness and justice when freedom is within one's grasp?"

He saw that he was again being rethreaded, normally an unpleasant experience, but this was the exception. "You are absolutely right," he came back as I paused, "I *did* have a mother-dependency problem when I was a child. My wife has often told me it has become my Achilles' heel today. She has a supervisory job in another company; they sent her to their one-week management course where she was taught that the supervisor must constantly plumb the depths of the innermost needs and wants of his or her subordinates, and you fit their description of the ideal supervisor to a 'T.' With your help I can overcome my dependency syndrome. Just let me know whenever it rears its head and I'll do the rest. Meanwhile, for my part, I'll never bring this project up again." I balked: "I didn't say *never* to bring it up, just keep me current on your progress, but not every day!"

What does "currently" mean now, he wondered? As a professional he had to hypothesize to find out. "A week seems not too risky; I'll give it a try," he decided.

Exactly a week later he called. It was another photo finish. And when I yawned he looked at his watch and mentally noted that it was eight minutes. The next week it took seven minutes for me to yawn. And the following week, six minutes. "This is where I came in," he beamed to himself. He hoped the extrapolation would come out with the same precision that it had the first time around. It did. On the eighth call eight weeks later I again ripped into him with the same criticisms, and he came back with a response as empathetic and accommodative as before, ending with, "… and for my part, I promise

I will never bring this project up again." And as before, I corrected him with, "I didn't say never, just not every week!"

This time he hypothesized a month as fitting my definition of "current." This was now to be the third time around, and was virtually a replay of the previous two cycles. However, on the eighth call eight months later I decided to put my foot down. "Look, young man," I said, "I've been beating about the bush on this dependency syndrome of yours, trying to use the sophisticated psychological concepts and techniques explained in a book on supervision my president gave me the day you reported to work. Where did it get us? It just dragged things out, that's all. So let me get it across to you the plain old way I know best. All I ever wanted from you on this project from the very beginning was a footnote in your quarterly progress report."

That was a boldfaced lie and he knew it. Had he been an amateur he would have felt it his moral duty to call me on it. But as a pro he knew that his moral duty in that regard would have to wait, for he had an even higher duty to attend to first. As soon as he and I hung up he immediately dialed his wife and exclaimed, "Get out your new dress, darling. We are going to celebrate tonight. I have just snagged the number-5 spot on my freedom scale!"

The Moment of Truth for the ManagEE

How long did it take him to climb one rung (from level 4 to level 5) on his freedom ladder? It was done in three cycles: eight months for the third cycle, two months (eight weeks) for the second cycle and eight days for the first, for a total of ten months and eight days. Why so long? Several reasons: (1) A lot of money was at risk, (2) I, his boss, was on very unfamiliar ground and (3) bosses, in their managER roles tend to change very slowly. The professional knows this and uses patience and persistence as his two most useful allies.

Amateurs in management, on reading the above account, will react typically: "Sure it worked. But if the young man's boss, the vice-president, had been a competent manager, the young man would not have had to use the manipulative approach in order to be allowed to do a job that, in any event, he was hired to do. If management would just let people do their jobs, this kind of shadow boxing would not be necessary." Notice the pejoratives that amateurs so typically rely on, "manipulative," "allowed," "shadow boxing" and so on. It is the vocabulary of the also-rans whose lexicons are authored by their favorite utopian management theorists.

If I let the story end here it would lose its credibility. The number-5 spot on the freedom scale is a high risk position to be in. Although it may take a comparatively long time to get there, the trip down to the number-1 spot can be sudden, violent and fast, as every experienced manager knows. Let's see how it can happen:

The Management Trap Door

During the following week I decided that I had matters sufficiently under control to risk being away for three weeks on a long-delayed field inspection trip. About two weeks after I departed, Murphy's three Laws ganged up on my young data-processing manager and created a problem so severe that our president, in my absence, had to get deeply involved. As hindsight would show, the young man was in no way at fault, but our president had not known enough about the project to be certain who was. The young man tried to reach me for several days before our president became involved, but to no avail. Upon my return I entered my office unaware that anything was amiss until I saw a note on my desk in our president's handwriting addressed to me. It said: "See me at once upon your return."

Perplexed, I called him to ask what it was he wanted to see me about. He replied that considering the size of my salary, I had better know what it was about before I walked into his office. On my way there I checked with some of the other vice-presidents for some hint of what the problem might be, but I encountered only sealed lips. On entering the president's office he greeted me with, "What has that young data-processing manager been up to over the last few weeks?" "How should I know?" I replied. "I am a vice-president, so I delegate. The executive development course you sent us to taught us to delegate! They taught us that to delegate, you have to trust. I trust that young man. So, I took a field trip. That's why I don't know." The president's eyes bored into mine like two laser beams as he said, "That young man works for you, not for me; yet I know what he's been up to and you do not. So give me just one reason why I need you."

While I was standing there trying to think of a reason, my president turned ninety degrees in his overstuffed leather-upholstered executive swivel chair toward the blacksmith's forge he had bolted to his office floor and kept at a white heat night and day. With the eye of a connoisseur, he reached toward it to grasp one of the dozen pokers he had stashed there. It was an ebony-handled poker from a medieval castle in central Europe, vintage eleventh century A.D. As he withdrew it the hot end momentarily illuminated that corner of the room, and before I knew what was happening he drove it up through the most sensitive orifice of my body until it singed my tonsils. I leaped ten feet in the air and hit the floor running. In no time at all I entered the young man's office with the cold end of that poker dragging on the floor behind me. I withdrew it and did unto him as I myself had just been done unto. When he landed after his ten-foot leap he cried, "Boss, you're not being fair. This is downright unjust. You've jumped to conclusions after hearing only one side of the story. That's not what you and I were taught when we were sent to the company's course on problem solving for managers. We were taught to state the problem, weigh the evidence and arrive, like two reasonable people, at a rational and balanced conclusion. You're not just! You're not fair!"

"I resent that," I retorted, "because you know my reputation for having the keenest sense of fairness and justice of anyone in this corporation *except* on those rare occasions when my innards are a boiling cauldron—when I temporarily lose all sense of fairness and justice. However, three months hence when we are both released from the hospital my sense of fairness and justice will return. Then you and I will sit down calmly and arrive at a rational, dispassionate conclusion; but between now and then it will be freedom level 1 for you, Junior!"

Management's Occupational Hazards

Every occupation has its hazards. Prudent persons carefully weigh the hazards of the occupation of their choice before they commit themselves to it. But once committed, they take those hazards in stride. In most instances when a manager is dramatically knocked down from number 5 to number 1 on his freedom scale it happens spontaneously without malice aforethought as a reflex from a sudden and severe blow to the corporation's balance sheet, to its public image, to its competitive position, to its employee relations, to its legal status, or whatever. However, if in your company these things happen more often than not as a result of malevolent premeditation, then it would appear that in your company at least, they cannot be classed as just an occupational hazard; and you would do well to direct the rest of your career elsewhere. In my own experience I have rarely encountered premeditated, malevolent intent behind such knock-downs. But forewarned is forearmed; so when your turn comes you will be prepared to make your decision either to pick yourself up and start over again in a spirit of good sportsmanship or to seek a position with another team.

In the case of our young data-processing manager, of course, what happened to him was "just one of those things." And I am glad to report that was his conclusion, too; its memory will surely linger long and serve him well!

The Casualty Insurance Policy

The five-point freedom scale serves as the managEE's measure of how much *freedom* he will enjoy in using his own judgment and influence on an assignment, program or project he is responsible for. Simultaneously, it serves as his managER's measure of his exposure to risk. It is the casualty insurance policy the manager takes out on that responsibility at a "deductible"—from 1 to 5—appropriate to his anxiety index.

As in its analogy, the conventional casualty insurance policy, the higher the deductible the lower the premiums and vice versa. At the highest deductible, number 5, the managER's exposure to risk is highest (high deductible) and his premium in supervisory time and attention is low. As the deductible is lowered, so is his exposure to risk but his premium in supervisory time is raised accordingly. Deductibles 2 and 1 do not reduce exposure to risk but nonetheless dramatically raise the premium in the amount of supervision they require, so they are not economic and are therefore avoided by professional managers.

Hindsight on the red-hot poker incident tells us that I erred in going on a three weeks' field trip insured at the highest deductible level. Although my confidence in the young man warranted that level, the reliability of Murphy's laws did not. At a deductible level of 4 my president's involvement would have been avoided, but at the cost of my managing to be reachable at any time. A deductible at level 3 would have required that I cancel the trip entirely, a premium I was unwilling to pay. However, the young man had worked so hard to achieve the number 5 level on his freedom scale, I apparently did not have the heart to lower it to 4 during my absence. It was a judgment call that I had time in the hospital to think hard about.

As it turned out, the incident brought us much closer together, for as luck would have it, we shared the same hospital room!

YOUR INTERNAL PEERS

At 4:30 P.M. Friday, a half-hour before quitting time, a phone rang in the Purchasing Department. A long-service employee, five times a grandmother, glanced at her wristwatch, picked up the phone and said wearily, "Purchasing Department." The voice on the other end said, "We want five more Type Y castings delivered on the receiving dock outside Building 3 at 8 o'clock Monday morning." This woman had been taught in the department's training program never to say yes at the outset to any such request from Manufacturing. Instead, as she was taught, she asked, "Who wants them?" "Mr. Smith," was the reply. Glancing through a list of names in her little black book, she replied (as she had been taught), "In that case we must have the request in writing."

At 4:45 P.M., fifteen minutes later, the same phone rang again with an identical request, but for delivery on the receiving dock outside Building 9. The originator of this request turned out to be a Mr. Jones, who also was listed in her little black book. But in this case she was taught to reply, "Please tell Mr. Jones that he will have what he wants, where he wants it, when he wants it, because we are banking on his perfect track record of catching up with and straightening out the paperwork within twenty-four hours of delivery."

For Mr. Jones it was "fly now and pay later" while for Mr. Smith it was "pay now and fly later—if ever." Why the difference?

Your Intracompany Credit Rating

It all goes back to what happened three years earlier just after both Smith and Jones had been hired as new manufacturing superintendents, one in Shop 3 and the other in Shop 9. It was at 4:30 P.M. on a Friday way back then when this same woman answered two identical calls—fifteen minutes apart—from these same two men, for some materials they wanted delivered early the following Monday morning. The call from Smith went as follows:

SMITH: We want [whatever it was] delivered here at Shop 3 Monday at 8:30 A.M.

SHE: Who wants it?

SMITH: I want it. The name's Smith, Superintendent of Shop 3.

SHE: I've worked this desk steady for twenty-eight years and this company has no superintendent named Smith.

SMITH: I was just hired a couple of days ago, that's why you don't know about me yet.

SHE: In that case you will have what you want, when you want it, where you want it because it is the Purchasing Department's policy always to give a new superintendent an even break at least once.

The exact same dialogue followed fifteen minutes later between her and Jones.

She then went to her supervisor to inform him that, in accordance with department policy, she had made a "rush" commitment to these two men. After checking into it, her supervisor discovered that the usual sources of the requested materials were out of stock, and that the department would have to work over the weekend to locate alternate sources, arrange transportation, etc., to make good on the commitment. By 5:30 P.M. the woman had missed her carpool and was trying to get hold of her daughter-in-law to let her know that she would be unable to spend the weekend with her grandchildren. At 7:00 P.M. her department head gave her a lift home.

The following morning she was at work with her coworkers putting in overtime for Jones and Smith. The sacrificial blood of loyal and devoted employees was oozing through the cracks in the floor between the desks as these people gave their all for the good of the company. The head of the department was sweating out the overrun this was causing in his overtime budget and the certain trouble the union steward would give him when he found out how he had picked the employees for overtime work.

The sun rose the following Monday morning at the start of what was to turn out to be an eventful and fateful week—eventful for Jones but fateful for Smith. Although Smith's and Jones' week obviously ran concurrently, our purpose will be best served by describing Smith's week first and Jones' week second.

Above and Beyond the Call of Duty

At 8:25 A.M. Smith stood with one of his foremen on his receiving dock awaiting delivery. Exactly five minutes later a tractor-trailer roared through the gate and pulled up and backed up to the dock. Smith supervised the unloading of seven crates, checked them against the invoice, and signed it off. Purchasing had made a three-point landing! As the truck pulled away, his foreman said to him, "Lousy luck! I just got word that the parts that were being sent to us by our Indiana plant won't be here for a month—the plant's on strike. Without those parts we can't use these materials." "You just can't win them all," replied Smith, "so we might just as well let these crates sit here till they arrive." With that, the two men went each his own way.

Three days later the woman in Purchasing, on her way to the company cafeteria for lunch, passed the receiving dock outside Building 3 and saw those crates still sitting there, untouched. Although it was clearly none of her official business what Manufacturing did with its materials, she wheeled around at once and ran back to the Purchasing Department, ascended three flights of stairs and burst into the Department Head's office. Breathlessly she told him what she had just seen. He gasped in disbelief. "Thanks, Matilda," he said. "Spread the word to everyone in the department to drop everything and come here. I have an important announcement to make."

The Short End of the Stick

Ten minutes later his office, far too small to accommodate that many people, was three deep in human flesh, with the overage draped on chair backs, coat racks and windowsills. He rapped for order and announced that Matilda had something of importance to share. When she had finished, a stunned hush swept across the room. The Department Head broke the silence: "All right, guys and gals, get out your little black books and take down the name of one Horatio Smith, Superintendent of Shop 3. We are hereby assigning him an intracompany credit rating of zero. In the future when he wants anything from us, he'll have to go strictly by the book. Meeting dismissed!"

Jones was also standing beside his foreman at 8:25 A.M. Monday waiting for delivery. At 8:45 A.M. the truck that had just made its delivery to Smith rolled up. Jones duly checked the seven crates and signed off on the invoice. A three-point landing for Jones, too! Jones' foreman then informed him about the strike-bound plant and the nondelivery that would result from it. The conversation then went like this:

FOREMAN: It's just one of those things. You have to take the bad with the good. This dock is as good a place as any to store these crates until we get the other delivery.

JONES: We have no time to lose. We have to get these crates out of sight fast.

FOREMAN: Why? They're well protected where they are.

JONES: There's no time to discuss it. Just take my word for it: We'll have a crisis on our hands if we can't make these crates disappear at once.

FOREMAN: Disappear? The warehouse is loaded; we can't put them in the shop or Safety Engineering will get upset. We're cramped for space. But did you say disappear? I'm only half kidding but how about ducking them into the mill pond behind the shop—it has eighteen feet of water in it.

JONES: You're *not* kidding. See those new waterproof tarpaulins
            yonder? Round up some strong backs, wrap these crates
            in them so as to keep the water from getting to them and
            lower them into the pond out of sight. Swear all witnesses
            to secrecy. You have ten minutes to get it done.
FOREMAN: They'll think we're crazy.
JONES: Remember, mum's the word.

Twenty minutes later the last of the tarpaulin-wrapped crates
disappeared below the water's surface just in the nick of time as one of
the Purchasing Department's employees rounded the corner of the
shop on his way to work. He saw nothing amiss.

Jones then went back to his job.

Wednesday morning his secretary ran into vague rumors in the
cafeteria that some mysterious objects were lying at the bottom of the
mill pond. Although no one had seen them, the rumor was persistent.
She happened to mention it to Jones. He sprang into action. He
dictated a letter to the head of the Purchasing Department, the essence
of which went as follows:

> There is a rumor going the rounds to the effect that something—no
> one knows what—is at the bottom of the mill pond. Don't believe
> anything you hear. Where there's smoke, there's fire, so let me give it to
> you straight.
>
> The seven crates of materials your people worked all weekend to get
> for us were sorely needed in order to hold onto one of our most valued
> customers—you know the one I'm talking about. If we had failed that
> customer without a good reason, it would have meant the loss of many
> jobs, some of them in your Department. So the effort you all made was
> worthwhile just on its merits alone.
>
> However, when the delivery was made Monday morning the word
> came that the other plant was on strike so we could not make use of the
> materials. I knew our customers would understand our predicament and
> not make us suffer for it. But I panicked when I thought about what
> your people had gone through for what turned out to be a false alarm. I
> didn't have time to think about how to level with you all before you found
> out, so I just made those crates disappear in order to give me time to
> think. Yes, that's where they are. They're well protected and I am having
> my boys raise them as soon as I finish dictating this. I hope your people
> will understand.
>
> (Signed) Algernon Jones

The memorandum arrived in Purchasing early Wednesday afternoon shortly after the meeting in the Department Head's office had

broken up. He stapled a buck-slip to it and routed it to all the supervisors in his department requesting that they show it to their employees. He added the cryptic comment, "Top Rating," across the buck-slip and dropped it in his out-basket. He then called Jones and told him there was no use to worry and hoped he'd have better luck next time.

As the weeks and months rolled on, Smith and Jones were steadily earning their respective, but opposite, credit ratings with the other internal peer elements on their molecules. Smith, as you might expect, had developed similarly low ratings with Building Maintenance, Personnel, Accounting, Administrative Services and others. Since all of his business within the intracompany economy had to be on a cash-in-advance basis (i.e., strictly by the book), he was slowly succumbing to administrative paralysis. He was, in effect, being beaten down by the system into blind conformity, strangled by administrivia and red tape. His system-imposed time had grown to the point where he had lost the initiative in his managee role, lost control of his managER role to the up-needle phenomenon, thus swamping him with subordinate-imposed time. His job, in short, was out of control, which he hoped to remedy with the seventy-hour week he recently started putting in. All this was taking an alarming toll on his production unit costs, his safety record, his spoilage rate, his QC reject rate and his personnel turnover rate. Although I would be tempted here to quote the Biblical proverb, "Whatsoever a man soweth, that shall he also reap," I must resist because it severely understates Smith's predicament. Although Smith was reaping he was also continuing to sow, with the result that the harvest engulfed him, after which he could sow and reap no more. Smith, in short, had turned his molecule into a career liability.

"Whatsoever a Man Soweth . . ."

Meanwhile, Jones was moving around his shop relaxed, but with a spring in his walk, wondering what Smith could possibly be complaining about. He had long since earned top credit ratings with his molecular internal peers and maintained them by using them as sparingly as possible. Whereas in the private sector economy you have to use your credit often to keep and improve it, the opposite is true in the intracompany economy. So whenever he could he "followed the book," so that when he couldn't he was able to use his credit rating to get the flexibility he needed. In short, unlike Smith, who had been forced by the system into *blind* conformity, Jones had earned the right to practice *flexible* conformity.

Needless to say, Jones had the support of his molecule, enjoyed a high average level on his freedom scale and had coached his subordinates in achieving a relatively high level on theirs, thus leaving him relatively free of subordinate-imposed time. All this had its impact on his performance record as Superintendent, a matter not unnoticed by the Manager of Manufacturing and his boss, the Operations Vice President.

But these two men were also troubled over the fact that Shop 3 was a failing operation. Although Jones and Smith had been competing for the same limited organizational resources, Smith has been getting less than his fair share, simply because Jones had been getting more. Yet top management regarded Smith's operation as having a higher priority than Jones'. They were thus faced with a classic example of the misallocation of resources in spite of corporate priorities to the contrary. What should they do?

There are those who would advise them to tell Jones to back off, that he is too greedy, resulting in Smith's poverty in resources. They would add that teamwork must replace competition so that Jones and Smith could "each get according to his needs and contribute according to his abilities." But the professional managers among my readers will be reassured when top management rejects such advice out of hand and instead considers two other alternatives:

1. Tell Smith that he is going to have to compete or seek a more suitable career elsewhere, or
2. Arrange for Jones and Smith to swap jobs and give Smith an opportunity to redeem himself with the company

But that still leaves the possibility that Smith can anticipate top management and extricate himself successfully before they are compelled to act. It would clearly be to his advantage to do so. Since his situation was three years in the making, no quick fix is available to him. Even in the private sector economy it takes time to rehabilitate one's credit rating. Molecules, like the proverbial elephant, have long memories that change very slowly. For Smith, the most practical resolution of his tragic circumstance would be to have a fresh start in a similar job supported by a totally different molecule whose members have little or no association with his past. (This would eliminate the option of swapping jobs with Jones.) If his company could not arrange that within the corporate family, he would have to make a career decision on his own and take his chances on the labor market.

Opportunity Is No Guarantee

This is my advice for my younger readers: Maximize your molecular assets. If this means that others who are competing with you for the same limited resources end up consistently with less than their fair share, do not succumb to a guilt complex because of it. Help the weaker brother to be more competitive if you wish, but do not allow your own molecular assets to weaken in the process. You do not owe it to him or to your company (and I hope not even to your conscience, although this is your private affair) to do so.

For those of my readers who are about to change jobs, remember you will never again enjoy as much molecular support as will greet you during your first few days on the job. Notice that both Jones and Smith were even at the starting line during their first week with the company three years earlier. It is characteristic of management molecules that they initially give each new nucleus the benefit of the doubt at the beginning. Your job is to see to it that the doubts do not mount. The time you devote to this you can charge off to the administrative overhead cost of molecular maintenance, a necessary part of your cost of doing business within the intracompany economic system.

YOUR SUBORDINATES

Why is it that managers are typically running out of time while their subordinates are typically running out of work?

The management of time necessitates that the manager get control over the timing and content of what he does. Since what the boss and the system impose on him are backed up by penalty, he cannot tamper with those requirements. Thus his self-imposed time becomes his major area of concern.

The manager's strategy in the role of managER is, therefore, to increase the "discretionary" component of his self-imposed time by minimizing or doing away with the subordinate-imposed component. That is, he must first rotate the needles to the down position. He will then use the added increment of discretionary time in his managEE role to get better control over his boss-imposed time, and in his role as molecular peer to get control over his system-imposed time. Most managers spend much more subordinate-imposed time than they even faintly realize, preoccupied as they are with upward-pointing needles. Hence we shall use a monkey-on-the-back analogy to examine how subordinate-imposed time comes into being and what the manager can do about it. A monkey, as we shall see, is whatever the next move is when dialogue between two parties breaks off.

Where Is the Monkey?

Imagine that I, a manager, am walking down the hall and that I notice one of my subordinates, Mr. A, coming up the hallway. When we are abreast of one another, Mr. A greets me with, "Good morning. By the way, we've got a problem. You see...." As Mr. A continues, I recognize in this problem the same two characteristics common to all the problems my subordinates gratuitously bring to my attention: I know enough to get involved, but not enough to make the on-the-spot decision expected of me. Eventually, I say, "So glad you brought this up. I'm in a rush right now. Meanwhile, let me think about it, and I'll let you know." Then I and Mr. A part company.

Let us analyze what has just happened. Before the two of us met, on whose back was the "monkey"? His. After we parted, on whose back was it? Mine. Subordinate-imposed time begins the moment a monkey successfully executes a leap from the back of a subordinate to the back of his superior and does not end until the monkey is returned to its proper owner for care and feeding.

In accepting the monkey, I had voluntarily assumed a position subordinate to my subordinate. That is, I had allowed Mr. A to make me his subordinate by doing two things a subordinate is generally expected to do for his boss—I had accepted the responsibility from him, and I had promised him a progress report. The managER and managEE roles had been "swapped" thus rotating the needle to the up position.

My subordinate, to make sure I do not miss this point, will later stick his head in my office and cheerily query, "How's it coming?" (This is called "supervision.")

Imagine again, in concluding a working conference with another subordinate, Mr. B, my parting words are, "Fine. Send a memo on that."

Let us analyze this one. The monkey is now on my subordinate's back because the next move is his, but it is poised for a leap. Watch the monkey. Mr. B dutifully writes the requested memo and drops it in his out-basket. Shortly thereafter, I pluck it from my in-basket and read it. Whose move is it now? Mine. If I do not make that move soon, I will get a follow-up memo from him (this is another form of supervision). The longer I delay, the more frustrated he will become (he'll be "spinning his wheels"), and the more guilty I will feel (my backlog of subordinate-imposed time will be mounting). The needle is up.

Or suppose once again that at a meeting with a third subordinate, Mr. C, I agree to provide all the necessary backing for a public relations proposal I have just asked Mr. C to develop. My parting words to him are, "Just let me know how I can help."

Now let us analyze this. Here the monkey is initially on my subordinate's back. But for how long? Mr. C realizes that he cannot "let me know" until his proposal has my approval. And from experience, he also realizes that his proposal will likely be sitting in my briefcase for weeks waiting for me to eventually get to it. Who's really got the monkey? Who will be checking up on whom? Wheelspinning and bottlenecking are on their way again.

My fourth subordinate, Mr. D, has just been transferred from another part of the company in order to launch and eventually manage a newly created business venture. I have told him that we should get together soon to hammer out a set of objectives for his new job, and that I would draw up an initial draft for discussion with him.

Let us analyze this one, too. My subordinate has the new job (by formal assignment) and the full responsibility (by formal delegation), but I have the next move. Until I make it, I will have the monkey and my subordinate will be immobilized.

Why does it all happen? Because in each instance I and my subordinate assume at the outset, wittingly or unwittingly, that the matter under consideration is a joint problem. The monkey in each case begins its career astride both our backs. All it has to do now is move the wrong leg, and—presto—the subordinate deftly disappears. I am thus left alone with another acquisition to my menagerie. Of course, monkeys can be trained not to move the wrong leg. But it is easier to prevent them from straddling backs in the first place.

Who Is Working for Whom?

To make what follows more credible, suppose that these same four subordinates are so thoughtful and considerate of my time that they are at pains to allow no more than three monkeys to leap—whether by phone call, memorandum or personal encounter—from each of their backs to mine in any one day. By the end of the first day (say, Monday) I will have accumulated twelve screaming monkeys.

I am an amateur in other respects, too. In my managEE role I am forced to practice abject compliance, subject as I am to my boss's harassment via phone, memo and personal encounter all day long; and in my peer-user role I am forced to practice blind conformity, thwarted as I am by the low credit rating I have earned with the internal peer elements of my molecule, forcing me to "go to the top" too often for the three-point landings I need, so I have just about worn out my welcome there.

Thus robbed of my discretionary time, I cannot make even a dent in this menagerie, so I decide at 4:30 P.M. to get organized. I reach for a book I have been reading entitled *Time Management*. It begins by saying that one must first set one's priorities. So I start stacking the monkeys in a priority hierarchy but get only halfway through by quitting time, so I sweep the twelve monkeys into my "monkey cage" (my briefcase) and take them home to finish my priority pyramid in the quietude of my den.

When I arrive home, my wife greets me on our front doorstep with the words, "Bill, you're home just in time to get cleaned up." "Cleaned up for what?" I ask. "Have you forgotten again?" she pleads. "It's our wedding anniversary." Another evening blown to bits.

The next morning I trundle them back to work for another day of harassment by the boss, frustration by the system and of being up-needled via the acquisition of twelve more monkeys from my subordinates for a total of twenty-four. I try to stack them in a new priority pyramid but am defeated by the ambiguities. With as many as twenty-four monkeys, it's impossible to discriminate significantly between priority 5 and priority 6, for example, or between 14 and 15.

So I reach for that book again and in Chapter 2 I find that when the population is that large you should grab three, four or five monkeys that look alike and talk to each other and put them in one pile; put another armful of monkeys that look alike and talk to each other in another pile, and soon you will wind up with five or six generic piles. That number is sufficiently small for meaningful discrimination. But as I stack them I seem to be getting farther and farther away from individual monkeys and closer and closer to the academic abstractions of subject matter classification. Meanwhile, I have been inadvertently up-needled by my four subordinates with twelve more monkeys for a total of thirty-six.

So I throw them all in my briefcase and take them home; but this time I'm greeted on my front doorstep by my creditors in the other roles I play in life, namely, father, neighbor, citizen, church member, etc. My seven-year-old daughter, I am advised by my wife, is having a Brownie point pinned on her at 6:30 tonight. The photographer from the local daily newspaper will be there to document the event for tomorrow morning's edition. There is no way I can duck out of this. She added that the church consistory is meeting tonight and as Treasurer I must attend to explain how the extension to the Sunday School building was constructed without funds. Moreover, the local political action group that I helped organize about a year ago to throw the "thieves" out of office is going to meet tonight, too. Being a charter member and founder, I must be there. I am thus paying off my creditors in the other roles I play in life so that when I settle with the last one in line, the undertaker, I'll be solvent forever. And that, they tell me, is what heaven is all about!

That evening I pin the Brownie point on my daughter, rush to the church meeting where I say, "Brethren, I haven't time to spend with you tonight; but let me say in all earnestness that my prayers are with you and that any decisions you make I'll back to the hilt. If you need help, don't hesitate to call on me." With that I'm off to the next meeting. And then to the next. And the next. ...

The following morning I dump those thirty-six monkeys on my desk, but once again—while harassed by the boss and crippled by the system—I pick up twelve more monkeys from my subordinates for a cumulative total of forty-eight. But Friday is different. On Fridays I always get delivery of my last monkey of the week at noon sharp because my subordinates like to clean off their desks by noon on Friday so they can get a running start for the hills to get in a little fishing.

So there I sit, in my office, with sixty screaming monkeys. Too many for my desk top, several have fallen over the side and are playing tag across my carpet. Trying to chase them down, I lose about two for every three I catch. If somebody asked me, "Oncken, what is your monkey inventory count?" I would have to say, "I've got about twenty, give or take thirty, or close to it." I finally say to my secretary, "Mabel, I'm locking my door from the inside for privacy. I'm so far behind I just have to get caught up. Hold all phone calls, except from you know who; and I don't want to see anybody, either, except you know who. I need privacy."

She says, "Yes, Mr. Oncken." Hanging up, she mutters under he breath, "I can't understand how Mr. Oncken can have any privacy locked in an office with sixty screaming monkeys. His office is so full of monkeys that he has neither time for himself nor for anyone else."

Outside my locked door sit my four subordinates still waiting to get a last chance before the weekend to remind me that until I return or otherwise dispose of their monkeys they are stymied. Luckily I don't hear what they are saying to each other about me as they wait: "Bottleneck Oncken. He just can't make up his mind. How anyone ever got that high up in our company without being able to make a decision we'll never know."

Obviously, the reason I have not been able to make any of these "next moves" is that my time has been almost entirely eaten up in meeting my own boss-imposed and system-imposed requirements. To get control of these, I have needed discretionary time that has in turn been denied me because I was preoccupied with all these monkeys. I have been caught in a vicious circle.

But time is a-wasting (an understatement). I call my secretary on the intercom and instruct her to tell my subordinates that I will be too preoccupied to see them before Monday morning. At 7:00 P.M. I drive home, intending with firm resolve to return to the office tomorrow to get caught up over the weekend. I return bright and early the next day only to see, on the nearest green of the golf course across from my office window, a foursome. Four up-needles pointed directly at me! Guess who!

And if by magic I could be transformed into a fly and buzz about their heads, I would overhear them remark to one another: "Things are finally looking up! Did you see whose car just pulled into the company parking lot? Looks like the boss has finally decided to earn his money!" Spoken like four competent "supervisors" about a loyal, hard-working "employee" who has just decided to put in an honest day's work. My mind now rolls back to my first job at Amerada in 1934 when I and my buddies spent many a Saturday in the plant getting caught up. We all knew where our bosses were: On the golf course! And that was as it should be, for that was how the incentive system of the American Dream had been explained to us.

But now, many years and countless Saturdays later, I am still in the plant and a whole new generation is on the golf course. "Just when," I ask myself, "did the American Dream pass me by?"

That does it. I now know who is really working for whom. Moreover, I now see that if I actually accomplish during this weekend what I came to accomplish, my subordinates' morale will go up so sharply that they will each raise the limit on the number of monkeys they will let jump from their backs to mine. In short, I now see, with the clarity of a revelation on a mountaintop, that the more I get caught up, the more I will fall behind.

Getting caught up is a valid solution to a vocational time management problem but a disastrous solution to a problem in managing management time. When an accountant is behind in balancing the books, he can spend the weekend at the office to get caught up, and he will be rewarded in kind. So can the engineer who is behind in his drawings and the salesman who is behind in his trip reports. But whose work am I behind in? Their work! I haven't been behind in my work since I became a manager because I never had the time to get it started. And with four of them generating it and only one of me working it off, I can no longer keep up by just working longer and harder at what I have been doing all along.

I leave my office with the speed of a man running away from a plague. My plan? To get caught up on something else I haven't had time for in years: a weekend with my family. What had started out to be a weekend of subordinate-imposed time had suddenly been transformed into a weekend of discretionary time. Some switch!

Sunday night I enjoy ten hours of sweet, untroubled slumber. So soundly do I sleep that twice during the night my wife feared that I was dead. She beamed the flashlight in my face to find out. There she saw, spreading from ear to ear, a serene, angelic smile. What am I smiling at? I have plans for Monday. Never before had I gone to bed at night with plans for the morning as clear as I have them now. Tomorrow I will prepare the ground for moving my fulcrum over. The needles will be rotated to the down position, which will rid me of my subordinate-imposed time. In exchange, I will get an equal amount of discretionary time, part of which I will spend with my subordinates in my managER role to see that they learn the difficult but rewarding managerial art called "The Care and Feeding of Monkeys." I will now, for the first time, be working *with* them rather than *for* them.

I will also have plenty of discretionary time left over for getting control of the timing and content not only of my boss-imposed time but of my system-imposed time as well. All of this may take months, but compared with the way things have been, the rewards will be enormous. My ultimate objective is to manage my management time.

Getting Rid of the Monkeys

I return to the office Monday morning just late enough to permit my four subordinates to collect in my outer office waiting to see me about their monkeys. As I walk past them toward my office door, I sense a profound change in this trip from what it had been when I had made it many, many times before. In the past I had been tormented by guilt feelings resulting from a condition described long ago by Benjamin Franklin's grandfather: "The surest way to lose a friend is to become indebted to him!" I had owed these men countless monkeys and would never be able to meet my payments. Worse still, I had seen in each of these men the principal source of most of my time management problems and that hardly endeared them to me. They, in turn, did not try to hide, in their expressions, the fact that they saw in me the principal source of most of their time management frustrations. Since my guilt and their frustration were feeding upon one another, we had become like five drowning men in a death clutch in the middle of an organizational sea, dragging each other down to management's Davey Jones' Locker. But today, for the first time, my disaffection toward them has turned to love, for I now see in each of their backs a potential repository for several monkeys. No longer the source of my problems, they have just become the only available solution to them. They sense a dramatic change in my demeanor as I walk by and, taken unawares, they burp in chorus. My secretary also, caught unaware as I forget for the first time to shut my door behind me, punctuates the chorus with a burp of her own. The air has become filled with uneasy expectation.

I call them in, one by one. The purpose of each interview is to take a monkey, place it on the desk between us, and figure out together how the next move might conceivably be his. For certain monkeys, this will take some doing. His next move may be so elusive that I may decide—just for now—merely to let the monkey sleep overnight on his back and have him return with it at an appointed time the next morning to continue the joint quest for a more substantive move on his part. (Monkeys sleep just as soundly overnight on subordinates' backs as on superiors.')

As each of my subordinates leaves the office, I am rewarded by the sight of a monkey leaving my office on his back. For the next twenty-four hours, he will not be waiting for me; instead, I will be waiting for him.

Later, as if to remind myself that there is no law against my engaging in a constructive exercise in the interim, I stroll by his office, stick my head in the door, and cheerily ask, "How's it coming?" (The time consumed in doing this is discretionary for me and boss-imposed for him.) I don't really care how it's coming; I just want to be the one to ask the question.

When he (with the monkey on his back) and I meet at the appointed hour the next day, I explain the ground rules in words to this effect:

"At no time while I am helping you with this or any other problem will your problem become my problem. The instant your problem becomes mine, you will no longer have a problem. I cannot help a man who hasn't got a problem.

"When this meeting is over, the problem will leave this office exactly the way it came in—on your back. You may ask for my help at any appointed time, and we will make a joint determination of what the next move will be and which of us will make it.

"In those rare instances where the next move turns out to be mine, you and I will determine it together. I will not make any move alone."

I follow this same line of thought with each subordinate until at about 3:30 P.M. I realize that I have no need to shut my door. My monkeys are gone. They will return—but by appointment only. My appointment calendar will assure this.

Transferring the Initiative

What I have been driving at in this monkey-on-the-back analogy is to transfer the initiative from manager to subordinate and keep it there. I have tried to highlight a truism as subtle as it is obvious, namely, before a manager can develop initiative in his subordinates, he must see to it that they *have* the initiative. Once he takes it back, they will no longer have it, and he can kiss his discretionary time goodbye. It will all revert to subordinate-imposed time, consumed by the upward-pointing needle.

Nor can both manager and subordinate effectively have the same initiative at the same time. The opener, "Boss, we've got a problem," implies this duality and represents, as noted earlier, a monkey astride two backs, which is a very bad way to start a monkey on its career. Let us, therefore, take a few moments to examine what I prefer to call "The Anatomy of Managerial Initiative."

As pointed out earlier, there are five degrees of initiative that the manager can exercise in relation to the boss: (1) wait until told (lowest initiative); (2) ask what to do; (3) recommend, then take resulting action; (4) act, but advise at once; and (5) act on own, then routinely report (highest initiative).

Clearly, the manager should be professional enough not to indulge himself in initiatives 1 and 2 in relation to his boss. A manager who uses initiative 1 has no control over either the timing or content of his boss-imposed or system-imposed time. He thereby forfeits any right to complain about what he is told to do or when he is told to do it. The manager who uses initiative 2 has control over the timing but not over the content. Initiatives 3, 4 and 5 leave the manager in control of both, with the greatest control being at level 5.

The manager's job, in relation to his subordinates' initiatives, is two-fold: first, to outlaw the use of initiatives 1 and 2, thus giving his subordinates no choice but to learn and master "completed staff work"; then, to see that for each problem leaving his office there is an agreed-upon time and place of the next manager-subordinate conference. The latter should be duly noted on the manager's appointment calendar to ensure that the monkey does not eventually starve to death.

Seven Rules for the Care and Feeding of Monkeys

In order to further clarify my analogy between the monkey-on-the-back and the well-known processes of assigning and controlling, I shall refer to the manager's appointment schedule as "Feeding Time for Monkeys," which calls for seven hard-and-fast rules governing their care and feeding (violations of these rules cost discretionary time):

Rule 1

Monkeys shall be fed or shot. Otherwise, they will starve to death and the manager will waste valuable time on postmortems or attempted resurrections.

Rule 2

The monkey population shall be kept below the maximum number the manager has time to feed. His subordinates will find time to work as many monkeys as he finds time to feed, but no more. (It shouldn't take more than five to fifteen minutes for the manager to feed a properly prepared monkey.)

Rule 3

Monkeys shall be fed on the initiative of the subordinate at the time and place specified in the feeding schedule. The manager shall not be hunting down starving monkeys and feeding them on a catch-as-catch-can basis.

Rule 4

Monkey-feeding appointments may be rescheduled, in case of conflict, at the suggestion of either party but shall not be indefinitely postponed. Failure to make progress on a monkey shall not be accepted as a reason for rescheduling its feeding appointment.

Rule 5

Monkeys shall be fed face-to-face or by telephone, but never by mail. (If by mail, the next move will be the manager's, remember?) Documentation may augment the feeding process, but it cannot take the place of feeding.

Rule 6

Memoranda or reports running to several pages or more shall be covered by a synopsis of one page or less to facilitate instant dialogue.

Rule 7

Every monkey that leaves a manager on a subordinate's back shall be covered by a casualty insurance policy with a deductible (level of initiative) appropriate to his anxiety index; otherwise the monkey will either starve to death or wind up on the manager's back.

"Get control over the timing and content of what you do" is therefore appropriate advice for managing management time. The first order of business is for the manager to use his self-imposed time to enlarge his discretionary time by eliminating subordinate-imposed time. With the needles now firmly in the down position, the second is for him to use a portion of his new-found discretionary time to see to it that each of his subordinates possesses the initiative without which he cannot exercise initiative, and then to see to it that this initiative is, in fact, taken. The third is for him to use another portion of his increased discretionary time to get and keep control of the timing and content of both his boss-imposed and system-imposed time.

The result of all of this is that the manager will increase his *leverage*, which will in turn enable him to multiply, without theoretical limit, the value of each hour that he spends in managing management time.

5

Maintaining Molecular Stability

More damaging than wheel spinning is slippage of time, caused by collisions between priorities based upon two independent criteria, namely (1) temporal priorities based on relative *urgency* (often subjectively determined) and (2) logical priorities based on relative *importance* (usually objectively determined). Knowing the rules of the road in management and knowing when and to whom to yield is the fifth precondition to effective time management.

THE PARAMETERS OF THE PROBLEM

Where does the manager's time go? That was our opening question in Chapter 1. Four chapters and 60,000 words have gone by since, and the answer we gave then is still as far as it went. But we now know that *how* the manager's time goes is different for the amateur from what it is for the professional.

Molecular Stability

Let us, then, distill from the four previous chapters the answer to both the *where* and the *how* for the *professional* manager, and its implications for molecular stability.

His or her time goes in three directions:

1. *Boss-imposed time,* the time he or she spends doing the things he would not be doing if he were not committed to (a) practicing *anticipatory compliance* by improving or at least maintaining his position on his freedom scale, and (b) encouraging his subordinates to do the same in relation to him at their level.

2. *System-imposed time,* the time he or she spends doing the things he would not be doing if he were not committed to (a) practicing *flexible conformity* by improving or at least maintaining his intracompany credit rating and (b) encouraging his subordinates to do the same at their level.

3. *Self-imposed time,* the time he or she spends doing the things he would not have been doing if he were not committed to (a) maximizing his discretionary time so as to make full use of his innovative talents, and (b) encouraging his subordinate managers to do the same at their level.

Failure in any of these three areas is, as we have seen, destabilizing to the manager's molecule, causing him to surrender control of the timing and content of what he does.

The penalty for failure in boss-imposed time is to become frustrated; the penalty for failure in system-imposed time is to become thwarted; and the penalty for failure in self-imposed time is to become inaccessible to subordinates and with little time to oneself. When these penalties become sufficiently severe and persistent to adversely affect one's performance record, tenure in the job is in jeopardy.

Destabilizing Influences

Failures in the boss-imposed and self-imposed areas are, as we have also pointed out, caused by imbalances at the managER/managEE role interfaces, which can exist in four possible combinations:

1. *When pro works for amateur:* In this situation, as illustrated in the parable of the young data-processing manager, the pro will either (a) deal with his amateur boss in such a way that it causes the latter to act like a pro or, failing that, (b) find another boss.

2. *When amateur works for pro:* In this case the pro will either (a) develop his or her subordinate by coaching him up his freedom scale or, failing that, (b) replace him.

3. *When pro works for pro:* In this case both will simultaneously seize their respective initiatives, the subordinate in *assuming* responsibility and the superior in *delegating* it. These initiatives are complementary and together bring about the ideal resolution to the managER/managEE role conflict.

4. *When amateur works for amateur:* This situation will be a standoff until one or the other becomes a pro, as illustrated in Chapter 4 in my Saturday-morning-at-the-office episode and in several earlier sitcoms. At that point the situation becomes either 1 or 2 above. If they both become pros, then it becomes situation 3.

Failures in the system-imposed area were also shown to be destabilizing and are caused by overlooking, at the peer-to-peer interface, the following four rules:

1. When you interface with a nonmolecular peer (one who is not on your molecule), the monkey is his until he can prove to your satisfaction that it is yours.

2. When you interface with a molecular peer (one who *is* on your molecule), the monkey is yours until you can prove to his satisfaction that it is his.

3. When you and an interfacing peer are each on the other's molecule, the disposition of the monkey must be negotiated to your joint satisfaction.

4. When neither you nor an interfacing peer are on the other's molecule, the monkey must be returned to its proper owner or referred to an authorized executioner.

The occasions for following these rules are (1) chance encounters (in hallways, stairwells, parking lots, cafeteria lines, scheduled meetings, washrooms and "drop-ins"); (2) daily in-basket administrivia and (3) telephone conversations and call-back slips. Benefiting from following these rules requires, of course, a currently up-dated molecular list that should, for obvious reasons, be kept confidential. The penalty for failure in correctly assessing the above relationships is to end up with monkeys you don't need or want, or sharp reductions in your intra-company credit ratings with those people, or both. All this will be spelled out in more detail later in this chapter.

Molecular Damage

Although the above three sets of circumstances are destabilization-prone, an additional circumstance for which there is no theoretical model ("matrix management" excepted, which is yet to be dealt with), can result in ruptured molecules, because it undermines the Unit President Concept and breaches the molecular structure of the management organism wherever it occurs. Some examples: (1) when managER bypasses one of his managEEs on monkey business one or more skip-levels below him, and (2) when managEE bypasses his managER on monkey business one or more skip-levels above him (see Figure 5). The damage done to the authority, responsibility and accountability of the bypassed nucleus of the molecule may become crippling. The only solution is to institute repairs at once. Fortunately, molecules can, entirely on their own, develop an adequate defense from this kind of damage, as we will show as this chapter unfolds.

INTERMOLECULAR GUERILLA RAIDS

Conventional management-training courses drum into our heads that one of our duties as managers is follow up! Follow up! Follow up! This conjures up an image of the boss as chaser and the subordinate as chasee. This is not follow-up—it is harassment, and it can have deleterious consequences as the following illustration of the application of rule 3 on the "Care and Feeding of Monkeys" will now make clear.

In this scene imagine that I, a plant manager, come to work on a Thursday morning at 8:00 and by 10:00 have disposed of most routine matters and handled a few run-of-the-mill crises. I then get an uneasy

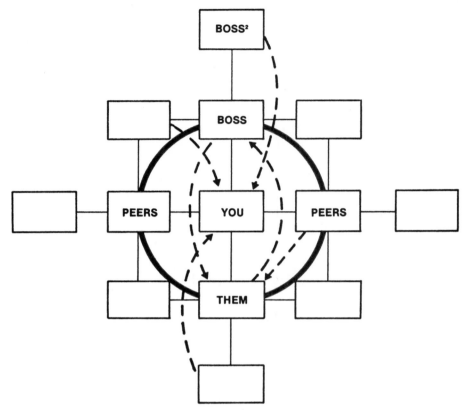

Inter-molecular guerrilla raids

Figure 5

feeling that the supervisors on the shop floor are balling things up again. So I decide to visit the shop to uncover the ingenious method they have devised this time. (I am about to become living proof of what Benjamin Franklin's grandfather once observed: "When Trouble Is What You Are Looking for, You Will Be Handsomely Rewarded.")

I first encounter Ed, a first-line supervisor in charge of a section of the Shipping and Receiving Area, who was appointed to that job out of the hourly ranks six months ago, and who is trying to do the job as best he sees it. He reports to a foreman, who in turn reports to a superintendent, who in turn reports to me. Clearly he is not listed on my molecule; nor am I listed on his, not even on his boss's molecule. Our two molecules are twice removed. This means, among other things, that he is not directly accountable to me for his performance. Since I am an amateur, I take these considerations to be irrelevant to the practice of management.

As I look past him through the shipping and receiving room to the shipping dock I spy a crate marked, "RUSH SHIPMENT." I had seen it there last Monday, and now it's Thursday and it still hasn't moved. To say that I am burned up would be putting it faintly. Ed is standing right there, so what could be more predictable for me, the amateur, than that I jump on him? I do just that.

"For goodness' sake, Ed, you know I'm doing everything I can to hold myself in, but there come times that try men's souls. Why don't we ship something around here once in awhile?

"Last Monday as I walked past here I was heartened when I saw that crate, consigned to one of our most valued customers, because I knew that the crew had got it out here within minutes after it came off the production line. That afternoon, though, it was still there, but I decided to say nothing. I'd been taught that if you give a man a responsibility, don't keep bugging him; give him his head. Douglas MacGregor said that most people would rather take initiative than not, that they would rather work than not, and I was believing it. It is called 'theory Y.'

"On Tuesday as I walked past, it was still there. It took all of the self-restraint I could muster not to say anything, so I bit my lip and involved myself in other things. I said to myself, 'Look, Oncken, if you're going to delegate, then delegate. If you're going to let a man run the shipping room, then let him run the shipping room.' When on Wednesday I saw it again, I suffered an attack of gas pains, heartburn and nervous twitches, but I reined myself in. Now it's still here, and it's Thursday!

"Ed, maybe you're not aware of the part that shipments like that play in our operation. We ship products to our customers to get the money to pay our wages. Or perchance you thought we had a printing press in the basement that grinds out dollar bills? Wrong! We *earn* our wages only after the customer gets delivery. Last year when customers weren't buying, you got paid anyway with money we borrowed from the bank. But you wouldn't know anything about that, either. You ungrateful, fringe-benefit squatters may think that the world owes you a living, but I'm proud that my character was formed in the crucible of the Great Depression, that I learned the value of a dollar and the dignity of hard work. It's high time you got a taste of those things. Now *let's get that crate shipped!*

"Are you listening, Ed? Ed?"

Ruptured Molecules

Let's stop now and analyze what was happening. I, the plant manager, just encountered a monkey that was almost dead of starvation. I grabbed the little creature in one hand, force-fed it with the other, slurp, slurp, slurp. I flexed its little muscles, nursed it back to vigor and returned it to Ed. Without realizing it, I had temporarily (1) fired his foreman but left him on the job, (2) taken his place and (3) deprived the company of one plant manager. The scene ended as I went off in search of another monkey, leaving Ed and his foreman to repair their ruptured molecules.

Next I encounter Art, a "bean counter" in the Accounting Department: "Art, you're an ole-timer around here. You know I don't go looking around for trouble; but just look at those invoices: sixty days old! I know that the policy of your department is to get invoices out within thirty days so please spare me your excuses. I've had it up to here all day so keep your promises to yourself. All I want is a little evidence of that loyalty and devotion to duty that our founder talked about in his annual New Year's messages to employees. Remember?"

"Are you listening, Art? Art?"

What happened? I found another monkey, almost dead of starvation; grabbed it and force-fed it; slurp, slurp, slurp; flexed its little muscles; nursed it back to vitality; handed it back to him; and ran off in search of another one.

Managers who do this every day have a name for it. They call it *supervision* or *follow-up*. It isn't any of these things. It's behaving like the warden of an insane asylum driving the inmates crazier than they were the day they qualified for admission, leaving behind him a trail of ruptured molecules that, were it not for their self-healing properties, would eventually undermine the viability of the management organism itself.

But the worst is yet to come. That night I, the plant manager, go home after everyone else has left; after a big steak dinner, four cans of beer and two TV shows, I pour myself exhausted into bed. I am kept awake all night tormented by the thought of all the monkeys that must have gotten away that day. Not having a monkey inventory, I had no way of knowing whether I had caught 20 percent or 40 percent or 60 percent of them, so the next morning I rush back to the plant to hunt down the ones I must have missed the day before plus the ones that no doubt will be due to be fed today.

Wednesday I go through the plant at triple-time to catch the remaining monkeys I have probably missed since Monday, plus those I must have missed on Tuesday, plus those I should be tracking down today. This continues daily thereafter in an ever-spiraling crescendo, until on the twenty-fourth of the month I call in sick. This is my regular monthly collapse. I am out now for an entire week, and this happens every month on the twenty-fourth so regularly that the employees plan on it.

Chasing Trouble to the Bitter End

On the wall calendars in the shop they have encircled the twenty-fourth of every up-coming month. That's the day of the month that "the Old Man loses his last marble." They use the week I'm absent to (1) get caught up for all the time they lose when I am on the job and (2) repair their ruptured molecules and get them back into stable equilibrium in preparation for withstanding the next onslaught.

What I seem not to understand is that no plant manager can hold himself responsible for tracking down, catching and feeding every starving monkey in the plant. In the interests of capitalizing on the leverage potential of his position, he must limit himself to feeding the monkeys that are on the backs of his immediate subordinates. They, for the same reason, must limit themselves to feeding the monkeys on the backs of their own immediate subordinates and so on. This is our second important application of the Unit President Concept introduced earlier. I was violating this concept by my daily intermolecular guerilla raids. This threw into unstable equilibrium the molecules I had breached, disrupted monkey-feeding schedules already in force at those levels, thus increasing daily the number of monkeys about to starve to death.

But I was doing the right thing in making those unannounced excursions around the plant, for I am responsible and accountable for everything that goes on, whether I am there or not; and general managers of three-shift operations are acutely aware that they are as responsible for what goes on when they're home in bed at three o'clock in the morning as they are for what goes on when they are on the job. Because of that responsibility, I have to inform myself, and one way of doing that is by practicing ubiquity.

Ubi in Latin means "everywhere." Ubiquity means the practice of "everywhereness." I have to get around, and if you wonder how I can be everywhere at once, let me show you how it is done without doing damage to the management organism below me by rupturing one molecule after another. I will now replay the above skit, but this time as a *professional* manager.

Unit President Concept and Stable Molecular Equilibrium

When I get to work, the first thing I see on my appointment calendar is that I'm scheduled to feed six monkeys today. Four of them I'll feed in staff meeting because I've learned from experience that if you have three or four monkeys that look alike and talk to each other they can be fed together, because they are of general interest to most of those attending. But occasionally there will be a monkey that is a "loner," and it would be a waste of a lot of people's valuable time to feed it in a staff meeting. So two of these monkeys are fed privately, as it says on my calendar: "Feed Keith's Monkey Number 2 at three o'clock, and feed Pam's Monkey Number 7 at three-thirty."

I then tackle my in-basket, and having cleared my desk by 10 o'clock, I walk down the hallway toward the shop floor; but being a pro, my purpose this time is quite different. I will not go through the shop and office spaces in order to track down and feed starving monkeys. All *my* subordinates' monkeys are already on feeding schedules, so my mind is free to do what only I, as plant manager, can do.

As before, I run into Ed, our supervisor of shipping. I am three molecular levels removed from him, so our molecules are not even tangent. I look past him to the shipping dock and, as before, see that unshipped crate. Of course I'm burned up about it, but I don't let on to Ed. This time I'm a pro, so instead I bid Ed good morning and reach in my inside coat pocket for my "Monkey Inventory and Feeding Schedule." I look down my inventory to see whether there is a live monkey or gorilla entitled "Shipping and Receiving Procedures." There *is* one, a live gorilla, a project for reviewing shipping and receiving procedures that has been underway for some time. This gorilla is right now on the back of the superintendent who has responsibility for shipping and receiving (among other things), and who reports to me. That's where it belongs, because I cannot place a monkey or gorilla any lower than the people who are the lower rim of *my* molecule without violating the Unit President Concept.

Without saying a word to Ed, I walk over to the house phone to call Roger, my superintendent: "Good morning, Roger. With regard to your gorilla Number 9 entitled 'Shipping Room Procedures,' when is its next scheduled feeding time?" (I know, of course, but I'm just testing him.)

He looks it up in his little black book and says, "According to my schedule, it is two weeks from today."

"I have news for you, Roger. We're feeding that gorilla tomorrow morning at 8:30 instead."

"Where are you calling from, Boss?"

"I'll give you one guess," I reply, as I hang up and head back to my office.

Changing Priorities Without Rupturing Molecules

Within a few seconds, miraculously, Roger shows up in the shipping room, having let himself down a fireman's pole he had specially constructed for occasions of this kind. All the while, I'm heading serenely toward my office, happy to let human nature take its predictable course.

On hitting the deck, he says to Ed, "Was Oncken here?"

"Yes, he was here."

"Ah. What did he see?"

"I'm not sure."

"Hmmmm," says Roger, "that considerably enlarges the scope of the problem."

Roger gets hold of Ed's boss, the foreman, and the three of them huddle. Roger says, "I have a problem. Tomorrow morning at 8:30 I have to answer Oncken's question, 'How's it coming?' For monkeys I get five minutes for the answer, but for gorillas, I get a half-hour. We will have to get this place in such shape that when he asks me how's it coming, I can tell him how it is tomorrow morning and not how it is now. What might he have seen when he was here?"

First they notice that crate. Within three minutes it is on a truck and out of the gate. (Monday they couldn't ship it because the truck was up on jacks having the transmission fixed; Tuesday they couldn't do it because it was in the body shop having a crushed fender straightened out; Wednesday they couldn't do it because they had some other rush orders ahead of it.) Hourly workers and supervisors who toil in the blue-collar vineyards have an uncanny ability to do the impossible once they make up their minds to it! No one will ever know how; that's their secret.

They then turn the shipping room upside down to find what else I might have seen so they can bridge the gulf between how it is and how it would have to be by 8:30 A.M. All of this activity was triggered by my "routine" visit!

At exactly 8:30 the next morning Roger walks bleary-eyed into my office. I, however, am rested, for I had nine hours of sleep knowing full well what was happening. "How's it coming?" I ask him. As he answers, I take a pad and start writing down what he tells me. Because I don't write fast, I ask him to slow down and repeat some things. (He knows why I'm writing it all down: When he's through, I'll walk with him through the shipping and receiving room and, using what he reported to me as a checklist, see for myself.)

How the Professional Practices "Follow-Up"

So when he is through, I say, "Fine. Now let's go down and have a look at it." When we arrive on the scene, I am astounded. The whole appearance of the place has changed. The floors are swept, the crate is gone, the pallets are neatly stacked and much, much more.

The difference between the results I got as an amateur and the results I have now are quite apparent. When, as the amateur, I told Ed to get the crate shipped, the crate got shipped, but that was all. But when instead, as a pro, I advanced the date of the next gorilla-feeding appointment, the shipment of the crate was only one of the many actions that were initiated as a result. Because they didn't know what I saw, they took care of everything that *three pairs of eyes* could see, working (I imagine) all night long. So many self-assignments were created and executed as a result of my one initiative that my organizational leverage must have been impressive by any standard. This was possible because I confined my own initiative within the boundaries of my own molecule and dealt with the gorilla at that level (superintendent). My leverage had previously been severely restricted by my insistence, as an amateur, on breaching both the superintendent's and the foreman's molecules in order to take my initiative directly to Ed, the supervisor. And since three pairs of eyes can see a lot more than one pair can see, I was much closer to being "everywhere at once" than when I insisted on doing all the looking myself.

All this was based on the prior existence of gorilla Number 9. Had there been no such gorilla (project), one would have been established at once to review the on-time performance record of current shipping procedures.

So much for one kind of intermolecular guerilla raid, namely, the monkey-feeding type. But there is one other—the monkey-dropping raid—in which the amateur manager will skip one, two or more levels below the lower rim of his own molecule to find backs to put odd-ball monkeys on—monkeys that do not fit comfortably on the backs of their own immediate subordinates.

This can best be illustrated with a story about Jack, an executive vice president of a Chicago manufacturing company employing about 2,500 people at the time I knew him. He was starting on his second year of a two-year contract to turn that company around. People in that position are often referred to unflatteringly as "hatchet men"! He had retained me to do some consulting work.

Jack was a brilliant man with an IQ of 160, had earned his bachelor's degree when he was nineteen and his MBA when he was twenty. His career subsequently experienced a rocket-like rise as an industrial engineer in the business world. But his prima donna behavior drove his managers first to distraction and eventually to administrative paralysis. He regularly came to work a half-hour before anyone else showed up, dove into his in-basket and devoured the facts and figures relating to the previous day's sales and operations. He had incredible powers of retention and recall, and armed with these figures, he would make a daily series of raids on the office and shop spaces. He would announce each raid with an opener like, "Joe, just looking at you reminds me of something." Joe was building maintenance manager, reporting to the plant superintendent who, in turn, reported to the general manager who reported to Jack.

The Ubiquitous Hatchet Man

Joe would likely be in the middle of adding up a column of figures, trying to carry 249 in his head, but that wouldn't stop Jack: "Joe, I don't want you to stop anything you're doing, but in Shop 3 there's a pillar that's squarely in the path of the dollies that the men move between the head of the production line and the receiving dock; you know how they keep bumping into it, bruising elbows and shins. It's a safety hazard. Now don't stop doing anything else, but when you get a chance I'd like you to come up with a layout that'll solve that problem." Distracted, Joe would grab a piece of paper on which he then would write his personal reminder: "Shop 3, pillar, safety hazard, new layout; don't stop anything else I'm doing." He would say, "Jack, I'll get right on it."

Jack would leave and walk into another office and blurt out, "Henry, are we ever in luck! In Shop 6 there are eight tool cribs serving the machinists; now, I don't recall if it was you or someone else who came up with another layout about a year ago showing that four tool cribs could support those machinists just as well as eight. Remember? We were looking at the burden we could eliminate, but we couldn't do it without violating the union agreement. If we'd cut out half those tool cribs we couldn't have utilized or fired the surplus personnel, so we had to keep them on. But Personnel told me just yesterday that half those fellows are beginning to retire, so we can now accomplish this reduction with attrition. As they retire I want you to snatch out first one tool crib and then another and still another, until we're down to four before the union has a chance to wise up. But don't stop anything else you're doing."

Henry would grab a piece of paper and mechanically write this reminder to himself: "Shop 6, eight tool cribs, reduce to four, cut down the overhead, mum's the word, but don't stop anything else I'm doing." And as Jack walked out, Henry would reassure him with, "I'll get right on it!"

Jack was like a human beer mug, with the "beer"—his expertise—up to his ears and the "foam"—the ideas he was generating—bubbling, boiling, frothing out of the top of his head. As he moved about, he slopped an idea on one person here, another idea on that person there; here a slop, there a slop, everywhere a slop, slop! And the recipients would respond each time with, "I'll get right on it, Jack. It's as good as done!"

When cautiously criticized for his disruptive behavior, he would justify it with this self-serving homily: "Companies don't stand still; if they are not moving forward, they are slipping backward; those companies that will survive are propelled by creative ideas; someone has to generate them, and I was hired to do just that."

One particular manager in the Product Development Department gave me, over a lunch table, his own experience with Jack's proclivity for monkey-dropping:

The Prolific Monkey Dropper

"He drops about seven on me a week by phone, by memo and by chance encounter; and every Friday night I add the ones I got that week to a typewritten list that I keep from the weeks before." He showed me a list of four weeks' accumulation. "Since I get roughly seven a week, this list is about twenty-eight items long. Next Friday evening I'll add to the top of the list the ones I got from him this week and, in order to keep the list from growing any longer, I'll drop the bottom seven off. I'll do that each Friday because twenty-eight is all I think I can handle at any one time. This means, of course, that the list turns over 100 percent every four weeks. No matter what item I work on, in less than four weeks it will have tobogganed down the list and off the bottom before I can get a handle on it; so I replace it with another from the top of the list and the same thing happens again. That is why I have never accomplished anything for Jack. Meanwhile, I've become tired of giving my own boss the same old excuse for falling behind in my regular job, namely, that I'm working off assignments I'm getting from Jack. I'm sure it won't help my upcoming annual performance rating that my boss will soon turn in to Personnel and, since I've done precious little for Jack, it won't do me much good when promotions and raises are authorized. It's a catch-22, and I see no way out."

Wanting to be of some help I suggested, "But at least you can throw Jack a sop: Poke a pencil into the list at random and work on the item it hits; then follow through on it to the end even if it falls off the bottom. Give Jack at least *something*."

"I'll be glad to do that, Oncken," he said, "Provided you take this list back to Jack and ask him to cross off all of those items he has by now either forgotten about or no longer cares about. Bring me back the list and I will be happy to work on the six that are left. Six out of twenty-eight is roughly twenty percent. That means that if, as you suggest, I work on an item picked at random, the chances are four out of five that I'll be wasting my time; I'm far too busy with my regular job to work against such odds, and that's why I'll never do anything for Jack. You can explain *that* to Jack, too."

I wasn't about to explain anything like that to Jack, unsolicited. My experience as a consultant has convinced me that managers will not change their management styles in response to advice consisting of "shoulds" and "oughts," any more than the rest of us will change our everyday behavior on that basis. Benjamin Franklin's grandfather underscored this truth when he defined nagging as "the persistent reminder of an unpleasant truth." Only a heuristic event in the right context will bring about the needed conversion, and, in Jack's case, it was clear that such an event could not be far off. The most I could do in the meantime was to be prepared to help Jack when that event moved in on him with apocalyptic force.

Stripping Gears

Meanwhile, even the untrained observer could assess what is happening. Referring to our gear train analogy, gears are becoming disengaged from gears immediately above and below them, thus resulting in slippage with the attendant loss of traction from top to bottom. In addition, the gears with which Jack is thus, for brief moments, engaging his own gear are being stripped (e.g., "that's why I will never do anything for Jack"), leaving his own gear spinning freely—all unbeknownst to him.

Academia, too, has its way of describing what is going on: it would say, and correctly so, that Jack is undermining the *authority* of each manager upon whose subordinate's back he lays a monkey; that he is diffusing *responsibility* and making a mockery of *accountability*. You will recall that we identified these as the three essential properties of management and that the management molecule was the smallest unit that exhibits all of them in an independent, stable mode. Thus, the atomization of management molecules in this manner on a sufficiently extensive basis over a sufficient period of time will result in the breakdown of authority, responsibility and accountability in the organization as a whole. The management organism is only healthy when its molecular structure is, not the other way around.

Thus, a most useful insight on what's happening can be gained by looking at it from the molecular perspective and the Unit President Concept that is an integral part of it. Frequent and persistent intrusions of this type upon a manager's time from a higher extramolecular source (1) weakens that manager's managEE role, causing him to drop one or more levels on his freedom scale, and, on the reverse side of the coin, (2) weakens his boss's managER role resulting in his lowering his insurance deductible on his subordinate's regular monkeys and incurring the higher premium cost in closer supervision. This almost-automatic lowering of the freedom/deductible level is a defensive reaction to a destabilizing influence. However, once such extra-molecular intrusions cease, the freedom/deductible level normally reverts toward its former level as molecular stability restores itself. Thus, a company, most of whose managers are professional in both their managER and managEE roles, is adequately fortified against the most damaging effects of intermolecular guerilla raids of this skip-level variety, because of the self-defensive and self-healing properties such molecules are likely to possess.

Self-Defense and Self-Healing Mechanism

An interesting parallel can be drawn to the self-healing mechanism of the human body. If I, for example, slam my car door shut on my finger and rupture my flesh, the normal activities of the cells in the injured area are suspended. In our imagination let us attribute to these cells human intelligence and emotions; they might then be content to do nothing about the rupture, saying to one another, "This was not our doing. This is the fault of top management (the brain). We cannot take responsibility for top management's self-inflicted wounds, so let them worry about it. It's *their* body!" Sound familiar? That is what we so commonly hear from molecules manned by amateurs.

Fortunately, you and I have delegated, for reasons programmed into our genes, responsibility to the appropriate cells of our bodies for minimizing damage from such intrusions and for repairing such damage as may occur. Management molecules, too, can accept such delegation; their instinct for survival insures this. And this is management's opportunity.

But I am not by any means absolving Jack, and others at his level, of culpability. Of course they *should* alter their management style and *ought* to do so at once. But a ruptured molecule must not be allowed to bleed to death waiting for those "shoulds" and "oughts" to take hold; it is the responsibility of the nucleus of each molecule to see that it does not.

The professional manager, knowing that even in the most professionally managed of organizations some molecules will from time to time be inadvertently breached or even ruptured, will engage in "fire-prevention drills" with his subordinates to limit the damage of such intrusions. This might be called "preventive molecular maintenance." Normally this is done in a manner not nearly as formal as the one I am about to describe, but it is done nevertheless.

Preventive Molecular Maintenance

Imagine that you in your managER role have just called such a fire prevention drill session with your immediate subordinates. Here is how the meeting might well have gone:

"Gentlemen," you begin, "We are here to review your responses to the skip-level intermolecular guerilla raids that are inevitable in even the best-managed companies. As we know, they are of three kinds:

1. *Direct*, that is, by someone organizationally in the line above me, who therefore has the Golden Rule going for him;

2. *Indirect*, that is, by someone at or above my own boss's level but *not* in the line above us who, although he cannot wield the Golden Rule over us is very influential with someone who can;

3. *Matrix*, that is, by a product manager who, by virtue of his responsibility for a product line from inception to marketing is authorized to place monkeys on your back and run feeding schedules without regard to formal lines of administrative authority and responsibility.

"Since we are in manufacturing, you and I are frequent targets of the third type of raid with respect to new products in the pilot production stage, and since they fall under our matrix management system, are legitimate. The other two are legitimate only in emergencies and crises, as we all understand. But legitimate or not, you must be prepared to deal with those that are directed at you just as I must with those that are directed at me, and we must do it in a manner that does not damage higher management's images of us as managEEs.

"Between now and our next meeting on this subject tomorrow at 3:00 P.M., I want each of you to list *by source* the nature, number and duration of the raids on your time that occur habitually enough to warrant our planning on their frequent recurrence. Then place opposite each the freedom scale level with respect to me on which you feel you should base your response. To take an example: If the controller asked any one of you, as he occasionally might, to act as a part-time temporary member of one of his own task forces, that might rate a number 3 freedom level, which would mean that the next time he came to you with a request like that, you would tell him that you would be only too glad to do so (the truth here won't matter), but that you'll call him back tomorrow after you have talked to me.

"If I decide against your participation, *I'll* call the controller and tell him; if I decide in favor of your participation, *you'll* call him. This will protect *your* relationship with him and will remind him who's in charge *here*. Either way, I will be strongly influenced by your recommendation.

"After your part-time participation on the task force gets under way, occasions will arise when the controller's demands and my demands on your time cannot be met to both our satisfactions. You will be tempted to decide, on your own, whose satisfaction to give priority to. Let me be clear about it: That decision will be mine to make, not yours. And if my decision creates a problem, that problem will also be mine and not yours.

"There will be other items on each of your lists that you will no doubt propose to handle at the number 4 and number 5 levels on your freedom scale, since some recurring intrusions will likely be low on my anxiety index and of routine import to you.

"At tomorrow's meeting we will discuss and iron out any issues you ran into in making up your lists. Thereafter, I will negotiate privately with each of you the freedom levels you proposed so that we can proceed from a common understanding.

"If later an unforeseen, substantial demand is made upon your time as a result of a skip-level intrusion, add it to your list and respond at the number 3 level; if it recurs, then negotiate the proper level with me for future guidance.

The Fundamental Principle of Molecular Stability

"The fundamental principle involved is this: As long as higher management holds me responsible for the viability and stability of my molecule (that's the Unit President Concept, remember?), then I must hold you equally responsible in the same way for yours. I am the principle member of each of your molecules, which means that (1) you are *accountable* to me and to me alone for the use of your time; (2) your job *responsibility* is first to me and only then to others and (3) your *authority* to act is defined by your position on your freedom scale as you and I understand it, regardless how anyone else may understand it.

"As on prior occasions of this kind, I am requesting each of you to conduct a similar "fire prevention drill" with your own molecular subordinates so that all levels can operate on similar understandings. See you tomorrow at 3:00."

In a matrix, regardless of the advantages that may be claimed for it, managEEs will always give priorities to their line managERs; that is the strength of the Golden Rule. That is why the principal manager in a matrix (i.e., the manager with the ultimate responsibility for three-point landings—right product, right time, right place) is in a position of risk. Higher (Golden Rule) priorities will always creep in ahead of his.

It is common in organizations delivering a complex product—like, say, a computer system—that various line groups (like Sales, Software Support, Hardware Maintenance) will have to come together under one manager to effect the installation. This is trivial enough if that one manager has the first authority over these groups; however, it is more common in the matrix organization that he does not! The only solution is to either negotiate up front for the required authority, or to shift the organizational structure from a profession-specific or product-specific structure to a market-focused structure. The dotted (secondary) lines of authority would then pertain to the professions; the solid lines, to the market-focused manager.

But this leaves us with this question: If it is important that you conduct such periodic drills with your own subordinates and that they, in turn, do the same with theirs, then shouldn't your boss do the same with you and his boss with him? The answer is, they *should*. But if your boss is an amateur managER, he probably won't. In that event it devolves on you as a professional managEE to assume the initiative and involve him as he would be involved if he were a professional.

When the timing is right you ask him for a half-hour appointment to consider a plan you have to make yourself and your organization more responsive to his priorities and other important concerns. The amateur manager hasn't yet been born who wouldn't snap up that kind of offer.

At the appointed hour you show up and make your proposal to him in words to this effect:

"You have in the past rarely complained to me about the adequacy of my responsiveness, or that of my people, to your priorities and other concerns, and that's what makes you a great person to work for. But we will not let that kid us. We are aware of too many instances where we had not been properly accountable to you for the use of our time, or shouldered our full responsibility for meeting your requirements, or used our authority to your best advantage. The reason in most cases is that we have let others take control of our time to the extent that, when we needed it to respond to your needs and wants, it just wasn't there. Yet our time is your time, and I and my people want to make that statement more of a reality.

"Here is a list I just had typed up of the managers at and above your level in the company who periodically usurp our time for reasons that, in their own minds, are legitimate enough. Since they deal directly with us, you are rarely involved in or aware of these intrusions, nor do you need to be. Although I can foresee that they will continue to use up our time regularly in the future, I cannot predict with accuracy when their next demands will be or how much of our time they will consume. But I can predict that if, as in the past, we give them all the time we can, you will, as in the past, wind up taking your place in line along with them. And this is what we have to change.

The Negotiated Freedom Scale

"Opposite each item on this list I have placed a 3, 4 or 5 representing the degree of initiative I propose to take in response to the related potential demand on our time. A 3 would mean that we would not take action on that demand before advising you of it in advance with our recommendation. A 4 would mean that we would respond but keep you informed of the trend it was taking. A 5 would mean that we would respond but would inform you of it routinely only. All this would enable you to have far better access to our time, and probably enable us to turn down a number of such demands upon our time that heretofore we had been too willing to accept."

You would have put it differently no doubt. But the essence of the matter would still be there. And amateur managER that he is, he'll know a good thing when he sees it and fall in with your plan as a professional would if he were one; but he isn't. You and he will then examine and discuss each proposed freedom level number, some of which he will agree to and some of which he will raise or lower. As you leave, you promise to send him a copy of the list when you have had it retyped so he can place it under his glass desktop by his phone for ready reference.

The Pole-Vaulting Monkey

We come now to dealing with the "pole-vaulting monkey"—the one who jumps from one of your subordinate's backs over your head onto your boss's desk. This sort of thing can make you very nervous indeed, so don't be surprised if your boss becomes emotional when one of *your* monkeys leaps over his head onto *his* boss's desk. If you are fated to make your boss nervous anyway, this is *not* the way to do it, for you will surely lose altitude on your freedom scale forthwith. There are no hard-and-fast rules to follow in this regard since so much depends upon your own judgment and influence. But if you understand the nature of the managER/managEE role conflict discussed early in Chapter 2 and the destabilizing effect of failure to resolve it, the damage done by a pole-vaulting monkey can be limited.

Let us now review the classic "worst-case" scenario of the pole-vaulting monkey:

Imagine that, for whatever reason, you find yourself with no choice but to go over your boss's head for a decision or judgment that is clearly his prerogative to make. Since this is an action of last resort you are, as it were, firing the last bullet in your chamber. If you miss, not only will your boss not be worth working for after that but the marketability of your talents elsewhere will be appreciably diminished. Whether such an outcome is as it should be is a matter on which reasonable persons can differ; but that it may be safely assumed to be inevitable can be attested to by eye-witnesses galore. And I present it here in much the same spirit as your local public safety department presents worst-case highway accidents on your TV screen from time to time with the admonition, "A Word to the Wise Is Sufficient." My admonition is "The Pole-Vaulting Monkey Must Look Before It Leaps."

You are free, of course, to communicate directly with anyone in the company, regardless of level, in furthering the company's interest. Your boss need be informed of such contacts only if there is a possibility that he could suffer embarassment from not knowing about it. You must also be careful that in your wide-ranging intracompany contacts you neither usurp nor compromise what your boss regards as his prerogatives. For example, he may accuse you of "leaking information," when he is only insisting on his own prerogative to decide when, how and to whom such information is to be disseminated.

All this applies equally well to your subordinates in their relationship to you.

The Hazards of Ubiquity

I will conclude this discussion with a warning about the pitfalls that lie in wait for the manager while engaged in even the most innocent and benign of activities—the practice of ubiquity. Imagine that you, as a *professional* plant manager are walking through the shop and notice an employee whom you do not recognize and so assume him to be a new hire. In order to make him feel a part of the "plant family," you walk over to him, lean over his shoulder and find that he is working on a new instrument with which you have not yet had time to become familiar. You introduce yourself, welcome him to the "family" and ask him to explain to you what he is doing. It isn't long before you realize that his thing is way over your head, but you nevertheless feign knowledgeability by punctuating his explanation with "Very interesting," or "Yes, I know," or "That's a good point," and so on. Presently you excuse yourself with, "Keep up the good work," and continue on your way. Minutes later the employee's supervisor comes over to his work station, glances at what he is doing and criticizes him for doing poor work. The employee responds with, "Wise up, Boss. The plant manager came by a few minutes ago and complimented me on my work. It's about time you got with it."

Even in the innocent practice of ubiquity molecules can be severely ruptured. So, watch your step!

INTERMOLECULAR MONKEY CONVEYOR BELTS

Up to this point we have dealt with molecular stability at the managER/managEE role interface; now we will deal with it at the peer-to-peer role interface, which involves monkeys that move laterally in the organizational continuum rather than vertically. Such monkeys are usually transported on continuous intermolecular administrative conveyor belts where they are dropped and picked up at fixed points along the way. These points are on every manager's desk: (1) in- and out-basket, (2) telephone instrument and (3) desk-top computer terminal. Since what follows can be applied equally to all three points, I will select the in-basket for our attention as it will serve as proxy for the other two.

You no doubt tackle the accumulation in your in-basket at a certain time every day. Some of the material is addressed to you by your boss or someone else with Golden Rule clout and is thus classified as boss-imposed. Some of it is from your subordinates and is self-imposed. How you dispose of the items in these two classifications has already been covered in earlier chapters, so your guiding rule is that, however you dispose of them, the needles are left firmly in the down position.

The remainder is addressed to you from individuals in a peer (both external and internal) relationship to you and is therefore system-imposed. For the amateur manager much of this ends up in his monkey cage (briefcase), or in his "pending" file, or in his "tickler" file, or in his "hold" basket or stacked on the work table behind his back. Generally it accumulates more rapidly than it is disposed of. The ultimate frustration is that no item can be located on demand, and these files and stacks become graveyards of lost opportunities. But some of it consists of peer-originated demands on the manager's time to which he tries conscientiously to respond in order to maintain his coveted image of a "team player." But the demands are too onerous and the hours too few for him to be effective in that aim. What to do?

The next time you tackle your in-basket in earnest, do as outlined in the next section.

Sideward-Leaping Monkeys

First lift the day's accumulation of *inputs from your peers* out of your basket and apply to it our four "rules of the road" presented at the bottom of page 141 governing peer-to-peer relationships. The first step is to sort it into two piles:

1. The *nonmonkey pile,* for those missives whose originators do not require or expect you to take any action. These were sent to you for your information only and are often—but not always—marked, "Read and destroy" or "Read and file" or "Read and route";

2. The *monkey pile,* for those items whose originators do require or expect you to take some action.

The first pile is, of course, procrastinatable because it can, for the most part, be neglected with short-term impunity. But lest you overlook a timely nugget of information hidden somewhere in that "haystack" you will probably read it all just to make sure that you have overlooked nothing worth reading. Since this could take as much as an hour or more a day and the yield is likely to be small, I suggest you assign this task to a subordinate, holding him or her responsible for not allowing you to be embarrassed by having missed something that someone in your position should have been on top of. Other approaches are outside the scope of this book and may well be available from Evelyn Wood's rapid-reading course.

Second, sort the contents of the second pile into two subpiles:

1. The *nonmolecular pile,* for those missives whose originators are *not* on your management molecule, and

2. The *molecular pile,* for those whose originators *are* on your molecule

Note that this classification is political and not substantive, that is, it is based on "who it is from," which tells you how urgent it is rather than "what it is about", which would tell you how important it is. As noted before, urgency is a measure of temporal priority, whereas importance is a measure of logical priority.

At this point I will assume that most of my readers are managers in organizations too large to be classed as entrepreneurships and that the demands on your time contained in your *monkey pile* far exceed your ability to make good on them to the complete satisfaction of their initiators. I can safely assume, therefore, that you have been forced to neglect (a relative term) at least half of them. I will proceed, therefore, to show you which half to neglect.

But before I do, please do not misquote me elsewhere as advocating irresponsible neglect. Far from it. Instead I am advocating *calculated* neglect.

The Principle of Calculated Neglect

The contents of your nonmolecular pile can be neglected with a much higher degree of career impunity than those in your molecular pile because their originators have limited powers of retaliation. This means that, regardless of their relative importance, they are far less urgent for *you* than those in your molecular pile. These, then, are the ones to neglect, at least for the time being. But because some of the items may be important—and you don't yet know which are—you must practice this neglect in a calculated manner, as follows:

1. Remember whose monkeys they are: If they are yours, then you must assume responsibility for whatever is done with them; but since they are the originators', *they* must assume that responsibility. For those of you who, due to inexperience, have difficulty with this issue, perhaps this appeal to logic will help: The responsibility at the outset is the originators' and continues to be at least until the monkeys are dispatched to the interoffice mail system. But if thereafter they get lost enroute (not an uncommon occurrence) 'the responsibility for these monkeys is still the originators'. Considering the notorious unreliability of most interoffice mail systems, the actual delivery to you of those monkeys is too trivial and unlikely an event to constitute formal transfer of ownership. Hence, the responsibility is still the originators'. If this leaves you unconvinced, consider an age-old principle of management enunciated by Hammurabbi after he was submerged in papyrus work: "Responsibility cannot be transferred across organizational lines through the interoffice mail system." He reasoned that if such were permitted, every job description—whose function is to *fix*

responsibility—would be invalidated, and accountability would become unenforceable. Nonmolecular amateurs try to get around Hammurabbi's principle by simultaneously sending your boss a copy, hoping thereby to convert your nonconformity, if you would otherwise neglect it, into noncompliance so that you won't. That missive belongs in your nonmolecular pile if your boss regularly ignores such copies, but in your molecular pile if he regularly checks up with you on them.

2. Next, deal with this nonmolecular pile as my mother taught me to do as a child: "William, always be more careful of other people's property than you are of your own." Accordingly, I suggest you take these nonmolecular monkeys and lock them up for safe keeping in your lower-left-hand desk drawer, preferably with a combination lock, to protect them against marauders and such who have no respect for other people's property, and wait.

Why wait? Have you ever had the experience of being away from the job for as long as a couple of months, either sick or on an extended field trip, and then when you got back and plowed through all this accumulation, you found that precisely because you had been gone that long, two-thirds of it either went away or answered itself? Of course. You need little more scientific proof that if you just let this accumulation sit there long enough two-thirds of it will likewise either go away or answer itself. Since two-thirds of those monkeys are destined to die anyway, they deserve a fighting chance to meet that destiny. Give them time.

They will die because, although the people who originated these requests may have been "high" on them at the moment, they may now be having second thoughts. Let's say that one of those inputs is from someone in the Accounting Department asking you for a set of figures. That was Monday. By Wednesday, the one who wrote you the note is busy chasing other rabbits down other cabbage rows to which the figures he asked you for are not even relevant. So after you spent five hours getting him his figures, he'll pluck them from his in-basket and say, "Whoever asked for these?"

Let Time Do Your Work for You

In every organizational unit of your company, there are frequent shifts in budgets, priorities, projects and emergencies; and what any one of them may ask of you on a Monday, may become moot by Thursday because by that time they may be hell-bent on another task. But will they be considerate enough to tell you, "Don't bother with it.

We no longer need it."? Surely not. They know that it would compromise their credibility the next time they asked something of you. So they'll let you waste your time doing what's no longer necessary and upon receipt throw it in the shredder so you won't find out. That is why, after one week, the mortality rate of the majority of these nonmolecular monkeys starts going up exponentially.

Sooner or later, somebody (let's call him Steve) will be following up on one of his monkeys. He asks you, "Where is it?" You say, "Where's what?" He says, "What do you mean, 'Where's what?' I sent that memo to you three weeks ago! That should have been long enough for you to do something about it." You say, "Three weeks ago you sent that thing to me? What took you so long to call me about it?" (Put the man on the defensive! Any manager who will send a valuable monkey through the unreliable interoffice mail, fail to get a registered return receipt and not follow up on it for three weeks is guilty of gross criminal negligence and should be brought to justice.) Then you add: "Since you were consciencious enough to call me, Steve, I will breathe not a word of this to anyone—this time.

"Now, Steve, if you can explain to me how my time and energy on this matter will either (1) increase satisfaction to customers, (2) increase return to shareholders, or (3) increase economic security, provender and shelter for the dependents of thousands of employees, then I'm your dedicated servant. But if it won't do anything for any of those three worthy causes, forget it! I have no time for neurotic administrative hobbies."

Neurotic Administrative Hobbies

Any nonmolecular peer who seeks to tie up your time on some "feather merchant" project that has nothing to do with the principal reasons that the organization exists is definitely not going anywhere! He is an amateur in management.

If he cannot convince you, he'll hate you for cutting him off. (Benjamin Franklin's grandfather once observed that we are fated to make enemies. We know, he said, because we have so many. Therefore, we must pick them with care.) Enemies, if you must create them, must be from among nonmolecular managers who aren't going anywhere. So when you hang up, he goes to your boss and complains about your lack of company spirit—and your boss throws him out because he, too, knows he's not going anywhere.

If he can convince you, advise him that he can prevent such delays in the future by calling you before he dispatches such a monkey, so that you can be looking for it and give it your prompt attention. This way you will show yourself to be a cooperative teamworker. But it will also give you the opportunity to talk him out of it (the burden of proof is on the nonmolecular peer, remember?), thus aborting the monkey on the spot.

However, if his career is going somewhere (by my test of benefit of customers, owners and employees), you will do your level best for him, because he is a professional, and you thus will make a friend of him. This way, you will wind up making friends of people who are going places, making enemies (unfortunately) of those who are not; and is it not somewhere written that "You are known by the company you keep and that your company is known by the people it keeps?" Make common cause with nonmolecular *professionals* who make demands on your time, but give short shrift to the nonmolecular amateur. This does not mean, however, that his enemy status need extend to your out-of-hours relationships. Even if he were your beloved brother, you'd still say the same thing to him during working hours, and then make it up to him, if necessary, after working hours. That's how you must relate the management ethic—which is appropriate during working hours, to the social ethic—which is appropriate after working hours. One of the marks of the amateur is that he doesn't know the difference.

Responsibility for Other People's Property

Eventually, two-thirds of these things that you have deep-frozen in your bottom desk drawer you'll never get called about. Those who originated them will either have long since made do with bailing wire and twine or galloped off on other tangents with different priorities resulting, as always, from intervening events. All this inevitably gives you an aging problem in your nonmolecular pile, evidenced by the steady accumulation of "crap" in your lower-left-hand drawer. So you decide to throw out anything in that drawer that has not been inquired about for, say, at least eight weeks.

Do you think that in so doing you are engaging in irresponsible behavior? Wait a minute: Whose monkeys *are* these in your lower-left-hand drawer? The originators', remember? The responsibility is theirs, not yours, for deciding how important their missives are. And if they haven't followed up on them for as long as eight weeks, they are plainly telling you, by inaction, all you need to know about its importance: "Forget it!" Don't second-guess. Throw them out. (Don't read them; because if you do, you'll get interested; if you get interested, the vocational work ethic will make you do something about it.) The day after you throw a missive out the originator may still call you, saying, "Where is it?" You reply, "Where is what?" He says, "I sent that paper to you eight weeks ago, which should have given you plenty of time to handle it." You reply, "Eight weeks ago, Steve? That's so long ago I cannot remember receiving it." (Of course you *do* remember throwing it out because that was only yesterday!) We have already characterized the manager who will send a valuable monkey through the unreliable interoffice mail, not get a registered return receipt and not inquire about its welfare. Nevertheless he deserves a second chance, so you say, "I will breathe a word of this to no one this time, but next time it will be different."

What your nonmolecular peers will learn from this is that anything they *send* you goes into your lower-left-hand drawer unless they either call you about it in advance or walk it down to your office, sit down by your desk and say, "Look, I'm not on your molecule, but I want to interest you in something that is of obvious importance and on which I need your input." If he can convince you that the benefit to the company justifies your time, you will give him your best efforts. But he also learns that if he doubts that he can convince you, he might as well not send the missive to you in the first place. He'll find some other way to meet his need. Thus nipped in the bud, the monkey is aborted, and one less piece of paper will clutter the interoffice mail system and one less piece of paper will have to be taken home in your monkey cage!

One more time: In dealing with your nonmolecular peers, the burden of proof is always on *them!*

Many of our readers who have kept up to date with the attempt of computer companies to widen their market with "office of the future" technology will see that in the absence of adherence to these rules, electronic tools, such as electronic mail, will not create efficiencies but only speed up the inevitable chaos. If your electronic mail system permits a nonmolecular peer to send you a monkey electronically without your having any say in whether you want it or not, chaos is inevitable. Worse still if the system allows him to invoke an automatic follow-up every hour! Even with electronic mail, Hammurabbis' rule holds: "Responsibility cannot be transferred across organizational lines through *any* mail system."

Note that we are not taking a Luddite's view of modern office technology; we are only giving repeated emphasis to an old rule that data-processing people have known for a long time: Successful computer systems *follow* successful manual systems.

Monkey Abortion

In this fashion, then, you wind up not doing what you don't have to do, doing what you have to do, making friends among those whom you want as friends and enemies of those whom you can afford not to have as friends. This is the Principle of Calculated Neglect in action!

Those people who are made enemies must decide what their enlightened career self-interest is by reexamining their own priorities in the light of their objectives, goals, and budgets; and then either to get in line or make a career decision. That is one reason why many companies, yours no doubt included, are committed to *management by objectives.* MBO provides the necessary enlightenment.

Let us now look at the other pile containing your molecular inputs. The originators are in peer-user or peer-supplier roles to you on your molecule and, since you must maintain their support, you cannot apply the Principle of Calculated Neglect to their demands on your time. Instead, you call each one personally to determine its urgency.

Say that one such paper is from Steve asking you for assistance that would take at least five hours of your time. It is, moreover, an obvious neurotic administrative hobby and, on those grounds, a waste of your time. However, Steve is on your molecule, so you will have to charge your time to the overhead cost of molecular maintenance. You call him, acknowledging its receipt. Never before had another manager called him gratefully to acknowledge receipt of a piece of "crap." When he recovers from his surprise, you tell him that you notice he wants you to complete your effort within five days, that you can meet that requirement but that you could do a much better job on it if the date were extended. So you ask him, "What is the latest possible date that I can get it back to you without the lateness of the date detracting from the value of the result?"

He is so struck with your unprecedented cooperative attitude that he volunteers to meet you halfway. Swearing you to confidence he reveals that his department always sets tighter due-dates for other departments than necessary and that in your case fifteen days will be acceptable—but no longer. You thank him, hang up and make a penciled notation on his memo changing the due date from five days to fifteen days hence.

What you have just accomplished is to stretch out from five days to fifteen days the time period during which that monkey could drop dead. If that monkey's horoscope has fated it to drop dead anyway, do not interfere with destiny. Nature must be allowed to take its course. So you put it in your tickler file to pop up in thirteen days so that if then it is still alive and well you can do what is necessary in the two days remaining. On the thirteenth you call him, saying, "About this request of yours (you read it to him), do you still want what you are asking for by day after tomorrow?" If, in bewilderment, he asks, "Want *what?*" you quietly hang up and tear the missive slowly into bits and throw them in the wastebasket. Nature had been given time to take its course. This is just one more thing you won't have to do. Meanwhile, you have maintained Steve's molecular support because he sees you as one of the most cooperative teamworkers among his peers. And that is how you must have him see you, for he is on your molecule. And you can manage to maintain that image among the rest of your molecular peers by doing relatively little!

Under an electronic mail system (EMS), of course, the monkey lives until someone electrocutes it. Your EMS should allow you, the recipient, to kill the monkey in the same way you can drown it manually in the wastebasket. The rules of office automation (OA) must be compatible with our rules. Eager OA advocates will want to tie up managers with a control system whose inflexibility won't allow "politics" room to work.

Let the Inevitable Do Your Work for You

Let me close this discussion of maintaining the support of your molecular peers with this quotation from Benjamin Franklin's grandfather: *"Never put off until tomorrow what you can put off until the day after tomorrow, because you may not have to do it day after tomorrow."* But remember this adage applies *only* to your system-imposed time; applied to your boss-imposed time it will put your job tenure in jeopardy, and applied to your self-imposed time it will rotate your needles to the up position.

POSITIONING YOUR FULCRUM FOR LEVERAGE

Now that we have covered two of the three elements of molecular stability (boss-related and system-related), we shall proceed to what this book has been continuously leading up to, namely, maximizing your leverage, of which the gear-ratio was our first glimpse. In doing so, I will take you again through still another scenario featuring myself as a near-hopeless amateur who is saved by a secular counterpart of the "religious conversion" and, thus reoriented, got his fulcrum into a stable position for the leverage he needed.

For this purpose I'll cast myself in the role of a regional manager of a nationwide company that manufactures and sells souvenirs *from* any part of the world. We export them all over the world so that rich Americans who can afford to travel can buy them in India of the Taj Mahal or in Japan of the Kamakura Buddha, bring them back and adorn their homes with them. We also sell these souvenirs domestically through discount retail outlets so that the poor can adorn their homes with the same souvenirs as the rich do; in this way we make our humble contribution to the egalitarian aims of our society. Our slogan at our annual sales convention is, "Whether or not people are created equal, we will make them that way regardless." We feel that this is well worth getting up for each morning.

As regional manager in Atlanta I have four assistant regional managers, namely, George, Mike, Valerie and Dave, all amateurs in management. Our region comprises the Gulf states plus Georgia; we sell through J.C. Penney, Sears Roebuck and most of the other national retail outlets.

George, my Assistant Regional Manager for Traffic and Transportation, controls a network of warehouses and a fleet of trucks, some owned and some leased. His job is to make sure that customers get delivery as promised by our sales force. His workdays consist of incessant trouble-shooting; no two days are alike, which he says makes his job interesting. He keeps it that way by refusing to plan. But because I myself built this region practically with my bare hands back in the Great Depression years together with our "glorious founder" (God rest his soul!), my vast experience is more than equal to every crisis that George encounters. So when he runs into me in a hallway or parking lot with the opener, "Hi, Boss, we've got an *insurmountable* problem," I reply, "Think positively! There are no problems, only *opportunities.*"

The Compulsive Monkey Picker-Upper

"Then we've got an insurmountable opportunity; two of our truck drivers are crammed in a phone booth in Mobile, Alabama, waiting on long distance asking us what to do next. Sears Roebuck has turned the trucks away claiming they never ordered the merchandise. I need empty trucks like I can taste them. Our New Orleans warehouse won't accept these loads; Baltimore is too far away; Miami won't return my calls and we *need* the *trucks*. What do we do?"

Instantly I rise to the opportunity to demonstrate my vast experience in such matters. I hunt for a scrap of paper, and with pencil poised, ask him what the order numbers are. He tells me. I say, "Aha! I was on the committee ten years ago that *devised* the order-number system. Because you're young and inexperienced you couldn't have known, but those two middle digits tell me where the problem is. It's Pete Smith back in Chicago headquarters sticking his meddling fingers into our region. The telephone lines are sure going to burn hot between now and two o'clock this afternoon when I put Pete Smith in his place! Who does he think he is, telling our people what and when to ship?" And George says, "Don't let them walk over you; *we're* running *this* region! But what will I tell those truck drivers? They are still on the line waiting for an answer." I reply, "Tell them to take a coffee break. We'll get back to them as soon as we can." I picked up that monkey giving no thought to how many hours it added to my backlog of subordinate-imposed time.

One hour later he corners me in the elevator and says, "Bill, we've got *another* problem." I reach for the back of an envelope and a pencil. "We haven't shipped a thing from most of our shipping rooms since the energy crisis last week obsoleted our official priorities for shipping by air freight, rail or truck. Our field people must have policies to go by. What'll we do?" I say. "A directive about this just came in from headquarters. When I read it, I'll let you know." He says, "What will we tell the shipping rooms?" I say, "Tell them to sit on cracker barrels and eat apples. We'll get back to them this afternoon at three." How many more hours this added to my backlog of subordinate-imposed time no one knows.

Since these encounters happen about three times a day, by the end of the week I have fifteen plus a bonus for the weekend—sixteen altogether, scribbled on as many scraps of paper stuffed in my pockets. During the week I've been unable to do anything about them simply because, being an amateur, my time is being eaten up by my boss-imposed and system-imposed requirements.

Procrastination:
The Thief of the Corporate Balance Sheet

Next is Mike, whom I hired two years ago because our Corporate Market Research vice president insisted that each region hire a counterpart market researcher (whether it needs one or not!). The day he reported for work, I told him to get lost; so he got lost doing market research, which, as anyone knows, is fairly easy to do. As for me, his salary came out of *my* budget, which had forced me to fire two high-producing salesmen to free up the money to take on this "useless intellectual."

Six months later he asked for a raise. "A raise for what?" I asked. "For the research I've been doing," he replied. "Research, Mike? I haven't seen any." "Wait a minute, Boss," he said. "You came up through the Depression, going to work after quitting eighth grade, and missed the education necessary to understand what research is. *Research is an invisible, cerebral activity going on within the cranium.* That you can't see it doesn't mean it isn't there."

I replied, "Mike, my father and I, when I was little, kept a flock of fifty White Leghorn hens because we were poor and needed the money from selling the eggs. We told those hens that although we never doubted the invisible activity allegedly going on within their ovaries, none of it would count until we heard 'plop.' Now, where is the 'plop' that will tell me that something tangible has been germinating in that mental ovary of yours?"

What the Boss Cannot See Is Just Not Happening

Since any MBA could understand that, the following Friday I got the "plop." It was a memorandum in my in-basket entitled "Progress Report." I read it in the bus on my way home from work. My pulse quickened as this three-page memorandum of seven paragraphs bristled with obvious money-making opportunities. I could not resist: I pulled out my pencil and, between bumps, I wrote in the margin opposite the first paragraph, "Follow up on this." The second paragraph was so intriguing I was compelled to write, "Get the figures on this." Opposite the third paragraph I wrote, "Call Steve Smith at headquarters about this." And so on.

Each paragraph generated a "next move" I intended to make. Seven screaming monkeys added to my inventory just while going home on the bus! And if we assume an average of thirty minutes workoff time per monkey, this adds three and one-half more hours to my management time deficit. But I am taking no account of that.

How to Become Swamped in Your Subordinates' Initiatives

The next day, Mike thrust his head through my office door and said, "Hi, Boss. Did you get my progress report?" (Already he's *supervising* me!)

The following week I received another progress report from him. I didn't know there were going to be *two!* Since it would take me a month to work off the seven monkeys generated by the first one, I clipped the second on top of the first with a note saying, "Don't read this report until completing action on the first one." I now carried the *two* of them around, but being harassed by the boss and crippled by the system, I had no time even to work on the first one. The third week he sent me still another one, making me an unwitting victim of an unsolicited subscription to a weekly "magazine" in the intracompany "junk mail" system.

Meanwhile, I was still getting problems from George and receiving, on schedule, more weekly progress reports from Mike until, at the end of the quarter, I had a total of twelve. (I would have had thirteen but he was out sick for a week.) I held them together with a stiff, darkroom clamp on a clipboard under a cover sheet marked, "READ," and carried them between home and office in my monkey cage (my briefcase).

Although there are four people reporting to me altogether, I will not describe the other two here. That will be no loss to you because they are probably already working, singly or severally, for most of you, my readers. I will leave it to you to describe them to yourself in the same spell-binding, dynamic, suspenseful way as I describe George and Mike. The others will, however, play a role in Chapter 6, so we'll keep them in abeyance for the moment while we concentrate on George and Mike.

A short time later I experience the secular counterpart of a religious conversion when, attending a local seminar on managing management time (headquarters ordered me to attend), I decide that I have been a patsy long enough. That night I dreamed of nothing but up-needles, monkeys, trapezoids, molecules and the rest. And upon arriving at work in the morning I ask for George. I am going to act like a pro.

He came in. "George, sit down. What can I do for you?" "Everything is falling apart," he replies. "Those two truck drivers in Mobile have been living on straight coffee for six weeks and want permission to throw in a hamburger. As for shipping policies, nothing has been shipped out of Birmingham for three weeks." George is my most conscientious assistant regional manager, who would rather see the world go up in smoke than let our region show up badly compared to other regions. He eventually works himself into such a frenzy over the consequences of my procrastination that, by the end of the hour, he collapses in his chair dissolved in his own sweat.

I calmly put my feet up on my desk, smilingly fold my arms and say to him, "You may not believe this, George, but I'm more broken up over all of this than you are." For some strange reason he doesn't believe it. "Moreover, I have it all figured out." And with that I reach into my jacket pockets, retrieve the sixteen scraps of paper and lay them like a pile of confetti on my desk under his chin. He says, "What's *that*?" I say, "Don't you recognize them, George? Those are the sixteen decisions that are holding you up." He asks, "What do you want *me* to do with them?"

And I say, "Since this is a rather unsightly pile, you might begin by neatening it up. Get yourself sixteen three-by-five cards, and then take one of these scraps of paper on which you will find written in my handwriting to myself a decision or an action required and transfer it onto a three-by-five card written in *your* handwriting to *yourself.* Do the same with the remaining fifteen. You'll then have sixteen three-by-five cards, each carrying a statement of a decision or an action required, written in your handwriting to yourself. Next, deal those cards into two piles. If a given decision or an action looks like it goes with *your* job, deal it in *your* pile; if one looks like it goes with my job, deal it in *my* pile. If you want some help in judging in which pile a card belongs, I will loan you my job description. That way, you will wind up with two piles! By when will you get this done?"

"With everything else I have to do, it will take me at least two days." he says. I say, "That's fine. So when will you be back?" And he says, "About nine o'clock on Wednesday." Today's Monday so I reach for my appointment calendar, leaf it ahead exactly two days, and put a note there to myself, "Wednesday, 9:00 A.M., be here. George will show up with the piles."

A Case of the Piles

George grabs that pile of confetti, turns around to leave and, as he heads for the door, I take in a sight that is so electrifying that years are being taken off my life. I'm looking at a back retreating out of my office with the monkey on *it*, screwed on squarely between its shoulder blades, out the door, down the hallway.

Then, like a young dentist having successfully pulled his first tooth professionally for pay, my morale up, I stick my head through my office door and holler, "Next!" And in walks Mike.

You'll remember that Mike was my market research man in the reading of whose dozen progress reports I was far behind.

"What can I do for you?" I ask. "I am being seriously held up," he replies, "without your responses to the questions, suggestions and recommendations I put in those progress reports. Most of my counterparts in the other regions are ahead of me in getting their feet on the ground, and if you don't start making some decisions, our region will be way behind the pack."

I pull his twelve progress reports out of my bottom-left desk drawer and lay them on my desk under his chin.

"What's that?" he queries. "Don't you recognize them? Those are the twelve progress reports I am behind in reading." "What do you want me to do with them?" I say, "I want you to read them." He says, "Are you crazy? I wrote them." "All the more reason," I say. "I was taught in one of our company's training programs that when a manager is behind, the only way for him to get caught up is to delegate; and in so doing, to delegate to the person whose knowledge and experience best qualifies him to do the work. In this case, it is obviously you."

"You can't mean ..."

"Hear me out, for I have a very special way I want you to read them: with a two-colored pencil in hand. On your first reading, underline in red everything you asked me to respond to that someone else is already being paid to respond to, and write their names and phone numbers in the margins so that we can involve them at once. On your second reading, underline in blue everything that you asked me to respond to that the person in your job is right now being paid handsomely to respond to. The rest, then, will be up for grabs between you and me. This way, we'll get off dead center."

The Executive Coloring Book

It began to dawn on him that much of what he had been writing had been sent to the wrong address and that some of it should have been addressed to himself. "When can you be back to go over with me what you've done?"

"With everything else I have to do, it will take me at least three weeks," he replies.

"Why three weeks?" I ask testily inasmuch as he has been demanding of me much faster action on these same reports.

"Because they have become a fair-size book."

The injustice of this galls me. He demands that I read unfamiliar material in a matter of days, although he asks of me three weeks to read his own words! My resentment gives away to outrage.

"You've got one week. You wrote it, so dammit, you'll read it."

As he gets up to leave I reach for my appointment calendar, leaf ahead seven days, and write to myself this reminder: "9:00 A.M. Be here. Mike will show up with his executive coloring book."

Different as Mike's and George's jobs are, I am doing precisely the same thing with both of them—transferring the initiative. But because I am radically affecting our managER/managEE role relationships I have to select in each case as a first initiative one that is (1) nonthreatening to either of us, and that is (2) clearly the first in a logical series of initiatives that, too, will have to be theirs to take. The next several monkey-feeding appointments will have to be at relatively short intervals in order to see to it that their managEE role—that of reaching for responsibility—develops concurrently with my managER role—that of delegating it. Just as in football a forward pass, however skillfully executed, does not count until it has been caught and run with, so in management delegation does not count until responsibility has been successfully assumed. But, although, in football training in receiving is as important as training in passing, strangely, in conventional management courses, training is limited to delegating. The unintended implication is that failure in delegation is due only to the failure of the delegator. Although it is therefore not uncommon in football to see a badly thrown pass turned into a winning pass by an able and willing receiver, the parallel in management could just as often be witnessed if conventional management development programs would give equal attention to the skill required of the delegee in his managEE role.

ManagER "Passes," ManagEE "Receives"

Concurrently, of course, I am engaging in a similar initiative transfer process with Valerie and Dave. The differences in their jobs make no difference when it comes to transferring the initiative.

Once Valerie and Dave are included in the process, *I* have no "next moves" that any of the four are waiting for me to make. This eliminates me as a source of their frustration and makes me instead a source of their "overwork." But the job-related stress that usually burns out managers results not from overwork but from frustration. Thousands of managers every year are driven to untimely deaths from sheer frustration, but not one dies from overwork. This is because managers, as noted before, are paid not for their time and labor, but for their judgment and influence. Therefore, if you want to kill any one of your managerial subordinates, don't waste your time trying to work the person to death; instead, frustrate him by taking all his monkeys away and keeping them tantalizingly out of reach. Then watch him "twist slowly, slowly in the wind" and quietly expire. Perversely pleasurable as this might be for a sadist, it would hold out no appeal for any of my readers!

Even as I am being eliminated as a source of their frustration, they are being eliminated as a source of my guilt. Whereas I once owed them, they now owe me. I have thus literally turned my organization chart 180 degrees, right side up, with the needles all pointing down.

Even so, the rest of my day is not much different from what it was before, for neither my boss nor the system yet knows that I recently underwent a "conversion" from amateur to pro. Since their images of me have not yet changed, I'm still being harassed into *abject compliance* and ground down into *blind conformity*. But with my newly found discretionary time, I now can, with patience and persistence, win the freedom and flexibility I need; and failing that, there is always the career decision.

And now back to George, who, this Tuesday afternoon, is in his office trying to make that *next move* in preparation for tomorrow's monkey-feeding appointment. He has dealt all but one of his cards into piles but cannot decide where that one belongs. He had just read in my job description that I am responsible for helping my subordinates, so he decides to come upstairs to supervise me in that responsibility. Passing a row of empty chairs outside my office he concludes that I must be away on a field trip. He asks my secretary, "When will Mr. Oncken be back?" She replies, "Be back? He hasn't gone anywhere. His door is open. Walk in. He's sitting inside, and he isn't doing anything."

As George enters, I lift up my eyes and realize that it's been thirty-six hours since I've last seen him. "George! It's been a long while. Come in and sit down! We have a lot to get caught up on—old times." George says impatiently, "I have no time for windbagging, so let's get down to business." "You in a hurry?" I ask. He replies, "You bet I am. Fifteen monkeys are screaming for attention in my office, and I have to get back to them." And I say, "What do you want?" He says, "I need your help." Putting my feet calmly on my desk, I say, "For that I have all day, so pick my brains." He says, "I'm glad *you've* got all day, but we have just thrown away three minutes of *my* time. Let's get started!"

Thus, the more I get rid of subordinate-imposed time, the more time I have for my subordinates and the less time they have for me. I am aiming for the ideal of always having more time for them than they have for me!

Who Is Running Out of Time Now?

There are two ways in which I can achieve that aim: (1) enlarge the amount of time I have for them, (2) arrange to shrink the amount of time they can spare for me. It is not important how much "clock time" I spend with my subordinates. What is important is that I can always spare more time for them than they can spare for me; that way I will become more accessible and they will become more self-reliant. Eventually I'll be able to institute an open-door policy knowing that they will not need enough of my time to deprive me of adequate time to myself, and that every monkey that comes in through my office door on a subordinate's back goes out exactly the same way.

Besides, there is a high correlation between self-reliance and morale, a correlation that is most evident in what behavioral scientists call *participative management*, which in our imagery means "an agreed-upon back for every monkey and an opportunity for every monkey to climb the freedom ladder." So I can also look forward to a solid improvement in morale, as I persist in this initiative-transfer process.

Now back once again to George, who has just come to me for help. "What can I do for you?" I query. And he says (shoving that card toward me), "I've worked hard trying to decide in whose pile this card belongs. Which pile do *you* want me to put it in?" George has just led from freedom level 2, a most prolific source of upward-leaping monkeys; but as a *professional* manager my skill in instant recognition brings into play the reflex necessary to bat it right back. Watch me do it: "Look now. *Just* a minute, George." I push that card away from me.

He thrusts that card at me a *second time* and says, "Bill, which pile does this card go into?" He persists, simply because I, as an amateur manager, have for years reinforced that kind of behavior. Recall B. F. Skinner's principle that I quoted earlier: "Any form of behavior that you reward, you will reinforce." Even counter-productive behavior may be reinforced if you reward it. He does not yet realize that he is in this way surrendering to me control of the content of his time on this matter. That's why I must keep batting that little monkey back again and again until I can begin rewarding an entirely different kind of behavior.

Even though I have recently been converted to professional management I still don't walk on water, so I succumb to my curiosity and grab the card. "George, you wouldn't believe this, but I don't know which pile this card goes in, either; so now that's *two* of us who don't know, and that's one too many for a thing like this. "Does that mean that you cannot help me?" "It means nothing of the kind," I reply, "because I do know, rightly or wrongly, what I would do if I were in your shoes: I would deal that card into your pile."

Don't Put Yourself in
Your Subordinates' Shoes

He gets up, picks up the card, and with a sigh of relief, he says, "Thanks so much. I spent two hours in my office getting nowhere with this decision, and now, together, we have made it in just five minutes. Thank you!" And I say, "Wait, George, *we* decided nothing! All I said is what I would do if I were in your shoes. But I am not now in your shoes, nor have I any immediate career plans in that direction. So I just can't wait until tomorrow morning to see into which pile *you* will deal that card."

He gets up, walks out, and mumbles, "*That* was a *total* waste of time!"

When your subordinates come to you for help, in most cases they are looking not for help, but to get your fingerprints on their weapons, and that's not help! Any rifle coach will tell you that in building a winning rifle team you must do everything within your power to help your team members, short of touching their weapons. If you pull the trigger *for* any one of them, only *your* skill in marksmanship will benefit. *Their* skill in marksmanship must take precedence over yours.

Your subordinates must do *something* before you can improve their performance. You may feel that if you know the answer you should tell them. And so you should if it correctly falls in *your* job description, for example, a decision on policy. However, if it falls in *their* job description, get them to make a recommendation. If they can't do that because they don't know the policy, explain *that* to them, but don't make *their* decisions for them.

The following day he comes in with his cards. Eager to see how he dealt them, I say, "Lay the cards bearing your decision in a pile on your side of my desk and those containing mine over here." You wouldn't believe how he did it: three cards in his pile and thirteen in mine! (This would make even Douglas MacGregor roll over in his grave.) Naturally I don't reveal my disappointment to George; I'm in the business of building people up, not tearing them down.

So instead, pointing to what he did, I say, "George, that's a very interesting beginning! Now withdraw from your pile of three the card bearing the decision that you feel is in the most urgent need of being made."

When he does, I interrupt him: "You just created a vacancy in your pile. Take my pile of thirteen and between now and the next time we meet, find a suitable replacement for it, because I would not want you to run out of decisions." (That is called *production planning and control;* now that it has been decided by his own hand that decision making is indeed a regular part of his job, it would be tragic for him to run out of raw materials inventory.) Then I say, "George, by when will you have made that decision?" He looks at it again and says, "That is going to take me at least three weeks."

I didn't know there was a three-week decision in the entire original pile of sixteen, so I falter again. Letting my curiosity get the better of me, I grab the card to look at it. A grin of recognition spreads across my face, because this decision is an old friend; I've been carrying it around with me for nine months simply because it is one that I could make better and faster than anyone else; I could make it in thirty minutes. I've been carrying it around for nine months hoping for that thirty minutes to show up. But I've now been cornered into choosing whether to give it back to George and get *something* back in three weeks or try to make it myself and thereby guarantee that *nothing* will be decided for another nine months!

A choice between such alternatives is best made by the method of *comparative values:* If I ask George to make that decision, I know that in three weeks he will *not* have come up with nothing; to do so would make him guilty of insubordination, a charge he can be counted on to avoid. But knowing George, I can predict to the fourth decimal place what he will, in fact, come up with in three weeks, namely 0.0001! (Mathematicians have a name for it: "next to nothing.") But it surely won't be *nothing!*

But if, instead, I decide to make that decision myself, my past track record will give high odds that, in the same period of time, I will have come up with nothing, or 0.0000 to be exact. This brings me to the comparative values test: How much bigger is *next to nothing* than *nothing?* If you divide "nothing" into "next to nothing," you'll find that it goes *more* than an infinite number of times.

Next to Nothing vs. Nothing at All

This proves conclusively that no matter what George comes up with in three weeks, it will still be at least infinitely more than I will come up with in the *same period of time.* Since no businessman can turn down such a proposition, I seize upon it and return the card to him. "You will make that decision, George." I enthusiastically leaf ahead in my appointment calendar three weeks and put a note there to myself: "9:00 A.M. Be here. George will show up with his decision." He gets up to walk out with all sixteen cards, the same number he came in with*, and as I hear his footsteps trail off down the hall, I begin to wonder why it would take anyone, even *George*, three weeks to make a decision I could make in thirty minutes.

So I ask Mabel, my secretary, to call George back. As he thrusts his head around my door, I say to him, "George, I'm not going to change that date, but just as a matter of curiosity, why would it take anyone, even you, three weeks to make a decision that I could make in thirty minutes?" George replies, "For one thing, Oncken, half a million dollars is riding on this decision." (This was, I realized, why I myself had been temporizing with it for so long.) As he heads back down the hallway, I get one of my chronic attacks of heartburn.

I wonder aloud how I could have abandoned all sense of responsibility in entrusting a half-million-dollar decision to a man who hasn't made a two-dollar decision in years. If he should err, by the time I would get around to wanting to fire him for incompetence I would myself no longer have the authority. I suddenly feel an irresistible urge to pursue him down the hallway screaming, "George! George! Give me back that monkey!" But I resist, for the still, small voice of my recently converted gut feel warns me, "Keep your cotton-picking fingers off that monkey."

"Give me credit for something," I plead. "I don't have it; but what protection do you have for my loved ones?" And it whispers, "Leave the monkey on George's back, but affix thereto a *casualty insurance policy* with an *appropriate deductible.*"

---

*This confirms an age-old principle in physics: "When output equals input, there's no accumulation."

So I say to Mabel, "Call George back." She says, "What! again?" I say, "What do you mean, 'What! again?'" She says, "Why don't you sit down and explain it to him all at one sitting like the Personnel Department tells you to do?" And I say, "You can tell the Personnel Department that I don't think of these things at one sitting!"

Casualty Insurance for Monkeys

As he enters I say, "George, promise me that if you should arrive at your decision before we meet next time, you'll take no action on it until after we've discussed it." He says, "Scout's honor!" As he turns around and proceeds down the hallway, I slump into my chair relaxed and relieved, fanning my face, which is now drenched in perspiration. That monkey cannot hurt me now. No matter how George decides, he cannot act on that decision until after we have discussed it! I had just covered that monkey with a casualty insurance policy at a number 3 deductible level as specified in rule 7 on the Care and Feeding of Monkeys (see pp. 137, 138).

While I'm working similarly with my three other managers along similar lines, he comes to me fairly frequently for help. But it's not long before he realizes that my help, though generous to a fault, stops short of "pulling his triggers" for him, which leads him to the sobering conclusion that the boss's help—regardless how generous—is not all that the management textbooks have cracked it up to be. Accordingly, his visits trail off in frequency and in duration until, during the third week, he doesn't come in to see me at all. Neither do my other people, and I become alarmed.

I begin to wonder what happened to me the day I was "converted." Prior to that my people used to stand in line to see me, and now they don't seem even to need me. This brings on guilt feelings—phony of course—arising from a deep-seated human *need to be needed*. I then happen to glimpse George walking past my open door on his way to the cafeteria. Impulsively I shout, "George! George! Come in! Isn't there *some* way I can be of *help* to you?" "Yes, sometime when I'm not so busy," he replies as he quickens his pace.

Now let us see what has happened. Until three weeks ago, George was completely *boss-reliant*, since I had all of his monkeys. Now he is becoming *self-reliant*, and it's tormenting me! I have for so long had a paternalistic self-image in relation to my subordinates that I am devastated when I realize that my people are no longer dependent on me. If you have any such image of yourself, then for the sake of your own sanity and your subordinates' self-respect, shake it loose! (Psychologists have likewise for years been telling us parents that our need to be needed could be the principal obstacle to the development of self-reliance among our adolescent children.)

The Need to Be Needed:
What Happens to Self-Reliance?

George shows up on schedule Monday morning and I greet him with, "George, have you made your decision?" "Yes," he says, "and I even have it written up," which is quite a triumph for him because writing has never been among his strong points. It's typewritten and triple-spaced. (The very fact that it's triple-spaced should tell you how much confidence *he* has in it!) As I scan it, I wipe my brow and thank my lucky stars that this decision was covered with insurance at the number 3 deductible, because otherwise he and I would already be on the street pushing résumés. (I don't say that to *him*, of course!)

Instead I say, "This is a very interesting decision." (A perfectly true statement; it's just an understatement: It's frightening!) "Have you talked to the Accounting people about this?" He replies, "Are you telling me this decision is wrong?" I say, "Yes, I'm trying to tell you this is *wrong*." He says, "Okay, then what's right?" (Did you just see the monkey leap? He's leading from freedom level 2.) I bat it back with, "George, if I knew the answer to that question, what would I be paying you for?" He counters, "But if you don't know what you want, if you don't know what's right, how can you expect—or even pay me—to know?" I reply, "There is something you need to know about the management process: Managers rarely know in advance what they want, and I am no exception. But I promise you this: I'll know it when I see it—and this decision is not *it*."

Unfortunately, never had a boss talked to him *that* way before. The conventional management-training courses he has taken taught him that the manager's job is to "plan, organize, lead and control the work of his subordinates." To George that has always meant that the boss had better *know* what he wants; yet here I am telling him that if I knew what I wanted, that if I knew what was right, I wouldn't need *him!* His long-ingrained concept of what management is all about, nutured in management-training programs and other resources provided by academia, has just fallen off the wall like Humpty Dumpty, taking him along with it from the number 3 to the number 1 position on his freedom scale.

Although my purpose in this is to get him eventually to move above freedom level 3, it's likely to be painful for him at first if he's not been handled in this way before, just as it would be painful for you if your boss had not handled you that way before. Any sudden and unexplained changes in relationships between people can be painful, just as growing pains are experienced among adolescents when their bones and joints suddenly grow out of synchronization with one another. Since there is bound to be some pain involved, one must brace oneself for it.

My position that I don't have to know exactly what I want prior to beginning action may come as a shock to you as it did to George. As managers we need to have our broad aims in place; however, if we are to be creative and entrepreneurial in *how* we achieve them, then we do not have to know at the outset how we are going to achieve them. It is reasonable and desirable that as a manager you should be able to judge your subordinate's decisions as right or wrong; however, don't be discouraged or surprised if you keep getting wrong decisions—nor should your subordinates be concerned. George had his greatest freedom when I did not even know *what* I should achieve, let alone *how* to get there. Blessed is the manager whose subordinates suggest goals as well as provide the stepping stones.

I've thus set George and myself in a seller/buyer relationship; since he is coming to me with a recommendation, he obviously wants me to buy it because he can't move on it until I do. But since he hasn't ever consciously accepted such a relationship with one's boss as inherently valid, he has never consciously taken any steps to improve his skill in the "selling" end of that relationship. Hopefully, that is yet to come.

The less articulate I am on what I am looking for, the more options George has in influencing what I want. Likewise, the better I am at articulating what I want, the less control George has over the timing and content of what he does in his boss-imposed time. As long as I rarely give evidence of knowing what I want in advance, then to that extent, George retains both. But I had better be competent at knowing what I want *when I see it;* if I am not, I could make a bad "buy" and we both could eventually be in trouble. Unless, that is, George is skillful at subsequently heading off "buyer's remorse."

Salespeople are constantly reminded in sales-training courses that the salesperson and not the customer should be in control of the situation. If the buyer is in control, then the seller is reduced to becoming an order taker, a form of selling held in low esteem by professional salespeople (it corresponds to the manager who deals with his boss from levels 1 and 2 on his freedom scale). Although the salesperson must be in control, he or she must not use that control to give the customer misinformation or limit his choices, for this would make the customer nervous. Nervous customers either decide not to buy or they make poor buying decisions, which could later lead to buyer's remorse. That is why in selling, openness and honesty best serve the seller's interest. These considerations are, at this stage, still beyond George's perceptions of what management is about, but because I am proceeding from "theory Y" assumptions about George, I will continue working with him in this way until he either catches on or proves my assumptions wrong.

He starts to perspire as his pulse quickens. The symptoms are unnerving. When you deprive a person of the "roadmap" he has put his faith in and replace it with only scraps of an unfamiliar one, he loses the ability to communicate coherently about the terrain. So I try to rescue him: "Calm down, George, it's not all that bad; I know I've come on real strong, but I'm really 'theory Y' because if I weren't, I wouldn't believe in you. But because I do believe in you, I'm going to put you to the test. So be calm."

After a short breathing spell, I continue: "All right, George, so I don't know what's right; but listen to me: You and I are both fashioned from the same humble, common clay. We both have our strengths and weaknesses: You have yours, and I have mine. And let me assure you, George, that I am not sensitive about my weaknesses; so let's begin by talking about my strengths instead.

"I have a strength, George, for which I am known throughout this company: an uncanny knack for spotting a wrong decision at sight. I've saved our company millions of dollars a year this way for the last fifteen years. Whenever top management has come up with a decision they were not sure was right, they'd say, 'Show it to Oncken. If it's wrong, he will spot it immediately!' You have no idea what a track record I have on this. That's my strength—spotting wrong decisions.

"My weakness, George, is that I've never been able to come up with a right one. And that's where *you* come in. I'm sixty-two years old so I'm looking toward retirement in about three years. Therefore, I am not now about to cultivate a *new* strength. Nor would I have room for such a strength, encumbered as I am with this overwhelming strength that I have right now. But with you it's different: You're a young fellow; most of your future is ahead of you, and you still have a wide range of choice in selecting any strength you wish. Since you and I will be working with each other for the next few years, why not pick for a strength one that complements mine, namely, the ability consistently to come up with *right* decisions? Our complementary strengths would then weld us into an unbeatable team. And to open your eyes to the opportunity you have for choosing this particular strength, let me remind you of what I wrote nine months ago on the performance evaluation sheet that our company has me make out on you every year. On the back of the form, as you know, they ask me to list your strengths and weaknesses. Under your 'strengths' I wrote: 'George hasn't picked one yet.'

Complementary Strengths and Weaknesses

"So you see, George, unencumbered as you are with any strengths worth listing, you are free to commit yourself to the development of any strength you wish. Do you want into our partnership?" I extend my hand. He grasps it gingerly wondering whether he's being "taken." As we shake hands, I say, "Now then, when will you talk to the Accounting Department about this?" He says, "I'll see them this afternoon." "When will you be back with your decision as it will then appear?" He says, "Tomorrow at nine." So I leaf my appointment calendar ahead exactly one day and write, "9:00 A.M. Be here—George will be back with his decision (version number 2)."

I hope you realize that putting that appointment on my calendar pad each time is not for coercive purposes. Instead it's to enable him to know the precise time tomorrow after which he will be *insubordinate* if he either (1) doesn't show up or (2) shows up with *nothing*. Without such an appointment procrastination is invited, and monkeys start leaping.

George leaves the office, and I continue in the same vein with the other three managers.

At nine sharp the next day he shows me what he has. As I glance at it, I say, "Wrong again!" (He now knows better than to ask me what's wrong with it. If I knew that, I'd know what's right and that's not *my* strength!) He leaves and comes back the next day at nine by appointment, and each time I have to repeat, "Wrong again!" Every day thereafter at 9:00 o'clock he "pings" the ball to me, and at 9:01 A.M., I "pong" it back to him with the words, "Wrong again."

Although I agree that one should be of all the help one can to one's subordinates, it just happens that on this particular issue I am something less than omniscient and therefore of little help to him.

Even the Bible says that God does not expect anyone to do more than his best even if that best is nothing. So while George is complaining behind my back about the "incompetent" help he is getting from me, I am getting an "E" for effort from my conscience, because I *am* doing my best (which happens in this case, unfortunately, not to be good enough for George). I am exaggerating this example in order to emphasize that no boss can become such a paragon of intellect, knowledge and wisdom that he will always be of the help that his subordinates may feel they have a "right" to by virtue of his position. He, too, was fashioned from common clay.

After George and I have "pinged and ponged" his evolving decision day after day with my only comment being, "Wrong again," he gets a little impatient (an understatement). Nevertheless, the one thing that keeps us both enthusiastically in this game is our certain knowledge that there can be only a finite number of wrong decisions. On the nineteenth day the inevitable happens—he runs out of them! So when he shows up with his most recent version, I glance at what he shows me, and a smile of recognition crosses my face. He looks hopefully into my eyes and says, "Bill, do you mean that this is finally right?" I say, "I don't know about that, George. That's *your* strength. But according to *my* strength, I can't see a cotton-picking thing wrong with it."

Now that's teamwork! When two people put two complementary skills together that don't duplicate each other, that's teamwork!

But suppose instead that we were *both* good at coming up with right decisions. We'd then be competing with each other. (Everyone knows that, in management, there is always more than one right way to "skin a cat" and that you can't tell, by looking at a professionally skinned cat, which way it was skinned.) He and I might come up with two different decisions that would be just as "right" in terms of the *final result*, but in other respects at variance with each other. An issue would then develop over who's right, an issue that might fascinate intellectuals but would surely blind us to our common overriding objective. But because instead I'm depending on him to come up with what's *right*, and he's depending on me to spot what's *wrong*, we complement our strengths and, therefore, need not get into fruitless conflict. *That's* teamwork!

What's Right vs. Who's Right

So then I say to him, "George, how soon can you get this thing off the ground?" He says, "I can complete phase I in about eight weeks at which time we should have a progress review. That should take all day: the morning to review what I will have done so far and the afternoon to review my plans for phase II, because I don't believe that I should proceed with phase II until you have reviewed it." And I say, "George, you've got the job." After I leaf my appointment calendar ahead, not just a few days, not just a few weeks, but eight whole weeks, I put a note there to myself. "9:00 A.M. Be here. George's monkey has just become a gorilla!" This set the date for the first of a series of gorilla-feeding appointments (progress reviews).

Our picturesque terminology has, of course, its counterparts in the conventional rhetoric of current management literature. For our word "monkey" the conventional counterpart is "assignment," which is defined as "any responsibility that is executable at a given point in time and place," such as when I asked him to talk to Accounting, write a letter, make a phone call, attend a meeting, or make a quick, spotcheck field trip requiring only two or three days. Academia's counterpart to *our* word "gorilla" is the project, which is not executable at a given point in time and place; instead it is a process consisting of one or more phases executed over a period of time. In this case George estimated eight weeks for phase I.

Academia tells us that a *project* is the vector sum of many logically related assignments executed in pragmatic sequence. (Wow!) In our more picturesque terminology a "gorilla" is defined as the vector sum of many little "monkeys" laid nose to tail. (You can see that in contrast to theirs our language communicates. That's why management-training programs taught by academia must end with written final examinations. Students must be forced to memorize language they otherwise would have no compelling reason to remember.)

Let us now recapitulate my "ping-pong" game with George (see Figure 6). Starting with his first move ("See the Accounting people"), it must be remembered that I did not know *at the outset* what *result* we were headed for. But that did not prevent me from starting the "game." Some business school devotees of the management-by-objectives cult keep propagating a myth that until one can articulate in operational terms a desired management result, it is pointless to start taking any steps toward achieving it. This myth gets its credibility from its vocational origins: It is true, for example, that until the architect has completed his drawings, it is too soon to start laying brick. In management, however, it is sufficient that there be a compelling purpose toward which immediate steps be taken; the desired result can then be made to articulate itself as progress toward it gains momen-

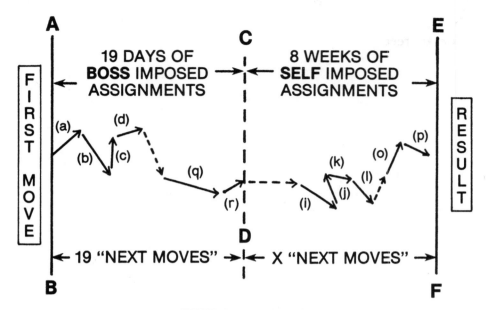

YOU HAVE DELEGATED ONLY WHEN
YOU HAVE TURNED OVER TO A SUBORDINATE FULL
RESPONSIBILITY FOR **SELF-ASSIGNMENT** WITHIN
A KEY RESULT AREA OF HIS JOB.

Figure 6

tum. Failure to see this distinction can cause unnecessary delay in initiating management action.

Purpose Precedes Objective

That's why I started *immediately* playing "ping pong" with George and on each of nineteen successive days *assigned* him a "next move," such as, "See Industrial Engineering," "Attend that meeting," "Make that inspection trip," etc. And when, at the nineteenth "pong," I set the date for the first gorilla-feeding appointment I implied (1) that between now and then all "next moves" will be assigned by himself to himself (I am now at dotted line C–D in Figure 6) and not by me and (2) that I would not need to know in advance either their number or their nature. I use "X" to indicate the unknown number and nature of *self-assigned* "next moves" it will take to get him from dotted line C–D to the interim RESULT E–F eight weeks hence. Foreseeably they will be made at freedom levels 4 and above (or at corresponding deductible levels 4 and above on my casualty insurance scale). The gorilla, however, is permanently insured at the number 3 deductible level, because he agreed that he would not proceed with phase II until I had given him my approval. This illustrates that *gorillas must always be more heavily insured than monkeys are.*

It must be remembered also that neither did I have *at the outset* (line A–B) much of a "feel" for my confidence in his competence, my rapport with his personality, or my respect for his character at or above freedom level 3 in this area of his responsibility. Our encounters, however, as we "pinged" and "ponged" day by day, steadily reduced my unknowns with respect both to the result we were aiming for and the confidence I could place in him for achieving it, until by the nineteenth "pong" my anxieties on both counts had got down to my threshold tolerance level. Only then could I finally let him move ahead on his own, confident that *he,* too, knew where he was headed and how he would get there.

Let me pantomime, for the sake of clarity, what happened on the nineteenth "ping": Without interrupting the "game," I turned my paddle over to George's free hand so he could play my side of the game while, with his other hand, he continued to play his side. His responsibility was to keep the game going in my absence and to see to it that I "won." This transition from boss-assignment to self-assignment is called *delegation. You have delegated only when you have turned over to a subordinate full responsibility for self-assignment within a key result area of his job.*

Observe, first, that delegation does not ordinarily occur at the outset of any important opportunity or problem having the dimensions of a project. Typically, delegation does not occur until somewhere down the road two conditions become evident: (1) Your confidence in the individual's competence, your rapport with his or her personality, and your respect for his or her character have grown sufficiently to reduce your anxieties to a level that will allow you to let him or her run for an extended period without your having to see him (you will be seeing him, no doubt, but not because you have to); and (2) the result (or objective, if you prefer) you are aiming for has come clearly into view, for, as we have noted, an ambiguous result can be anxiety-creating especially if much is at risk. Delegation neither requires nor justifies abdication.

There is a textbook name for these monkey-feeding appointments (a), (b), (c), etc.: *coaching* sessions. Thus, he came to me at (a) for one minute of coaching, at (b) for another minute of coaching, and at (c) for still another. They could each have lasted longer than a minute if I could have been of more help, but a minute's worth was all the help I was able to give him in this instance. The sole purpose of coaching *is to get yourself into a position where you can delegate with confidence.* Delegation is not a single administrative act as some business school textbooks seem to suggest; instead it is a state of affairs reached only after sufficient coaching. And when, in a managER's judgment, that state of affairs is out of the reach of an individual managEE, career counseling is indicated. Delegating is not giving someone something to do. A subordinate's monkey can never be delegated to him—it is his already. It may have been misplaced for a while, wandering around the organization, but it was always *his.* Giving it back is not delegating—it is assigning. Nor is delegating occurring if monkeys remain at freedom level 3. Delegating occurs only when a state of affairs occurs that lets monkeys live at level 4 and above.

The Purpose of Coaching Is Delegation

You may have felt that I must have had incredible patience to endure to the bitter end nineteen "pings" (coaching sessions or monkey-feeding appointments) at such a snail's pace. I exaggerated the situation, of course, but only to remind you that compared to this long, arduous, tedious coaching process, my only realistic alternative was to do virtually nothing—in short, to procrastinate. This tiresome coaching process was by comparison infinitely superior. But now let us suppose that next week, during *your* "ping pong" game with *your own* counterpart of my George, your boss loses patience and interrupts your game by demanding instant accountability for the final result. I hope you don't say to him, "Sorry, Boss. Bill Oncken's book says to 'play the "ping-pong" game out to the bitter end,' so you will just have to wait." You will have acted like an amateur, not a pro.

My rules are framed primarily to facilitate the kind of pragmatic, tactical footwork essential to career survival; not having a life of their own, they are not to be followed as if they did. It may be embarrassing to you and a morale setback for your subordinates to have to interrupt or even abandon a game because "the boss just hollered," but you must, by your own example, give them a short refresher course on the art of managEEship and the part that a sense of good sportsmanship plays. Such disruptive intrusions by your boss place you *de facto* in the number 1 spot on your freedom scale. Although these occurrences cannot be eliminated entirely, they can be kept at tolerable levels of frequency and severity through the practice, as discussed earlier, of anticipatory compliance.

Returning again to George:

Now that I have turned my paddle over to George in mid-game thereby delegating responsibility for its outcome, I am free to start another game, this time with Mike. I will stay in the game with him until my confidence in him and his confidence in himself permit me to turn my paddle over to him. I now will have two games going, which frees me up to start up games with my other people as well. When and if I am able finally to reach the *delegation* stage as well with them I will have four games going simultaneously but will not be actively involved in any of them. All four players will hopefully be doing their best to see that I win, for that is their responsibility. Each "ping" will be a *self-assignment* and each "pong" an act of *self-supervision;* and I will have four series (projects) of these going while *my* hands are in my pockets. I will be observing them closely at this stage, so all these *self-assignments* (or self-actuating monkeys) will be initiated at the number 4 freedom level. In textbook language, each will have been delegated responsibility for a project.

I will not be active in these games, but I will be still just as accountable for their outcomes as I was before I delegated. My role, therefore, will be occasionally to ask them individually, "What's the score?" If one of them replies, "Seventeen to fifteen, your favor," I may get nervous if that margin is too close for comfort. So I'll say, "Give me my paddle," and put myself back into the game long enough to spread out that margin. When I have done so, I'll return the paddle and check on the other games for the same purpose. These occasional intrusions I call *executive supervision* because I am not pulling anyone out of a game to take it over myself; instead I am entering it only when necessary and staying only long enough to get the score comfortably in my favor. To be sure, the freedom level of their initiatives gets dropped from number 4 to number 3 but that corresponds to lowering the deductible and paying a higher premium in supervision until the score justifies my returning the paddle. Although the players may be annoyed by such intrusions, they will have to accept them if they habitually let the score run at close margin, or even against me. Sorry about that.

What You Call It Makes a Difference

One final observation: although amateurs typically use the terms *assign* and *delegate* interchangeably, it is clear from the foregoing that the two are not even of the same genre. One often hears them say, "I *assigned* that to Judith and *delegated* that to Norman," meaning the same thing in both instances. The manager who doesn't know the difference will never understand leverage. But you may ask, "What difference does it make what you call it? What's in a name?" An electrical engineer who uses the terms *volts* and *amperes* interchangeably because "it's all electricity anyway" should be removed at once from company property before he causes incalculable damage. A manager can likewise never become a professional until he, too, learns how to think and talk like one. Larry Apply once made this point in saying, "If you don't think it, you won't do it." (Fortunately the opposite is not true; if it were, this would be a very interesting world indeed!)

Suppose, further, that as we continue in this way, each eventually acquires control of *four* projects apiece (quite possible in management but not in ping-pong—my analogy breaking down at last, but not before I had made full use of it!). This state of affairs will be a tribute to them no less than to me, for the needed modifications in our roles as managEEs and managER could not have been wrought without patience and persistence on both sides. And there is little chance that we will ever slip back into our old ways prior to my conversion, because the comparison between then and now makes it unthinkable for any of us.

The lower rim of my molecule is now in stable equilibrium with my managER role and will remain so as long as I can limit it to executive supervision. This requires that my subordinates maintain the upper rim of their molecules (i.e., myself) in stable equilibrium with their managEE roles, and will remain so as long as they can limit their freedom levels to number 3 and above.

In real life none of these people will be the equal of any other; one may be in the early stage of ping pong where I will have one of the paddles. With him I will be supervising his monkeys. But another one will be so far along that I'll need only to delegate responsibility for self-assignment. With him I will be exercising executive supervision. The development of these people will hopefully progress to the point where they all will be engaging in self-supervision. Their boss-imposed time will be spent practicing anticipatory compliance and my self-imposed time will be spent in executive supervision, while being accessible to them and with adequate time to myself.

Raising Your Gorilla-to-Monkey Ratio

To get an idea of the extent I am thus leveraging my time, let us make some more simplifying assumptions: Each of the sixteen projects runs concurrently for eight weeks to the completion of its phase I, and each project requires twenty "next moves" to carry it from the point of delegation (dotted line C–D) to the RESULT of phase I. This means that each of my sixteen acts of delegation triggers twenty self-assignments (or initiatives, or next moves—as you prefer) over the ensuing eight-week period, or a total of 320 self-assignments within the sixteen projects. Yet I myself am not working as long and as hard as when, before my conversion, I was trying to take all the required initiatives myself. My leverage—using these simplifying assumptions—is thus the number of subordinates times x, where x is the average number of projects per subordinate multiplied by the average number of next moves each makes per project in the same period of time. In real life such a formula would be useless for calculation, since self-assignments are not recordable and therefore not countable. But their number *is* related to the freedom level at which the subordinate is working, and *that* number, or one proportional to it, can be used for x. Thus, two of the critical elements in gaining leverage are (1) organizing the work into projects within each of which an act of delegation can trigger a chain reaction of self-assignments, and (2) coaching subordinates to work as high on their freedom scales as circumstances will permit. If my responsibilities increase beyond the capacity of my four subordinates to accept responsibility for additional projects, the addition of a fifth subordinate will create the potential capacity for four additional projects and, therefore, for eighty additional "next moves." This would only be possible for a *delegating* manager.

If I had remained an *assigning* manager (which is what I was to the left of dotted line C–D in Figure 6) my leverage would have been only four to one, because four people can do only four times as many things in a given period of time as one person (myself) can do. Thus limited to one project apiece, the addition of one more person to my staff would add relatively little to my capacity to take on more responsibility. This underlines the difference between the effectiveness of the *assigning* manager (low leverage) and the *delegating* manager (high leverage).

I will end this chapter with the following summary, in tabular form, of the three components of molecular stability:

BOSS-IMPOSED	SYSTEM-IMPOSED	SELF-IMPOSED
Degree of Freedom as ManagEE	Degree of Flexibility as Molecular Peer	Degree of Leverage as ManagER
Freedom 5 (Anticipatory Compliance)	*High Credit Rating* (Flexible Conformity)	*High Leverage* (Delegating)
Freedom 4		
Freedom 3		(Assigning)
Freedom 2		
Freedom 1 (Abject Compliance)	*Low Credit Rating* (Blind Conformity)	*Low Leverage* (Doing)

This chart will help you see where you stand in relation to your boss, your peers and your subordinates. Bear in mind the following:

1. You enjoy different degrees of freedom in different parts of your job.
2. Your credit rating will be higher in relation to some of your peer-suppliers, lower in relation to others.
3. You will be more fully delegated to some subordinates, less so to others.

As an exercise, rate yourself as of today on each of these three scales, using "average" levels. Then ask yourself these questions:

1. Is this the level at which I want to be?
2. If not, what level would objective circumstances require and permit?
3. What must I do to get there? How long should it take?

Although this chapter ends here, my scenario involving myself, Mike, Valerie, Dave and George does not. We will pick up their trail again in the middle of the next chapter, so read on!

6

Maximizing Leverage for High-Value Output

The concepts, principles, and values underlying the management of management time can be represented by a three-dimensional rectangular grid which represents holistically the real world of management in which managers compete. Any manager can, upon finishing this book, take five minutes each day to assess the relative value of the time he or she is, at the moment, putting in and to determine what, if anything, he or she must do about it.

FULCRUM-MOVING-OVERMANSHIP

If my foregoing discussion of gaining managerial leverage sounded simple, it was beause I tried to make it so. But that did not make it sound any easier. The long, arduous and painstaking "ping-pong" process I went through with Mike and George in Chapter 5 should strike a responsive chord among those of you who have gone through similar experiences with amateur subordinates who showed some promise of becoming professionals.

If leveraging your time by delegating is so simple—and it *is* simple—why is it not easy to learn? Part of the answer can be found in Chapter 3; for the rest of it, I will shortly resort to an allegory; but first a few words about the art of fulcrum-moving-overmanship.

Archimedes said, "Give me a place on which to stand and I will move the world." To move your management world that "place" is the center of your molecule—where you are right now. But it must be a *stable* platform, as Chapter 5 had made abundantly clear. Your fulcrum is your *discretionary time,* which, if you are a pro, will be adequate to the weight of responsibility on the output end of your lever. The position of your fulcrum is determined by the proportion of the time spent in your managER role that is at the executive level, that is, *seeing to it* that things get done and are under control, compared to the proportion you spend at the supervisory level, that is, *getting* things done and controlling what's being done. As hinted earlier, this position allows for far more leverage at higher organizational levels than at lower; therefore, the professional must be judged not by how much leverage he exercises, but whether he has fully developed the leverage available to him at his organizational level. In this sense both a first-line supervisor and the company's president can be judged by the same criterion: the *actual* leverage compared to the *possible* leverage at their respective levels. This is just another aspect of the application of the Unit President Concept.

Archimedes was also the first to give abstract definition to the leverage principle in physics, although the lever itself was no doubt used by prehistoric man. Archimedes' contribution was his mathematical law of the lever, namely, that if you want to lift, say, a ten-pound weight and you can muster only one pound of effort to lift it with, you must see that the fulcrum is at least ten times as far away from where the effort is applied as it is from where the weight is resting. The ratio of the greater length to the shorter length is called its *mechanical advantage*. In this example the mechanical advantage, or *leverage*, would be ten-to-one.

The mechanical advantage is not obtained scot-free. In physics it is obtained at the cost of the *mechanical disadvantage* of having to move the free end of the lever ten times as far. In management it is obtained at the cost of three *psychological disadvantages* that the user of the lever must learn to overcome, which brings us to my allegory:

Try to imagine the experience of the first prehistoric man to discover the use of leverage in lifting, say, a rock. Up until then he had lifted rocks directly with his bare hands. But his first crudely devised lever confronted him with these three psychological disadvantages:

1. He had to move the long arm of the lever × *units of distance* for every *one unit* he raised the rock;
2. He had to apply his effort *some distance away* from the rock;
3. He had to apply his effort in the *opposite direction* from that in which he wanted the rock to move.

These were indeed *psychological* disadvantages because his milleniums-old, bare-handed method had until then accustomed him to the following three experiences:

1. For every inch of lift, he could move the rock a *corresponding* inch.
2. He could apply his effort directly to *the rock itself* and thus be "on top of the situation" at all times.
3. His effort and the resulting movement of the rock were in the *same* direction.

Our imaginary prehistoric man faced, at this point, what every person in every age has faced when confronted with a technological breakthrough. He or she had to choose either to (1) retain his existing habits of rock-lifting and therefore forego a capability of lifting a rock many times his or her own weight, or (2) exploit his device by learning the new habits it required. Had he elected to retain the former method, he or she might have rationalized his choice as follows: "When I lift rocks I like to (1) raise a rock an *inch for every inch* of effort, (2) be right *on top of the rock* at all times and (3) apply my muscle in the *same direction* as I want the rock to move. This new gadget (lever) requires that I do everything the opposite way. My father used to say, 'The best way is the way you know best. Keep *improving* upon it!' He was right. I'll therefore continue to try to find *better* ways to lift rocks barehanded and throw this contraption (lever) away." His decision, therefore, would have been to "refine yesterday's solutions to last year's problems."

Is the Best Way the One You Know Best?

The analogy surely has not escaped you. Organization is to management what the lever is to physics and engineering. Indeed, it was not until I had my four subordinates managing four projects apiece at the number 3, 4 and 5 levels of freedom that I was enjoying real leverage. Let us reexamine, in this context, how I did it.

The Y-axis (see Figure 7) lays out three degrees of managerial leverage corresponding to three components of a manager's time that make up a typical day or week. We define them as follows:

1. *Employee time* is that component of our time that we spend *doing things*. The leverage is one to one, because one person can accomplish in a given time period only what one person can do in that time.

2. *Supervisory time* is that component of our time that we spend *assigning things* to each of our subordinates to do himself. Here were are getting things done. The leverage is n to one (where *n* is the number of immediate subordinates we have) because we can accomplish *n* times what we could have accomplished singly in the same time.

3. *Executive time* is that component of our time that we spend *delegating responsibility* for self-assignment. Here we are seeing to it that things get done. The leverage is nx to one (where *x* is the average level of freedom our subordinates are exercising in getting things done) because the result, through synergism, is greater than the sum, *n*, of its individual parts.

To see, therefore, how I was able to achieve this leverage through my own people, let us now proceed to examine in detail the three points on the Y-axis in the light of what we saw happening in the last part of Chapter 5.

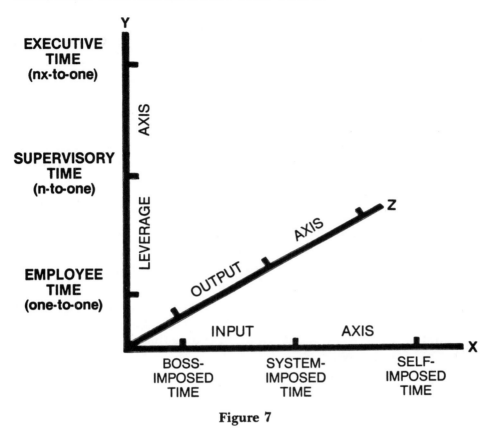

Figure 7

The Employee Time Component

Before my secular conversion in Chapter 5 I was swamped with monkeys, putting great pressure on the employee component of my time. Like our hypothetical prehistoric man I was trying:

1. Too see accomplishment *equal* to my own efforts;
2. Be *on top of* all the problems myself;
3. Work in the *same direction* as my job description implied, namely, to "direct the efforts of my subordinates."

The first of these was drastically limiting, the second unattainable and the third self-defeating.

There are, to be sure, occasions when time in the employee component can be justified. These situations occur when we are *training* our subordinates to do the things required by their jobs—just as a school teacher will solve a few problems *for* his students in order to get them to solve similar problems *for themselves,* or in a time of crisis when everyone is expected to pitch in and help regardless of his title or position. The professional manager knows when, and when not, to justify enlarging his employee component.

The Supervisory Time Component

The "ping-pong" (coaching) stage with Mike, George and the others in the last part of Chapter 5 brought into being the *supervisory component* of my time, which is governed by the seven rules for the care and feeding of monkeys listed in the latter part of Chapter 4. My struggles with the "disadvantages" of the *n*-to-one leverage that this component required were apparent on almost every page, to wit:

1. Each assignment I gave each individual could instead have been done *directly* by myself. That way, I'd have gotten the satisfaction of making an element of progress for each element of my own effort. *N*-to-one leverage, on the other hand, denied me this.

2. The problems moved to my *subordinates'* desks from *mine.* This *separated* the effort (mine) from the action (theirs). This denied me the satisfaction of being "right on top of things" all the time.

3. The greatest psychological disadvantage in leverage is, as noted earlier, that you apply the effort in the *opposite direction* from that of the desired result. Prior to my conversion, both I and my subordinates accepted literally to the point of naiveté the statement in my job description that it was my responsibility to "direct the efforts of my subordinates." Organizational leverage required that, in order to fulfill that responsibility, I move in the *opposite* direction, namely, to have my *subordinates* anticipate *my* thinking. By thus applying my efforts in the opposite direction, I wound up fulfilling that responsibility very well indeed. This did, of course, deny me the satisfaction of directing their efforts by attempting to govern *their* thinking. Amateur managers try to direct the efforts of their subordinates by attempting to think out everything *for them.* The result? Up-needle, one-to-one leverage, and a backbreaking assortment of monkeys.

The Executive Time Component

The *executive component* of my time came into being when I had the four "games" going without my hand on a single paddle. It reached its maximum when they were able to handle four projects apiece. In each case, the supervisory component was used for an extended period of time until each subordinate was able to relieve me of the onus of assigning specific things to him. Each one eventually assumed responsibility for *self-assignment*. The x factor in the leverage formula (nx to one) measures the degree of freedom in self-assignment. With four subordinates, my leverage can be far greater than four to one because of the number of self-assignments each individual takes on and completes without my knowing about it. Knowing *when to stay away* from your subordinates is a mark of the pro. The amateur never gets over the feeling that to stay away is to move in the *opposite direction* from where he or she should be moving. The fact is that "oppositeness," as noted already more than once, is one of the psychological disadvantages of leverage. The pro soon gets used to it. His or her subordinates, as they become increasingly professional, thrive on it because it gives them more elbowroom for getting control of their own boss-imposed time.

Having said this much and no more we would be guilty of overlooking the *control* factor in (1) assigning and (2) delegating. Both assigning and delegating invite the risks incurred in accepting the three psychological disadvantages that we must accept if we are going to enjoy the benefits of leverage. When you *assign* things, you must also *control things*. When you *delegate* responsibility for self-assignment you must also have *things under control*. Let us analyze these two kinds of control now in detail.

Controlling Things

Because there is no way for a manager to enjoy the high leverage available in the executive component of his time (in respect to any particular subordinate) without passing through the *supervisory component* en route, the "controlling things" concept must be mastered before the "things under control" concept can be implemented.

At this point the seven rules on the care and feeding of monkeys listed in the last part of Chapter 4 come into play. The *supervisory* component of my time, spent as it was in coaching Dave, Valerie, Mike and George, was dominated by two symbols: the monkey was the symbol for *assigning things*, and the monkey-feeding calendar was the symbol for *controlling things*.

Things Under Control

As noted before, I had to "ping-pong" my way up my leverage scale in my relationships with George, Mike, Valerie and Dave from the one-to-one leverage position *before* my conversion *through* the four-to-one leverage position (requiring many patience-trying months of attempting to master the art of "oppositeness") to the nx-to-one leverage position available in the *executive* component of my time *after* my conversion. This progression on my part up my leverage scale can be succinctly summarized as follows:

Employee time:	things out of control
Supervisory time:	controlling things
Executive time:	things under control

In the *employee* component of my time I am so overloaded with monkeys that I can't handle them. Things are definitely *out of control.*

In the *supervisory* component of my time I established a temporary division of labor. My job: to *feed* my subordinates' monkeys on individually established feeding schedules. My subordinates' job: to *work* the monkeys and bring them to my office on schedule for feeding. I have now shifted from *doing things* to *controlling things.* The techniques of control may vary, but the one element common to them all is the calendar appointment pad.

In the *executive* component of my time I achieve a permanent division of labor. My job: to feed gorillas on established feeding schedules and practice executive supervision in the interim. My subordinates' job: to feed their own monkeys and bring their gorillas to my office on schedule for feeding. I have now shifted from *controlling things* to having *things under control,* and my subordinates have shifted from *boss-control* to *self-control.*

My progress through these three components neither was nor could have been any more rapid than the concurrent progress of my subordinates up their own freedom ladders. This points up a truism of managerial experience: The component (employee, supervisory or executive) within which a manager deals with each of his subordinates depends on the level that particular subordinate has achieved on his own freedom scale. Subordinates who are rank amateurs in management literally drag their bosses down to very low leverage positions. The young data-processing manager was an outstanding example of a pro working for an amateur (myself) in such a way that, in my relationship with him, I was buoyed up like a cork in a rapidly filling bucket to a high leverage level. Subordinate managers have great difficulty in recognizing the degree to which their *own* mastery of managEEship influences their *boss's* style of managERship. Subordinate managers who complain most about bosses that cannot or will not delegate are often the primary causes of the very problem they complain about.

Let us now summarize the thrust of this chapter so far:

Leverage	Component	Action	Process	Control
nx:1	executive	delegating	seeing to it things get done	things under control
n:1	supervisory	assigning	getting things done	controlling things
.1:1	employee	doing	doing things	things out of control

In every management position, from first-level supervisor to CEO, all three components are present, either in actuality or potentially. At the top level the executive component may be as high, say, as 85 percent of the working day, whereas at the first-line supervisor level it may be as much as 20 percent of the working day if the supervisor has some workers who are willing and able to assume responsibility for more than just an honest day's work for a fair day's pay. This happens more often with knowledge workers than with production workers.

One More Time:
The Unit President Concept

Let us now resume the saga of the Southeastern Region, of which I am playing the role of Regional Manager in Atlanta. It is now two years since my conversion, my leverage is nx to one (or 4x to one since *n* is the number of subordinates I have); and to see that it stays that way I have had a legend hung on my office wall behind me lettered in Old English script two inches high on imitation parchment paper to this effect: "For every problem and opportunity facing this region there will always be someone who has it, and his name will never be Bill Oncken. What can I do for you?" Dave, Valerie, Mike and George are, as you may expect, up to their elbows in problems and opportunities; so much so that whenever I drive by the plant on a Saturday morning on my way to the golf course with the CEO of any one of our many key customers, I see their four cars in the company parking lot. "Workaholics!" I exclaim with patriarchal disdain, for are they not there of their own free will even as I had been in years gone by?

Let us now interrupt this scene to switch to another one in Houston where our company's Southwestern Region has its headquarters, and where John Baxter holds forth as Regional Manager. As it happens, our two regions are identical as to our markets and distribution patterns and so are our organization charts and staffing patterns. The job descriptions of John's four assistant regional managers are identical to those of Valerie, George, Mike and Dave, and we both are accountable to our Chicago headquarters under the same financial, operating and sales yardsticks. So similar are our two regions that our company's internal auditors half-jokingly remark, "When you've seen one, you've seen them both."

Indistinguishable but Different

But there is one difference that the auditors consistently miss: John Baxter is an amateur manager and I am a professional. John, being, therefore, an *assigning* manager, it trying to compete with me, a *delegating* manager. John's leverage is four to one, whereas mine is 4x-to-one and my x-factor is growing steadily as my people grow in judgment and in influence. Handicapped by his low leverage, he tries to make up for it by becoming trapezoidal to the right, putting in seventy hours a week. His operating and sales performance is steadily slipping behind mine, and he is fast becoming a physical and nervous basket case. His subordinates, likewise amateurs all, are beginning to show symptoms, clearly visible to the naked eye, of acute frustration. The situation between him and them is at a paralyzing standoff.

Finally, at the urging of his wife, John Baxter consults a psychiatrist, who informs him that his health is being endangered by extreme job-related stress caused by the unconscionable pressure the company is putting on him to close the growing gap between his region's sales and operating performance and mine. The conversation continues thus:

> BAXTER: I wouldn't be in this shape if the company would ease up on the pressure and give me some help in replacing my four assistant managers with qualified people who want to do an honest day's work. Whenever I bring this up to headquarters, I get a deaf ear followed by a diatribe on "catching up with Oncken." They have never given me an ounce of recognition for having sacrificed, for the good of

	the company, my home life, family life, church life and social life. What do they want, my soul, too?
PSYCHIATRIST:	You are just another casualty of the profit-hungry capitalist system that trods down all human values in its insatiable pursuit of material gain. You, like scores of others whom I counsel, are being used by these corporate monsters who, when they have wrung the last drop of blood out of you, will turn you loose to take your chances in the chattel market for used-up and burned-out executives. What then becomes of you will be your concern, not theirs. That's the *system*.
BAXTER:	But where do I go from here?
PSYCHIATRIST:	Before they rob you even of your sense of personal worth and human dignity, call them up and tell them that your pride won't allow you to be chattel to them any more; that you demand to be treated with the dignity befitting a human being and that if they don't, you will have to resign to preserve your self-respect.
BAXTER:	I'll do just that!

Bringing Top Management to Book

He returns to his office and calls Chicago. His boss, who is Vice President of Operations, answers the phone. Then this:

BAXTER:	I've given my life's blood to this company and what do I get in return? Corporate Personnel won't help me with my personnel problems and the pressure to keep up with Oncken has made me put in a seventy-hour week for more than a year now. My psychiatrist tells me that I've been pushed to the breaking point and that if the company does not come through for me, I won't last out the month.
V.P.:	I'm shocked that no one had even suggested to me that we had been doing this to you. How can we help?
BAXTER:	This time I'm not talking about a raise, or even a bonus, although I deserve both. I am not for sale any more. The only way the company can now show that it cares is to give me some relief from the burden I'm carrying.
V.P.:	How can we do that?
BAXTER:	By adding $30,000 to my annual budget so I can hire another assistant regional manager. The four I have now are just not enough.

> V.P.: That seems like a fair request. Decisions like that are made by our President. I'll see him right away and—sensitive and caring person that he is—I'm sure he'll authorize me to give you the relief you need.

They both hang up. The Vice President takes the elevator to the top of the John Hancock Building (where the corporate offices are housed), walks into the President's office and pleads John's case. The President listens earnestly and sympathetically. Then this:

> PRESIDENT: I have long felt that our regions were under-staffed at the assistant manager level and I intend to budget for an additional assistant manager for each region as soon as earnings are up. However, I can allocate at once the $30,000 requested, but before I do, I want you to satisfy my curiosity about one point: You and I know that the Southeastern and Southwestern Regions are identical in every respect. It would seem, therefore, that if Houston needs an increase in staff, Atlanta should too. Am I right?
>
> V.P.: You may be, but decisions like this have always been made on the "squeaking wheel" principle; Baxter is squeaking, Oncken is not—that's why Baxter needs the help.
>
> PRESIDENT: I did not turn this company around on any squeaking wheel principle and I am not about to base this decision on it either. But that has not changed my mind; I *am* allocating the money. There is, however, a technicality involved: Bill Oncken in Atlanta will get the money and not John Baxter.
>
> V.P.: But when Baxter hears this he will be outraged and will demand an explanation.
>
> PRESIDENT: I rather expect that he will, so if he requests it, tell him to take the next plane for Chicago to allow me the privilege of personally administering the explanation unto him.

Why the "Rich" Get Richer and the "Poor" Get Poorer

The Vice President leaves the President's office a confused man; he cannot follow the President's reasoning, which is why he will never become President. But my readers, no doubt, are ahead of the story: The President knows that Baxter, as an assigning manager, is trying, with four-to-one leverage, to compete with me, who is enjoying nx-to-one leverage. Other things being equal (which they are), the $30,000 would raise Baxter's leverage from four-to-one to five-to-one, whereas the same money similarly applied to Atlanta would raise my leverage from 4x-to-one to 5x-to-one. The President did not rise to where he is by being an economic idiot: For the same money he can buy x times as much leverage in Atlanta as he can in Houston!

Upon returning to his office, the Vice President realizes he has *two* phone calls to make: one to Baxter and one to Oncken. He decides first to make the less unpleasant of the two:

> V.P.: Oncken, I have unexpected news for you, so hold on to your chair. The President has just allocated an additional $30,000 to your annual budget to support an increase in your assistant manager complement from four to five.
>
> ONCKEN: To what do I owe this unexpected largess?
>
> V.P.: The reason you are getting the money is that Baxter in Houston asked for it.

With that I hang up. I know when I am ahead. I also suspect there may be some mistake; it doesn't make sense. Had I been thirty years younger, I would have asked for an explanation. But thirty years of experience have taught me that demanding explanations of higher management is strictly for losers. Anyway, how often does top management make a mistake in your *favor*? So I decide instead to use the money in such a way that my president will eventually be able to brag to the directors of the company about his uncanny genius for profitably allocating funds, using Oncken's region as a crowning example. If I succeed, I can look forward to an increasing frequency of such "mistakes." Remember B. F. Skinner's principle: "Any form of behavior that you reward, you will reinforce."

The Vice President now calls Baxter:

> V.P.: Baxter, I have good news and bad news. The good news is that our President saw your point and allocated the money. The bad news is that the money goes to Oncken and not to you.
>
> BAXTER: That does it! It only confirms what my psychiatrist says about the cynicism of big business when it comes to human values. I've been working myself to the bone twenty-four hours a day—and all night besides—while Oncken spends afternoons and weekends on the golf course with big shots; he hasn't done an honest day's work in the last two years.

And whom does the company help? Not the ones who need it! It helps people like Oncken, that smooth, fast-talking politician who can boot-lick and apple-polish his way to anything he wants. This company is shot through with politics—it's not what you know but who you know that counts, and this time I'm not taking it lying down. I demand an explanation!

V.P.:   Our President anticipated that you would want an explanation, so he has authorized you to come to Chicago so that he can personally administer it unto you.

Baxter took the next plane for O'Hare and grabbed a taxicab to the John Hancock Building, where he joined his boss for an elevator ride to the top floor and the President's office. As they entered, the President greeted Baxter with, "What can I do for you?"

BAXTER: I demand an explanation, and I am not leaving town without one.

One More Knock in the School of Hard Knocks

PRESIDENT: You will have your explanation. Fortunately, it is to be found in Holy Writ. I will therefore quote to you the applicable Bible passage, suitably amplified for management purposes: "For he that hath (leverage) to him shall be given (additional help); and he that hath not (leverage) from him shall be taken even that (job) which he hath." (Mark 4:25)

That happens to be among the most difficult of Biblical verities, especially difficult for losers, many of whom would prefer the utopian norm: "to each according to his needs and from each according to his abilities." But the difficulties it poses do not detract one iota from its credibility. Having survived the test of nearly 2000 years of human experience, it needs neither defense, explanation nor proof. It needs only to be taken as a warning that the dispensers of the gold can be trusted not to throw good money after bad.

So for Baxter, the long-overdue career decision has finally forced itself upon him and with it the opportunity for a fresh start in either a job in which he can compete as an assigning manager or a job in which he is willing to learn to become a delegating manager.

As for me, I'll let the reader construct his or her own scenario of *my* outlook!

OPTIMIZING VALUE

It was stated in Chapter 3 that management time, in contrast to other kinds of time, has two properties, duration and value; and that as a manager assumes increasing responsibility one or both of these must increase in response. We saw that the amateur's response is to increase the duration of his workday, whereas the professional's response is to increase the value of each hour he puts in. Unlike duration, value has no *absolute* limit, which makes it possible for managers to be competitive in overcoming the *circumstantial* limits on the value of their time. This was illustrated in many of the parables, anecdotes and sitcoms that followed, culminating in the Atlanta-Houston scenario.

All this was further illuminated by the analogy of the lever, in which the three variables were (1) input, which is defined as the work done on the lever; (2) output, the work done by the lever; and (3) its mechanical advantage (or leverage), the ratio of the weight at the output end to the force on the input end. So far so good.

But now we must remind ourselves that even our allegorical prehistoric man must have realized that merely being able to lift a rock many times his own weight was no more than an intriguing exercise unless he could make the phenomenon serve a useful purpose, namely, to enhance the value to himself, if not to others, of the time he had to spend lifting rocks. Once he had a purpose sufficiently compelling to motivate him to overcome the three psychological disadvantages of leverage, he used it to determine (1) the desired direction of the thrust, (2) the place on which the fulcrum should rest, and (3) the position of the fulcrum along the lever. He knew that his determinations were correct only after they had been confirmed by successfully serving his purpose. With practice, this empirical method no doubt sharpened his skill to the point where Archimedes' à priori method—had it been presented to him—would have added little to the cost-effectiveness of his rock-lifting activity

Until the behavioral sciences give us reliable à priori methods for maximizing the organizational value of a manager's time, trial and error will continue to be the accepted method. Some managers, by improving upon their trials and reducing the frequency and severity of their errors, develop intuitions and skills so reliable that what they don't know about behavioral science (in the academic sense) doesn't hurt them. They are students in what we referred to in Chapter 3 as the School of Experience. Others, the amateurs, whose random trials and mounting errors are forcing them trapezoidally to the right, would not be helped even if they were taught what behavioral scientists know today because, as students in the School of Hard Knocks, they don't even know what their problem is. And until they find out, no theory, however intellectually respectable, will be of any practical use to them.

Practice Makes You Competitive, Not Perfect

This leads us to Figure 8, a conceptual model of the organizational realities within which managers must manage their management time. It borrows from algebraic geometry some of the characteristics of a three-dimensional system of rectangular coordinates in that each axis measures a different value and that its value is zero at the origin and 3 at its positive extreme. It departs from the algebraic parallel in that the axes are finite and relate to discrete rather than to continuous functions. It thus becomes useful as a grid for assessing the value of one's management time insofar as it is affected by its input, leverage and output. As we will show later in this chapter, you will be able to place, within this reality matrix, what you are doing at any moment during the day, simply by determining its three coordinates. Thus (2,2,2) means that what you are doing is system imposed, that you are assigning it to a subordinate (supervisory time) and that it is a

The Management Time Cube

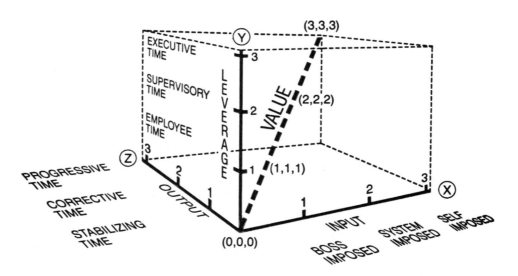

Figure 8

corrective action. Twenty-seven such points comprise the whole. But before we explore this further, we must explain the meaning of the z-axis, which we purposely postponed until now.

The z-axis designates the output of the manager's time, that is, the purpose toward which his action is directed. *Stabilizing time* is the time you spend refining yesterday's

- solutions to last year's problems, or
- responses to last year's opportunities

You use this approach when, in your judgment, the best way is the way you know best. If a rationalization is needed for not choosing a more innovative or creative approach, it will be the familiar "there is no point in rediscovering the wheel." The method is primarily routine, which conserves nervous energy for the nonroutine things that face you further out on the z-axis. Benjamin Franklin's grandfather's observation about the relationship between the routine and non-routine is worth quoting here:

> Let routine things be done in routine ways and let nonroutine things be done in nonroutine ways. Heaven help the one who insists on doing routine things in nonroutine ways, for he will soon run out of the discretionary time necessary to give nonroutine things the nonroutine treatment they deserve.

Don't Give Routine Treatment to Nonroutine Things

Most of a manager's stabilizing time is consumed in performing administrative functions that appear trivial (hence our term "admin-istrivia") when conscientiously attended to but can erupt into minor crises when *not* conscientiously attended to. Although managers get little pleasure from doing administrative work, they nevertheless endure it to avoid the pain from not doing it (the pleasure-pain principle again, remember?). The practice of blind conformity is helpful in this respect because it requires only a receptively reconstruc-tive (as opposed to a creatively constructive) approach, which, in turn, is conducive to routinizing the routinable. The principle value, then, of stabilizing time is to conserve your discretionary time for dealing with things further out on the z-axis that cannot be given routine treatment.

When misapplied, however, stabilizing time can impede progress. For instance, had a trained scientist been working for Thomas Edison, he would no doubt have come up with a brighter-burning candle.

Routine methods normally result in meeting routine expectations, or, in the words of a not-so-ancient philosopher, "Means are ends-in-the-making." On the other hand, not all progress is worth the cost, hence the adage, "If it ain't broke, don't fix it." Edison followed that maxim in wasting no time in improving upon the candle (stabilizing time) because it was already living up to all the claims its advertisers were making for it. Instead, he concentrated on making a kind of progress that would, if successful, be well worth the cost; and as we shall see several paragraphs below, this placed his efforts at the far end of the z-axis (progressive time), where they produced the first incandescent lamp!

Corrective time is the time you spend finding tomorrow's

- solutions to this year's problems, or
- responses to this year's opportunities

You use this approach when things are happening differently (either better or worse) from what was expected or planned. They result from the fact that luck plays a significant role in the outcome of a management action, for in management "Results always equal performance plus luck." Thus, the more professional a manager's performance, the less significant will be the role of bad luck in the outcome. But luck, as we all know, comes in *two* varieties, good and bad. Bad luck creates problems, and good luck creates opportunities. The professional, using foresight, seeks to be prepared to maximize the impact of good luck and minimize the impact of bad luck. In doing the former he plays the role of opportunist, while in doing the latter he plays the role of trouble shooter. In either case, time spent in this position of the z-axis is aptly described as "just one damn thing after another," and, because these activities are far more visible than those in the other two positions on this axis, the casual observer concludes that this describes *all* the manager's time. The noncasual behavioral scientist makes the same mistake, for his method requires that he give the greatest weight to the manager's most visible forms of behavior, a method that was valid enough when, as a graduate student, he studied the behavior of rats in mazes. It is hardly surprising, therefore, that when he applies these same methods to studying managerial behavior in the maze of organizational realities, he sees it only as an "executive rat race." But you and I know better.

The Executive Rat Race

In this area of your concern you are neither managing nor administering, but *operating*. The "compulsive monkey picker-upper" and "prolific monkey dropper" described previously were primarily operating, that is, taking corrective action. The approach called for in this position on the z-axis is (1) nonroutine, (2) innovatively adaptive and (3) tactical. In the vernacular of shops and offices, it is called the "fire fighting" part of the job.

When time spent in this manner becomes excessive the manager must watch for any problems or opportunities that exhibit recurring patterns, for they are predictable—at least statistically—and can therefore respond to more routine treatment. This, as noted, releases discretionary time for those events that, while foreseeable, cannot be predicted with accuracy and therefore require nonroutine treatment.

Progressive time is the time you spend anticipating the eventual

- solutions to next year's problems, or
- responses to next year's opportuities

This is the forward-planning part of your job. The future will arrive on time whether you do anything about it or not. Your career-competitive position at that time will very much depend on what you do now. The prudent manager will assume that (1) his future will not be like his past, (2) it won't be like he thinks it's going to be and (3) it will be here sooner than he thinks. He must, therefore, rely on foresight to anticipate future events that cannot be predicted with accuracy and over which he has no control. Crystal balls and Ouija boards aside, to foresee the future you must have an understanding of the present. For example, in planning a trip, a roadmap is useless if you only know where you want to go; it becomes useful the moment you find out where you are. Understanding the present helps you decide what your possibilities are, and planning serves to turn those possibilities into probabilities, that is, planning loads the dice. What you can foresee you need not predict; if you can foresee a heavy winter, you get ready for it so that even if it doesn't happen you still did the right thing. Your approach in this part of the z-axis is creatively constructive, and is strategic rather than tactical.

Each of the three outputs on the z-axis exists in every management position from the bottom to the top of the organization. The relative emphasis will be different from one job to the next, but the first-line supervisor no less than the president must, in his enlightened career self-interest, be alert to the possibilities of change in the circumstances of his own job so that he can respond creatively and constructively when events turn some of those possibilities into immediate probabilities. This is yet another application of the Unit President Concept.

We are ready now to turn to Figure 8, first to provide you with a simple exercise, or game, to help you internalize holistically the message of this book and, second, to give you a technique for making a three-minute audit each day of where you are in relation to where you want to be within this time management grid. This audit will be analagous to the mariner's "shooting the sun" with his sextant to determine where he is in relation to where he wants to be.

"Shooting the Sun"
with Your Managerial Sextant

To this end let us analyze some of the possible combinations in the grid. The combination most important to personal and organizational growth is (3,3,3) at the far corner of the grid. This combination is relatively high in both risk and opportunity and is full of problems unfamiliar to us because they lack precedent.

The combination least important to growth is (1,1,1) near where the x, y and z axes intersect. This combination is relatively low in both risk and opportunity, but its problems are familiar to us and have plenty of precedents. It is, however, important to survival.

There are, as noted earlier, twenty-seven such possible combinations, each with its own mix of risk, opportunity and familiarity. The diagonal (the heavy dotted line) connecting the point of least risk and opportunity but the greatest familiarity (1,1,1) to the point most novel and unfamiliar but has the greatest risk and opportunity (3,3,3) is the line of increasing value.

The time of most managers oscillates around mid-point (2,2,2) where he is, to pick a typical example, being prodded by the organization (system-imposed time) to prod his subordinates (supervisory time) to fight the day-to-day fires of the business (corrective time). Occasionally, he will slide down to (1,1,1) where he, for example, is being prodded by his boss (boss-imposed time) to perform a task (employee time) that will patch up an irregularity in the standard operating procedure (stabilizing time). Occasionally he will move to the far corner

(3,3,3) where, for example, he will call a meeting (self-imposed time) to delegate responsibility (executive time) for coming up with a new plan to anticipate competitors (progressive time).

Although we have thus far analyzed only three points on the diagonal, we will later leave it to you to thoughtfully analyze the remaining twenty-four within the rest of the grid. Meanwhile, remember that value increases as you move away from the intersection. Any rigid conceptualization of human affairs, such as this one, invites oversimplification with its attendant errors. For instance, a research scientist, working at point (3,1,3) may come up with a discovery so profitable to the company that his value, *that year*, may be far greater than that of his vice-president of R & D working at the far end of the diagonal (3,3,3). This would seem to invalidate our statement that the far corner is of the greatest value. However, if the vice-president is on top of his job, he will see to it that the eventual profitability of this discovery multiplies itself far beyond anything that the scientist himself could have foreseen. He must do this on his own initiative (self-imposed time) by involving many others (executive time) in the full exploitation of the discovery (progressive time). The far corner of the grid will thus come out ahead in the value scale. Should the vice-president fail to produce this value, he will no doubt be replaced by someone who promises to succeed.

The purpose of the grid is thus to provide a basis for self-examination as to how you are spending your time in relation to the expectations under which your job most logically falls.

But let us first go through a few more simulative exercises: Suppose that you are, at the moment, working at point (1,1,1). This means that you are working at your boss's discretion (boss-imposed time), doing it all yourself (employee time) and on a strictly routine matter (stabilizing time). The risk here is low, but so is the challenge. That is why the pay, too, is likely to be low. But you can still find people in highly paid positions working in the low-value end of their jobs (1,1,1) and people in low-paid positions working in the high-value end (3,3,3) of their jobs.

The Value Line

Suppose instead that you are spending your time at (3,3,3) on your grid; what you are now doing is self-imposed, which means that your boss does not yet know that you're doing it. As soon as he finds out, he's obligated either to approve or disapprove. If he approves, then it automatically becomes boss-imposed for you at the number 5 freedom level. It then becomes *his* idea. But until he finds out about it, it remains strictly self-imposed for you and is still *your* idea. Your z-axis coordinate (3) means that you are doing long-range planning that involves "guesstimates" about which you could be wrong. And because you are doing your planning on a self-imposed basis at the executive leverage level, you've got your people doing the actual work, which is tying up a lot of your payroll. That's very risky. Moreover, you could be accused of going beyond your authority, especially if your planning proves to have been wrong when the facts come in. Your neck is out, as the saying goes, three ways. If things now fall apart, you will read about your drop to the bottom of your freedom scale in the morning paper in your carpool on your way to work, and you will ask your driver to let you out so as to save your company the cost of de-hiring you. But if things work out, your boss will not criticize you for having exceeded your authority for he won't have time. He'll be too busy answering his congratulatory mail!

Or again suppose you are sitting behind your desk, your telephone rings and someone at the other end says to you, "Where is it?" You reply, "Oh, hi, Ken. What do you mean, 'Where is it?'" And Ken says, "That report I was supposed to have yesterday." And you say, "Oh my gosh! Haven't you got it?" He says, "That's why I'm calling." And so you say, "I'll take care of it." That is your input from the *system*. You immediately call one of your subordinates and say, "Pete, where is it?" Pete says, "Where's what?" You reply, "That report—you know, the one we promised to Ken." That's your leverage (n to one) for you just made an *assignment*. Pete replies, "I'll get right on it; it will be in Ken's hands tomorrow at 10:00." And that is the output—*corrective* time. Many managers, as noted, spend a good proportion of their day just this way, at point (2,2,2). Then if the boss is out of town, they can drop the boss-imposed orange. If their telephone cord is pulled out by its roots and they have no in-basket, they can drop the system-imposed orange. And unless they can have an original idea about what to do, they'll have to drop the third, self-imposed orange, and that would end the act. At that point their location on the grid would be (0,0,0)!

The No-Orange Juggler

There are some people who, after they've made about fifteen "round trips" like this at point (2,2,2) become so exhausted that when they go home, they can say, "This was one of the hardest working days I ever put in." The Protestant work ethic thus sanctifies a day of mediocre value. It is at (2,2,2), the midpoint of the grid.

But let us repeat now the above scenario among you, Ken and Pete, except that your time is now at (2,1,2) on the grid, which places your leverage at the *employee* level (one-to-one leverage) on your y-axis. Then instead of calling Pete and assigning it to him, you say to yourself, "With idiots like Pete working for me, I have to do it myself if I want it done right," so you do it, and will be working on it past quitting time. (And who walks by the office at quitting time bidding you a cheery weekend? Pete, of course, who should have been doing it in the first place.) *That's* spending your time in (2,1,2) fashion.

Now let us visualize a likely scenario for point (2,3,2). Here the input is still from the system, the output is still corrective, but the leverage is at the executive level. So now the phone rings, and Ken says, "Where is it?" And you say, "Where is what?" He asks, "Where's the report?" You say, "I'll see that you get it." When you hang up, you call in three of your subordinates and say, "There is something the matter with how we get reports out. What's your role? And yours? And yours?" Here a *managerial* decision is being addressed ahead of the immediate *operating* decision to make sure that future inputs of this kind from the system are directed at them and not at you. If instead you reacted *only* to the immediate operating matter, you may be sure that you would have to react to it again and again and again. (*Operating* as used here is equivalent to *corrective*.) You increase your leverage by making the managerial decision first, that is, by delegating responsibility for seeing to it these monkeys are in the future dealt with by their proper owners and not by you. Only then do you take the immediate corrective action.

Managerial vs. Operating Decisions

Next, suppose that you are working (3,1,3). It's your idea, you're acting on it yourself, and it's on a long-range planning matter. If this is what you *should* be doing, then you're obviously a staff planner replete with a green eye-shade and sleeve garters, sitting behind a corner desk up to your neck in computer printouts, a lone, creative contributor. But if your job is at the executive level of the company, can you imagine the harm you're doing your company and your people by doing long-range planning by yourself in your office without making them party to it? They will be whispering behind your back, pointing in your direction: "The boss is in a seance communing with the spirit of our late founder. We can't wait till the genie comes out of the bottle!" You may be sure that when you reveal your clairvoyant strategy you will meet resistance to the plan at every turn regardless of its merits. Involvement in planning is essential in order to make sure that you are not thwarted by noninvolvement when the implementation stage arrives. Although planning all by yourself is valid in vocational work, management planning in isolation is a contradiction in terms. So much for point (3,1,3).

I hope you have become sufficiently familiar with the time management grid in Figure 8 to appreciate the following story:

Back in 1961 I conducted a seminar on this subject within a high-tech corporation where the managers in attendance were primarily engineering and scientific types who, as you might expect, took to my time management grid like children to a toy. On one of my visits several months later the leader of the group told me how he had been using it: "I brought my secretary a cheap alarm clock and asked her to set it to go off at a randomly different time every day. Now, each time the alarm sounds, I stop what I am doing at the moment and ask myself three questions: (1) In which one of these twenty-seven grid locations am I now working? (2) Why am I working there? and (3) How do I like my answer to that last question?"

Five Minutes a Day That Could Move Your World

He continued, "After doing this daily for several weeks I noticed that I was beginning to do things differently. Although it takes less than five minutes a day, by now it's such an ingrained habit with me that on those few occasions when my secretary forgets to set the alarm, I feel that something in the day was missing."

I will never forget this; it's a classic example of a fact of experience that doing the right thing is never wasteful of time. We've all seen how the interminable drop, drop, drop of water on a block of granite will eventually create a distinct and permanent groove. Two to five minutes a day asking three *right questions* about what you're doing with your time will, I am convinced, beneficially change your orientation to what you're doing and will make a permanent difference in your career, because what you are doing determines what you are becoming.

And if there is one book I could recommend to my readers as a stimulant in dealing with these three questions, it would be Peter F. Drucker's *The Effective Executive*, published by Harper and Row in 1966. It is far more relevant today, for its time has surely come.

Appendix A
Parable on Organization

Once upon a time there was a baseball team, remarkable in many ways. Although it put in creditable performances against the competition, it fell short of what it believed it could do. What was remarkable was that it had more than its share of outstanding and versatile players and boasted of a highly informal way of playing the game, which, they believed, released the "feeling of belonging," "team spirit" and "good fellowship" so necessary to success.

It came to pass one day when the other side was up at bat, the first baseman asked to pitch the ball and burned one across the plate. The batter swung and missed. The umpire, instead of calling the strike, announced "time out" and censured the first baseman for having usurped the pitcher's responsibility.

He referred to violations of several basic "principles of organization"—of baseball in this instance—and warned him that he would be disqualified if he pitched from first base again.

The first baseman answered him and said, "It just so happens that I am an outstanding pitcher besides being a top-notch first baseman. Most of the men on this team can do more than one job well. We don't stand on bureaucratic formalities. They stifle initiative. When a special situation comes up, we throw the ball to the man best talented to handle that situation. So when this particular batter stepped up to the plate we all knew I was best able to strike him out. Did you see him miss my first pitch? Watch him on the next two!"

The umpire became wroth and retorted, "But pitching goes with the position and not with the man. If the man in the pitcher's box is not equal to the challenge, swap places with him between innings. But I won't let you pitch from first base."

"Well, who in thunder are you?" asked the first baseman.

"The voice of experience," answered the umpire.

"Do you know who I am? I'm the captain of this team, and I built up the club from bush league to what it is. I've played every position and I want my men to be able to do the same. Whatever experience you happen to be the voice of is irrelevant here. We're a unique kind of ball team. None of us limits his responsibilities to his own job description.

220

When there is a game to be won we all turn to and do what has to be done. That's our particular genius. I'll stack my men against those of any other team—player for player."

"Do you win many games?"

By that time the rest of the team had crowded around first base, listening eagerly to the conversation. They could no longer resist getting involved.

Catcher: "We could have won *a few more* if I had known where the next ball was being pitched from."

Fielder: "and if I had known where to throw the ball for the next pitch."

Pitcher: "and if I had thrown it to third to put out a runner instead of throwing it to the boss for the next pitch."

These comments from his men shocked the captain. He had never heard them talk like this before. His cherished beliefs in happy-family informality were apparently not shared by his men. His greatest source of pride seemed to go unappreciated.

"Ungrateful wretches," he thought to himself. "They don't realize how fortunate they are to work in the highly informal and unrestrictive atmosphere I have spent my life nurturing. Well, if they don't appreciate it, let them work for one of the other ball clubs where they stand on formality. As for me, we're going to play the game like a happy family."

And they continued to do so, for, as captain of the team and owner of the club, he was in a position to see that they did.

For the joy of playing first base according to his *talents* rather than according to the requirements of the *game* he was willing—unwittingly no doubt—to limit the effectiveness of his *team*. A costly luxury, as it turned out.

Eventually, the team leveled off its career at the minor league level. It tried to break into the big time by buying some big-league talent. This did not help. After several years of frustration the captain realized he had to make a choice:

1. Sell the team.
2. Be willing to accept a few hits in each game—and possibly even some errors—in exchange for building a winning major-league team.

How would *you* have chosen?

Appendix B
Authority, Responsibility and Influence

"I could really get things done if I only had the authority" is probably the most frequently used copout of the also-rans in management, because it has a ring of legitimacy. Management texts say that "if you give a subordinate responsibility you must also give him or her the authority to carry it out." Why, then, does American business rarely delegate authority commensurate with responsibility? It's simply a matter of risk.

How much authority will you, yourself, delegate to a person for whose character you do not have sufficient respect, or with whose personality you do not have sufficient rapport, or in whose competence you do not have sufficient confidence? ANSWER: *Less* than sufficient authority. And this will be *less* than he or she needs to do the job for which he or she is responsible!

However, as he or she earns more respect, rapport, and confidence from you and from others, you yourself will delegate to him or her correspondingly more authority. Eventually, he or she may acquire from you the authority that is, in fact, commensurate with his or her responsibility. We say "may" because he or she will no doubt be promoted before that happens and will have to start all over again with his or her new boss. This is one of the frustrations of success!

In Chapter 3 we have analyzed influence on the job into four components:

1. Influence of *competence*—which has to be acquired. It evokes *confidence*.
2. Influence of *authority*—which has to be delegated. It evokes *deference*.
3. Influence of *personality*—which has to be developed. It evokes *rapport*.
4. Influence of *character*—which has to be cultivated. It evokes *respect*.

You can, through any one of these components alone, get others to do some things you want them to do when you want them to do it. For example:

My doctor can hand me a prescription and "order" me to get it filled. He is not my boss, but he still has plenty of influence—of competence. I wouldn't risk disobeying him, so I comply with alacrity and jump into my car and speed to the druggist.

On my way I hear a siren and my rear-vision mirror tells me I am being "ordered" to pull up to the curb. The young rookie has nothing to work with but his influence of *authority* (his badge); and I won't risk not giving it the deference he expects.

He lets me go after giving me my traffic ticket, and I resume my trip to the druggist, who gives me a vial containing six tablets and charges me twelve dollars. I hit the ceiling at what seems an outrageous price. He asks me, as a friend, what price a man will put on his health, let alone his life. Brought instantly to my senses, I apologize and obey his "order" to pay the twelve dollars. Only a fool would resist the influence of *personality* so ably wielded by this man. He is so easy to listen to! He never fails to say the right thing at the right time to help you keep your values straight!

I return to the car and proceed to my home and go to my bathroom upstairs to take my dose. But I hesitate. I wonder whether this pill is really what it purports to be. For all I know, it could be sugar-coated chalk. If so, I've been "taken." What guarantee have I?

I read the "orders" on the vial and down at the bottom I see, in fine print, this statement by the pharmaceutical house that manufactured the ingredients: "Product of Smith, Konrad and Fletcher, pioneers in honesty and integrity in the service of the medical profession." You can't beat that! My respect for the manufacturer thus reassured, I yield to the influence of his *character* and swallow the pill.

Usually—especially on the job—we respond simultaneously to all four components of the influence exercised by other people and not just one. But this illustration helps us clarify the nature of each component independently.

The four components of influence have been listed intentionally in a particular order. From the top down they follow the order in which they are critical to our careers.

When we apply for our first job we are asked, "What can you do?" Thus *competence* is the earliest separator of the men from the boys, the women from the girls. We also get our first raise on this basis, if not our first promotion.

Having demonstrated our competence, we are eventually selected for promotion to a supervisory position in the hope that we can handle skillfully the influence of authority that goes with it. The person who understands the limitations of authority and how to overcome them can make the grade.

Having demonstrated success as a supervisor, we are selected for promotion to a middle-management position in the hope that we can succeed in a situation where authority has little influence. The middle manager is too far removed from the work to tell people daily what to do and how to do it, still too far away from top management to influence policies and priorities, too far away from the "action" levels in other departments to get quick response from them. He or she is a coordinator, an expeditor, liaison man, a trouble-shooter, a diplomat, a "revolving door" for daily crises, a "pulley" on an endless administrative transmission belt. If others find him or her hard to talk to, listen to, and work with, he or she will be ignored or even sabotaged. A middle manager in isolation is a contradiction in terms. To get things done above him, below him, and to either side of him, he or she must have the influence of *personality*. We do not mean a "personality boy" or "glamour girl," but the person must be considered easy to do business with by superiors, peers and subordinates alike.

Having achieved success as a middle manager, we are now up for promotion to the officer level in the company. At this point the trail we have left behind us in the administrative sands of time is the critical factor in our chances for this promotion. In short, what is being looked for is a person of integrity in the eyes of scores, if not hundreds, of people. At this point it is of no importance how certain we are of our own integrity. Many an honest person has *seemed* to be lacking in integrity merely because of a thoughtless, though possibly well-intentioned, act. He or she suffers, nevertheless, for the trail he has left behind him has already been interpreted by others according to their own lights.

Happy is the person who makes certain that his or her trail does not have confusing or misleading patterns, which may look crooked to others regardless of how they may appear to him or her. But his own opinion about this will carry scant weight at this crucial juncture. What higher management wants is a person in whom *others* respect the influence of *character*. His or her trail must already have spoken "loud and clear" to all whom he or she will be expected to lead and influence.

If we are finally selected for this top promotion, we will continue to cultivate breadth and depth of character while being careful also to continue striving for excellence in competence and personality.

From bottom up, likewise, these components of influence follow the order in which they must be *worked at*.

Character, although blooming in full *latest* in life must be worked at *earliest*. That's why we start little ones off in Sunday school. "As a twig is bent, so it will grow." "Train a *child* in the way he should go, and, when he is old, he will not depart from it."

Competence blooms *earliest* in life but is worked on *latest*. We often do not know what profession we want to follow until we are out of high school or even until the end of our college sophomore year. Yet a few years later, with our college diplomas in our hands, we are an engineer, accountant, architect, economist, or whatever.

In between, personality and authority get their respective emphasis in due order. Parents subject their children of high school age to training in the social graces using such devices as dancing classes and parties to assist in the process. What is being learned, hopefully, is the art of being easy to talk to, to listen to, and to be with. To many youngsters, paradoxically, this does not come pleasantly!

This does not mean that an older person is handicapped permanently in his or her business career by a lack of formal education or lack of social and communication skills. Some individuals have overcome both lacks through the cultivation of depth and breadth of character.

Now we come to answer the inevitable question: "So what?"

In getting others to do what you want them to do when you want them to do it, you must lead from that component of your influence appropriate to (1) what you want done, (2) whom you want to do it, and (3) the situation within which it must be done.

For example, let us say that it's the time of year when you and the other department heads are drawing up your budget requirements for the upcoming fiscal year. Your aim is to get your boss to approve your budget estimate and make it stick when the budget committee finally meets to put the overall company budget together.

From which of the four components of your influence will you lead? Obviously not from number 2 (your authority), as this is influential only with your subordinates. So you decide for the moment you'd better lead from *competence*.

After consuming a couple of weeks' worth of midnight oil analyzing and putting together all the relevant facts and figures, you evolve a case so complete, watertight, and incontrovertible that the sheer *competence* of your arguments should carry the day for you even if the boss is in one of his most skeptical and critical moods. So proud are you of your labors that you have the art department put your facts and figures on flip charts for detailed presentation to the boss.

Next you call him for an appointment and feel lucky to get one with him at 3:30 P.M. next Friday, an hour before he knocks off work for the weekend.

At 3:00 P.M. Friday you call him on the phone just to make sure the appointment is firm. He acts a little surprised and confused but, on checking with his secretary, he confirms the appointment. You congratulate yourself on having had the good judgment to call in advance and thus prevent him from having forgetfully gone home early and thus missed your presentation.

What you don't realize, of course, is that this is the end of his toughest week in months and what he needs now is NOT an involved and irrefutable technical presentation. And in you walk.

You begin your presentation at "A" with every sign of not stopping until you get to "Z," which appears to be an hour away at least. Realizing that he won't be able to take it much longer, he interrupts you:

> This looks fine, Joe. A lot of work behind it. Characteristic of your approach to everything you do. Give me the approval form. After all, you've never let me down in the past on these matters so I'll be happy to sign it now.

You're caught unprepared for this immediate approval. You don't have the form with you because in the past he has always taken a couple of days after your budget submission to make up his mind. What you don't realize, of course, is that he has just decided that the *character* component of your influence will be enough for him at 3:45 P.M. this Friday.

But you insist that he hear your argument to the bitter end. You just can't see a couple of weeks' work go for naught. As you plod your pedantic way through your charts and tables, he becomes inwardly more and more annoyed. Finally, he decides to beat you at your own game. Rising from his chair he purposely mistakes a fly-speck for a decimal point and asks you why you take up his time with material that hasn't even been proofread. With that he picks up his hat and unceremoniously leaves for the club and a long weekend.

You had all the influence you needed to get his approval the moment after you entered the office but on a different component than you had planned. You had it on *character* but then lost it because you insisted on having it on *competence*.

You did the right thing in coming fully armed with facts and figures. You did the wrong thing in not being willing to sense the man's mood, the timing and the situation—and in not switching immediately from one component of your influence to another.

But the situation might have been different had the presentation been scheduled for a Monday morning at 9:30 when he's alert and ready for a battle of facts and figures and *you* are fighting a wicked hangover. Now it's you who have no stomach (or head) for leading from *competence,* so you ask him rhetorically whether there's any point in going over the facts and figures with him since in the past he has always concurred and would probably end up doing so now. In other words, you desperately want to lead from the influence of your *character* and so get it over with. But, because *he* is the one now who's "shiny-nosed and bushytailed," he replies, "Joe, I don't doubt the integrity of your motives or the reliability of your conclusions, but your reputation will never be a substitute for facts. So proceed!"

This very same man wants you to lead from one component of your influence on one day and from another the next! On still another day he'll want it all on colored slides and sound effects, that is, leading from *personality.*

The professional manager is both willing and able to make the required shift on the spot and takes pride and satisfaction in being able to do so. This way he or she usually has enough of the right kind of influence on tap to get his boss to do what he wants him to do when he wants him to do it.

So much for the need for flexibility.

Second, be careful not to lead from one component to camouflage a weakness in another.

For instance, let's suppose that one of your own subordinates comes to you for a decision requiring a great deal of technical competence. Since he or she is far more qualified in the matter than you, he has brought along his homework with a strong recommendation as to what your decision should be. As you listen, you begin to get lost in the technicalities until you realize that this thing is way over your head. But, for reasons best known to yourself, you don't want him or her to know that you're just not competent to judge. So you reply, "Joe, we won't go ahead on this." He asks why. You answer, "Because that's my decision." Joe now realizes that you have substituted the influence of your *authority* for that of your *competence*—you've "pulled your rank." When a decision requiring competence is made on rank, it always turns out to be a "rank" decision.

Or, suppose you are in a conference where a matter of policy is being debated. Before long you find yourself a one-man minority fighting with your back to the wall. Your one reply to the pleadings and the arguments of the others is that you are against the proposition "as a matter of principle." This only aggravates them more, but you remain adamant. Eventually, communication between you and them breaks down completely and the meeting is recessed. You console yourself by laying the entire impasse to your own strength of character, identifying yourself with the early Christian martyrs who would die before giving in on a matter of principle.

Without realizing it, you may have trapped yourself into feigning strength of *character* to cover up a deficiency either in your *personality* or in your *competence*. There need be no conflict between gaining the other person's respect or confidence and, at the same time, maintaining rapport with him. The individual who cannot conquer this conflict within himself loses much of the influence his *character* may already have provided him. "Learn to disagree agreeably."

Or, once again, suppose you are talking alone in his or her office with one of your peers in another department who has just adopted a new system of order handling that is going to make the work in your department more difficult. In short, he or she has made it harder for you to do business and, in a moment of emotion, you decide to retaliate in kind. So you say, "To be absolutely frank, Henry..." and you let him have it, but with a halo. Frankness is an enviable quality of character through which you expect to gain a brownie point in one-upmanship. Such a halo costs its wearer much of the influence he already had before he donned it.

Third, do not lead from one component of your influence in such a way as to create a false impression about another component.

For instance, suppose you are stopping off in Las Vegas for a couple of carefree days on your way home from a company sales meeting. After a few drinks at the bar, you find yourself talking to one of the most delightfully interesting men you ever met. He's an off-duty priest in civilian clothes moving about the hot spots in order to give those who've got money a chance to put a little of it to God's use. He shows you a picture of himself surrounded by a crowd of poor orphans, and you slip him a $100 bill. That night you sleep the sound sleep of the righteous. But the next morning you see his picture in the paper over the caption, "Wanted by the FBI." He had led from *personality* in such a way as to create a false impression about his character. In the underworld he would be called a con man. In the business world the word is "fourflusher." Men of this type see no need for being honest when just seeming to be honest for the moment pays off. In the long run, however, it costs them whatever influence they had.

From time to time every supervisor, manager and executive has to choose between being liked and being respected. The choice, then, is between leading from *personality* or from *character*. Most readers will agree that when the choice is forced on them, they have always led from *character*. Lose a man's respect, and it's a long uphill pull to regain it if it can be regained at all. Lose a man's liking for you, and it is a relatively easy matter to win him back. This is particularly important in dealing with employees. The foreman who is out to win a popularity contest will lose his influence in the quicksand of compromise. If he is out primarily to win their respect, he can then go as far as he wishes in winning their friendship.

Or, again, a person who is easy to listen to, easy to talk with and easy to do business with (strong on *personality*) may be creating the impression that he or she is strong in *competence*. By picking up a few technical terms and borrowing a few statistics, he or she can double as a Ph.D. in economics to the point of fooling even the pros—for awhile. In business the one who habitually leads from personality in order to create an impression of competence is called a feather merchant. In the underworld he or she is called a phony. Either way he or she loses influence over the long run.

If you have not knowingly committed these errors, you may have been erroneously perceived by others as having committed them. This is just as damaging to your career as having committed them. This is why it is so necessary to develop a sensitivity to choose the appropriate component of your influence to use on the appropriate person at the appropriate time. It pays off in your ability to get him or her to do what you want him to do when you want him to do it. That's what management is all about; managers are paid primarily for what they get done through their judgment and influence, of which their authority is only one component and is effective only on subordinates.

Appendix C
Parable on Professional Management

Once upon a time there were two dormitory roommates on a university campus. One was embarking on a course of study leading to a professional degree in chemistry, the other on a course leading to a professional degree in management. Each was preparing herself for a career in industry.

The first of these two women understood chemistry to be both a science and an art. The *science* she would acquire primarily from lectures and texts; the *art* from the laboratory. Indeed, it was in her laboratory work that she expected to become skilled in doing the very things she was going to be paid to do when she went to work.

The second woman understood management, likewise, to be both a science and an art. The science she, too, would acquire from texts and lectures. But where would she acquire the art?

Management is the science and the art of achieving *planned objectives* through the efforts of *other people*. Her immediate objective was a doctor's degree in management. What better way to develop skill in the very field in which she was getting her degree than to form an organization whose objective would be to get her that degree?

She proceeded to hire a vice president for attending classes, a vice president for writing papers, and a vice president for taking examinations. She had no doubt she would thereby become so skilled in the art of management that she would be awarded her degree with highest honors.

It came to pass that she was expelled from the university for allegedly committing a serious ethical and procedural breach. After doing penance in sackcloth and ashes, she humbly approached the dean begging readmittance on the ground that she had acted in good faith, albeit in ignorance, and vowed she'd not repeat her error. The dean consulted with the committee and, with misgivings, they granted the request.

For the remainder of her course, she faithfully attended her classes herself, wrote her papers herself, and took her examinations herself. She graduated, receiving her doctor's degree in management—*summa cum laude*.

234

At the close of the commencement exercises, a reporter from a local daily paper approached her and asked, "What did you learn most during your three years of graduate training in management?"

Without hesitation she replied, "If you want it done right, you've got to do it yourself."

Appendix D
The Collected Sayings of Benjamin Franklin's Grandfather

"It's hell to work for a nervous boss—especially when you are the one who is making him nervous."

"Always do what your boss wants; if you don't like what he wants, change what he wants, but do what he wants."

"It is easier to help your boss to make up his mind than it is to persuade him to change it."

"It is better to occasionally ask forgiveness than constantly to ask permission."

"Your boss cannot *make* you do anything, but he can surely make you regret you didn't."

"The Golden Rule of Management states that he who has the gold makes the rules. Its corollary is that he who wants the gold cannot make the rules."

"If you don't want to follow your boss's advice, don't ask for it. But once having asked for it accept it like a good sport even if its not the advice you wanted. You asked for it!"

"To get promoted you don't have to be the best; you need only to be the least worst of all the known candidates at the time."

"Success in almost any field depends more on energy and drive than it does on intelligence, which explains why we have so many stupid leaders."

"The true test of the professional is not what he knows how to do, but how be behaves when he does not know what to do."

"Any philosophy is acceptable if it is affordable."

"Let your conscience be your guide; beware of him whose conscience is his accomplice."

"Maturity is the ability to do a job without supervision, finish a job once it is started and carry money without spending it."

"If you never step over the line, you'll never find out where it is."

"The surest way to lose a friend is to become indebted to him."

"When trouble is what you are looking for, you will be handsomely rewarded."

"Nagging is the persistent reminder of an unpleasant truth."

"Since we, as human beings, are fated to make enemies anyway, the least we can do is to pick them carefully."

"It is better to strike a straight blow with a crooked stick than to spend the rest of your life trying to straighten the damn thing out."

"Don't throw out the baby just because the bathwater stinks."

"If you are both in the same boat, the other guy won't put a hole in it."

"When your man puts his best foot forward, keep an eagle eye on his other foot."

"He who has the working papers has the initiative, and he who has the initiative has control."

"Mankind is divided into three classes: those who are immovable, those who are movable, and those who move."

"The difference between education and experience is that education is what you get from reading the fine print, whereas experience is what you get from *not* reading it."

"Our Maker gave us TIME to keep everything from happening at once."

"Never put off until tomorrow what you can put off until day after tomorrow, for you may not have to do it day after tomorrow."

"We will not learn how to create a more perfect world until we know how to live more perfectly in this imperfect world."

SERVICES AVAILABLE

Since 1960, The William Oncken Corporation has been providing business education, industry and government with quality management seminars throughout the United States and Canada. Its client list includes such Fortune 500 companies as Hewlett Packard, DuPont, Digital Equipment and International Paper Corporation. Government clients include the U.S. Internal Revenue Service, U.S. Department of Agriculture, U.S. Department of Labor and various Army and Navy installations in the U.S. and overseas.

Services available include: seminars (open-to-the-public and on an in-house, contract basis) ranging from half-day presentations for conferences and annual meetings to two-day seminars followed by a third day skill implementation workshop, keynote speakers, audio, video and computer-based training programs on such topics as, "Managing Management Time," "Managing Managerial Initiative," "Taming the Bureaucracy," "Motivation by Communication—The Extra Five Knots," "The Authority to Manage" and others.

The William Oncken Corporation's management seminars are presented by a staff of trained professionals all of whom had previously held executive management positions in large corporations.

For Further Information Contact:

The William Oncken Corporation
8344 East R.L. Thornton Freeway
Suite #408
Dallas, Texas 75228
(214) 328-1867

Index